NEW FOUNDATIONS
FOR ASIAN AND PACIFIC SECURITY

NEW FOUNDATIONS
FOR ASIAN AND PACIFIC SECURITY

Based on the Addresses, Papers, Reports, and Discussion
Sessions of an International Conference Held at Pattaya,
Thailand, December 12–16, 1979

Edited by
Joyce E. Larson

Published by
National Strategy Information Center, Inc.
Distributed by
Transaction Books
New Brunswick (U.S.A.) and London (U.K.)

New Foundations for Asian and Pacific Security

Copyright © 1980 by National Strategy Information Center, Inc.
111 East 58th Street
New York, N.Y. 10022

No part of this publication may be reproduced, stored in a retrieval system, or transmitted in any form or by any means, electronic, mechanical, photocopying, recording, or otherwise, without the prior written permission of the publisher.

Library Edition: ISBN 0-87855-413-0
Paperbound Edition: ISBN 0-87855-845-2

LC 80-82521

Printed in the United States of America

CONTENTS

PREFACE   *Joyce E. Larson* .... *vii*

FOREWORD
Perspectives on War and Peace: The United States and Asia at the
    Beginning of the 1980s   *Frank N. Trager* .... *xi*

CHAPTER 1: POLITICAL/MILITARY DIMENSIONS OF SECURITY IN SOUTHEAST ASIA

ISSUES AND QUESTIONS TO BE ADDRESSED: 1 3

The Continuing Struggle in Indochina: Editor's Introduction
    Joyce E. Larson 9

ADDRESSES

International Politics in Asia and the Pacific: Complexities and
    Uncertainties   *Ali Moertopo* 21
The Strategic Outlook for Thailand in the 1980s
    Upadit Pachariyangkun 25
Conflict and Cooperation in Southeast Asia: The New Chapter
    Thanat Khoman 33

CONFERENCE PAPERS

The Indochina Situation and the Superpowers in Southeast Asia
    Lim Joo-Jock 41
The Internal and External Dimensions of Southeast Asian Security
    Jusuf Wanandi 57

REPORT OF COMMITTEE #1 75

CHAPTER 2: POLITICAL/MILITARY DIMENSIONS OF SECURITY IN NORTHEAST ASIA

ISSUES AND QUESTIONS TO BE ADDRESSED: 2 85

Japan and the Security of Northeast Asia: Editor's Introduction
    Joyce E. Larson 89

ADDRESS

Northeast Asian Security: The Japanese Role   *Masao Horie* 97

v

CONFERENCE PAPERS AND COMMENTARY

The Japanese Defense Posture and the Soviet Challenge in
    Northeast Asia   *Kenichi Kitamura and Jun Tsunoda* 103
The Tensions on the Korean Peninsula   *Hogan Yoon* 121
Commentary   *Frederick Chien* 129

REPORT OF COMMITTEE #2 135

CHAPTER 3: ECONOMIC DIMENSIONS OF SECURITY IN ASIA AND THE PACIFIC

ISSUES AND QUESTIONS TO BE ADDRESSED: 3 143

CONFERENCE PAPERS

Toward Regional Cooperation and Prosperity   *Sun Chen* 151
Regional Security Through Trade and Investment   *Munir Majid* 163
Energy Resources, Raw Materials, and the Safety of the Sea Lanes
    of Communication: An Organic Approach Toward a New
    Security Framework   *Alejandro Melchor* 175

REPORT OF COMMITTEES #3 and #4 187

CHAPTER 4: POLICY PROPOSALS AND ASIAN AND PACIFIC SECURITY

ISSUES AND QUESTIONS TO BE ADDRESSED: 4 193
The Pacific Basin Community: Editor's Introduction
    Joyce E. Larson 197

ADDRESS

Toward a Pacific Basin Community: A Malaysian Perception
    Tan Sri Muhammad Ghazali bin Shafie 201

CONFERENCE PAPERS

Policy Proposals: A Southeast Asian View   *Sompong Sucharitkul* 215
Policy Proposals: A Northeast Asian View
    Jun Tsunoda and Kenichi Kitamura 223
Policy Proposals: An American View   *Douglas Pike* 233

APPENDIX

CONFERENCE PROGRAM 249

LIST OF PARTICIPANTS 253

NSIC PUBLICATIONS 257

EDITOR'S PREFACE

For most of the nations of the Asian/Pacific region, the post-World War II decades have been a period of significant economic growth and progress toward the development of viable and stable political institutions. As diplomatic interactions have become ever more complex, and as trade relations among the various countries have expanded, both the economic vitality and the geo-political importance of the region have gained increasing recognition.

Continued regional progress is dependent, in part, on the establishment and maintenance of conditions of domestic and regional security which allow attention to be focused on the requirements of orderly political and economic development. The latter half of the 1970s, however, brought changes in the international climate and in the regional balance of power which, when viewed together, carry disturbing implications for the prospects for peace and stability in the Asian/Pacific area. These changes include:

1. The perceived reduction of the American commitment to Asian security; the actual reduction of U.S. military strength deployed in the area; and the uncertainties characteristic of U.S. security relations with such major allies as Japan, the Republic of Korea, and the Philippines arising from American neglect or policy "shocks."
2. The rapid and extensive expansion of Soviet military power in East Asia and the Indian Ocean area, and the consolidation of Soviet military and political influence in Indochina.
3. The victory of communist forces in Vietnam, Laos, and Kampuchea; the emergence of Vietnam as the strongest military power in Southeast Asia; and the current Vietnamese domination of the entire Indochinese peninsula.
4. The intensification in East Asia of the Sino-Soviet conflict, and the outbreak of actual hostilities between the People's Republic of China (PRC) and Soviet-backed Vietnam.

5. The emergence of strained political and economic relations between and among the region's developed and developing nations arising from various pressures to restructure trade policies and tariff regulations.

The Asian/Pacific area has become a crucial arena of great power rivalry, for it is in this region that the interests and ambitions of the U.S., the Soviet Union, Japan, and the PRC intersect and often clash. At least partially in response to these realities, new or strengthened alignments or relationships—most of them tentative and not yet fully formed—are developing in the region, including the Sino-American and Sino-Japanese rapprochements, growing unity among the Association of Southeast Asian Nations (ASEAN) states, and improved relations between ASEAN and the PRC. Whether these developments will serve to modify significantly the currently heightened uncertainties, tensions, and strains in the region remains to be seen.

Careful consideration of these varied and complex concerns has led a number of observers to conclude that today's international environment requires greater emphasis on security-related matters in Asia and the Pacific Basin. Acting upon this conviction, the National Strategy Information Center and five cooperating organizations co-sponsored a conference on "New Foundations for Asian and Pacific Security" at Pattaya, Thailand in December 1979. This book contains the addresses, conference papers (some in slightly altered form), and committee reports which constituted the formal substantive aspects of the conference.

The organization of any conference requires often difficult decisions with respect to the range of issues to be approached, the formulation of specific topics, and the choice of participants—i.e., the determination of parameters which are neither too broad nor too narrow and which serve to define a framework for effective discussion of the matters at hand. In the view of the organizers and participants of the Pattaya conference, an adequate approach to security concerns must include attention to the political, economic and military dimensions, and the reader will find this recognition of the complex and multi-dimensioned nature of what comprises security reflected both in the book's organizational format and in its substantive analyses.

Editor's Preface

Conference participants included public- and private-sector leaders and scholars from eleven nations—Japan, the Republic of Korea, the Republic of China, the Philippines, Singapore, Indonesia, Malaysia, Thailand, Australia, New Zealand, and the United States—located in the area broadly referred to as "Asia and the Pacific Basin" or, alternatively, the "Asian/Pacific region." It is obvious that not all nations geographically situated in this region were represented at the conference. For the purposes of the Pattaya meetings, it was determined that the countries invited should share certain common foundations and outlooks, as reflected in their non-communist political and economic systems, general friendliness toward one another, and demonstrated commitment to cooperative regional endeavors. There exist a variety of approaches to the establishment of this particular parameter, and future conferences may well involve a different configuration of participating states.

It is the hope of the National Strategy Information Center that the essays contained in this volume will serve to focus attention on crucial issues of security and stability in an area of the world which has moved increasingly toward the center of international politics and economic relations. We wish to take this opportunity to offer our appreciation to the conference co-sponsors, the conference participants, the staff of the Thai Oil Refinery Company in Bangkok for their administrative assistance, Dr. Thanat Khoman for his special help, and the Institute of Southeast Asian Studies in Singapore for its cooperation in publishing an Asian edition of this book.

> Joyce E. Larson
> *Managing Editor*
> *National Strategy Information Center, Inc.*

August 1980

FOREWORD

Perspectives on War and Peace: The United States and Asia at the Beginning of the 1980s

I.

At the beginning of the 1970s, key persons associated with the National Strategy Information Center became convinced that, in important respects, the flow of international developments was moving in directions contrary to the interests of the United States and other free nations which aspire to independence and self-fulfillment.

To begin a program of cooperative action in response to these troubling realities, NSIC—in liaison with concerned leadership and like-minded non-governmental groups in Europe, Asia, and the Middle East—convened a series of four international conferences:

—"Economic and Political Development in Relation to Sea Power

Along the Routes from the Indian Ocean" (London, May 25-28, 1972)
—"The Emerging Era of the Pacific: Economic Development, Stability, and Rivalry" (Honolulu, Hawaii, February 4-7, 1975)
—"New Dimensions for the Defense of the Atlantic Alliance" (Winchester, England, November 18-21, 1976)
—"NATO and the Global Threat: What Must Be Done" (Brighton, England, June 1-4, 1978)

At the Brighton Conference, it was recommended that more attention be turned in the near future to the region of Asia and the Pacific Basin. Recent trends and events in this area have clearly indicated that the challenges to the security, stability, and economic well-being of non-communist states around the globe have by no means receded, and may in fact have escalated—thus making imperative an intensified search for the policies and pathways which can lead to a better and more secure future as we enter the decade of the 1980s. In an attempt to contribute significantly to this search, the National Strategy Information Center and several co-sponsoring groups convened a fifth international conference focusing on "New Foundations for Asian and Pacific Security" at Pattaya, Thailand in December 1979.

Approximately sixty government officials, parliamentary leaders, university scholars, members of the business community, and labor representatives from eleven Asian/Pacific Basin nations were in attendance.[1] The co-sponsoring groups included the Center for Strategic and International Studies (Indonesia), the Faculty of Political Science of Chulalongkorn University (Thailand), the Institute for Pacific Affairs (Japan), the John F. Kennedy Foundation of Thailand, and the Pacific Institute (Australia).

II.

The seriousness of the occasion and of the participants was intensified by the several crises which weighed heavily upon international and regional politics at the time the conference was convened. These included:

---
[1] The full list of conference participants will be found in the Appendix, pp. 253 to 255. It will be readily apparent that conferees were invited from Northeast Asia, Southeast Asia, Australasia, and the United States.

Perspectives on War and Peace

1) The Vietnamese invasion of Kampuchea and the subsequent war in that country between the ousted Khmer Rouge regime and the Vietnamese-dominated Heng Samrin government. This conflict has seriously endangered the peace and security of Thailand, and has heightened the ominous rivalry between the People's Republic of China (PRC) and the Soviet Union, which are respectively supportive of the warring communist regimes in Kampuchea.
2) The ever-present dangers in the Korean peninsula, which at the time of the Pattaya conference were exacerbated by the dislocations in South Korea subsequent to the assassination of President Park.
3) The increasing Soviet involvement in Afghanistan, leading ultimately to the Soviet invasion of that country in late December, less than a fortnight after the conference. The anxieties engendered at the conference by such Soviet actions were intensified when viewed from the perspective of the Soviet military buildup in the Indian Ocean and along the USSR's Pacific Coast.

Many other issues at a critical if not crisis level demanded and were accorded attention at the conference. Among them were the problem of assuring a continued supply of oil and other scarce mineral and agricultural resources; the need to better protect the vital sea lanes of communication; the challenges of trade and further national and regional economic development; and the difficulties arising from world-wide inflationary pressures. Last but certainly not least, much attention was paid to the enormous scale of human suffering caused by the forced exodus of the ethnic Chinese "boat people" from Vietnam and by the devastation and famine arising from the war between the rival communist regimes in Kampuchea. Firm statistics were impossible to obtain with respect to the many thousands of Kampuchean refugees in Thai and Malaysian holding camps. If, as is often estimated, the population of Cambodia totalled between six and seven million people at the start of the infamous Pol Pot regime, perhaps 10% of the survivors in the current war between the rival communist governments have now become refugees seeking to escape from both regimes.

III.

The crucial nature of the relationship of the United States to the above-mentioned concerns, ostensibly located comparatively far from American borders, was apparent throughout the conference, and the need for a carefully formulated and clearly articulated U.S. policy with respect to the Asian/Pacific region was an undercurrent which flowed through much of the conference deliberations, often rising to the surface and itself becoming a topic commanding considerable attention. That such a policy is lacking hardly reflects a newly emergent inadequacy in American foreign policy. Twenty-five years ago Edwin O. Reischauer embraced this very problem in the title of his book, *Wanted: An Asian Policy*. Reischauer's request is even more appropriate today than when it first was stated, and it is not without reason that several American analysts of Asian affairs have recently echoed his plea.

Time and again many observers of the Asian scene have charged successive post-World War II American administrations, and most particularly the Department of State, with being Europe-centered and spasmodic, if not neglectful, in attending to the Asian interests of the United States. The refrains of this lament have been phrased in such variations as:

1) The development and implementation of America's Asian policy are frequently sacrificed for European policy. The U.S. policy for Asia is "dictated" by the London and/or Paris "desks" of the State Department.
2) Americans, being descendants mainly of European (or "Western") cultures, tend to downgrade Asian (or "Eastern") cultures. In so doing, they ignore the Asian origins and roots of the Judaeo-Christian and early Greek philosophical traditions, and otherwise neglect the richness, diversity, and vitality of Asia's cultural and historical heritage.
3) U.S. administrations tend to rush into and suddenly announce policy decisions or "doctrines" relating to Asian affairs without full examination of their merits and defects, without making proper provisions for dealing with the potential consequences, and frequently without undertaking reasonable consultation with other friendly regimes affected by such decisions.

Although such criticisms are often characterized by a certain amount of exaggeration, they nevertheless carry both substance and significance.

There is a great deal which must be known and understood

about Asia before reasonably satisfactory U.S. perspectives can emerge regarding issues of war and peace in that area of the globe. Asia is the largest of the continents, containing roughly one-third of the earth's land surface and probably 65% of the world's population. The continent abuts on the Arctic, Pacific, and Indian Oceans and a number of their adjacent seas. Asia's diversity of physical characteristics is accompanied by a seemingly endless variety and complexity in the distribution of ethnic, religious, and linguistic groups.

To some extent the distortions, errors of political judgement, and conflicts which have arisen in U.S. policy on Asia since World War II can be traced to the insufficiency of American knowledge with respect to our friends, allies, and adversaries. There exist few, if any, short-cuts to learning, and while Americans have acquired well-earned reputations for many notable attributes, they are not as yet known for the thorough study and patient acquisition of experience which is required for the formulation and execution of effective foreign policy. If the U.S. is to develop supportable perspectives and policies with respect to Asia, it must begin with an enlarged data base to serve as a foundation for responsible deliberation and debate. In international as well as domestic affairs, analysts and policy-makers alike are never faced with a *tabula rasa*—i.e., a clean or empty slate from which to start. With this in mind, it is useful now to review in summary form the essential aspects of U.S. Asian policy as it has evolved since the end of World War II.

IV.

The so-called Cold War may be seen to have its origins in the failure to sustain the "grand alliance" of 1941-1945 into the postwar years. In response to the actions of the Soviet Union in Europe, the U.S. developed over a five-year period (1945-1950) a policy which can be summed up in the concept of the "containment" of communist expansionism. The twin operational means designed to carry out the policy of containment in Europe were the implementation of the Marshall Plan (1947) for the reconstruction and economic redevelopment of the war-devastated European states and the establishment of the North Atlantic Treaty Organization (1949) for Europe's defense.

In contrast to its stance regarding Europe, the U.S. during the same five-year period pursued a course of disengagement and partial withdrawal from Asia.[2] However, the eruption of several communist insurgencies (supported by the Soviet bloc) against the newly independent Asian regimes, the fall of the Nationalist regime on the Chinese mainland and its removal to Taiwan in October 1949, and—most importantly—the invasion of South Korea in June 1950 decisively altered the content and direction of U.S. foreign policy in Asia.

For the next twenty years, encompassing the administrations of Presidents Truman, Eisenhower, Kennedy, and Johnson, U.S. policy in Asia—in principle, if not in quantity and quality of supporting means—paralleled U.S. policy in Europe. The concept and implementation of containment was extended to Asia at the beginning of the 1950s by means of a series of bilateral and multilateral mutual security treaties, which—according to U.S. constitutional law—imposed legally binding commitments on succeeding U.S. governments (until such time, if ever, as the treaties were properly terminated). Containment continued to imply the protection or extension at home and abroad of vital national values vis-a-vis potential and existing adversaries. The national and international objectives of the policy were the ensurance of security, the furthering of stability, and improvement in the conditions of living.

The seven U.S. "containment" treaties applicable to Asia included: the Mutual Defense Treaty with the Philippines (August 30, 1951); the Security Treaty with Australia and New Zealand [ANZUS] (September 1, 1951); the Treaty of Mutual Cooperation and Security with Japan (September 8, 1951); the Mutual Defense Treaty with the Republic of Korea (October 1, 1953); the Pacific Charter and Southeast Asia Collective Defense Treaty [SEATO] with Australia, France, New Zealand, Pakistan, the Philippines,

---

[2]Perhaps the best exposition of this essentially negative policy of disengagement or noninvolvement in Asian affairs can be found in Secretary of State Dean Acheson's masterful but evasive "Defensive Perimeter" speech given at the National Press Club in Washington, D.C. on January 12, 1950. In many ways, this speech by the distinguished but Europe-oriented Secretary defined a policy which was already passing. See the Department of State *Bulletin*, January 23, 1950, pp. 111-18.

Thailand, and the United Kingdom, and the Protocol for Cambodia, Laos, and the State of South Vietnam (September 8, 1954); the Mutual Defense Treaty with the Republic of China (December 2, 1954); and the Baghdad Pact and Middle East Treaty Organization [later CENTO] with Iraq, Iran, Pakistan, and the United Kingdom (1955).[3] In addition to the treaties, a supportive set of statements of lesser constitutional status, known as agreements, resolutions, or doctrines, were developed. These included the Eisenhower Resolution on Formosa (1955); the Eisenhower Doctrine on the Middle East (1957); the Rusk (Kennedy)—Thanat Khoman Agreement on Thailand (1962); and the Johnson Resolution on the Gulf of Tonkin (1964).

The policy of containment, however, did not survive the testing ground of Indochina. In the wake of the 1968 North Vietnamese "Tet Offensive," the eventual U.S. defeat in Vietnam, and what has been called the American "Vietnam Syndrome," containment as a focus for U.S. foreign policy disappeared for more than a decade. In its place the Nixon, Ford, and [at least until the December 1979 Soviet invasion of Afghanistan] Carter administrations adopted and adapted the basic elements of the "Nixon Doctrine" (more accurately termed the "Nixon-Kissinger Doctrine") first enunciated at Guam in July 1969.

The new policy thrust rested on a revised analysis of world power, which held that the duopoly of power formerly shared by the U.S. and the Soviet Union had given way to a multipolar or polycentric world in which there no longer existed—if there ever was one—a communist monolith. Advocates of the new policy argued that the U.S. should enter into negotiations with the Soviet Union so as to achieve a state of detente based on a linkage of strategic parity, arms control, economic and cultural exchanges, a general relaxation of tensions, and other factors which were expected to lead toward behavioral restraints. It was similarly

---

[3]Since 1949 the U.S. has also instituted some sort of economic aid agreement with most of the nations in Asia. For a fuller treatment of the various treaties and agreements mentioned in this essay, see Frank N. Trager, "American Foreign Policy in Southeast Asia," in R. K. Sakai, ed., *Studies in Asia* (Lincoln: University of Nebraska Press, 1965), pp. 17-59; and Frank N. Trager with William L. Scully, "Asia and the Western Pacific: A Time of Trial," *Royal United Services Institute and Brassey's Defense Yearbook 1975/76* (London and Boulder, Colorado: Westview Press, 1975), pp. 165-212.

stressed that negotiations with the PRC should be undertaken in pursuit of the goals of friendly relations and mutual recognition. With respect to Indochina, the new view held that the U.S. should seek to end the war in Vietnam through a process of "Vietnamization," i.e., turning the war in Vietnam back to the Vietnamese.

Apparent progress along these lines was made regarding detente with the Soviet Union (the SALT I treaty, the Vladivostok agreement, and the Helsinki agreement) and expansion of relations with the PRC (the Shanghai communique). In 1973 the U.S. took the final step toward disengagement from Indochina when the Nixon administration yielded to the North Vietnamese terms for peace.

Elsewhere I have written that:[4]

> Generally the Nixon Doctrine was received by our Asian allies with doubt, developing into shocks and suspicion, especially after the February 1972 U.S.-PRC meeting and its accompanying Shanghai communique. To wind down the war in Vietnam was "good," but was it wise to withdraw American and other forces before an *effective* cease-fire and peace agreement was accepted by *all* parties to the conflict? To maintain our nuclear shield for our allies was "good," but was this compatible with the decline in U.S. power in the Pacific and Indian Oceans and the paralleled rise of Soviet power and Chinese power in the same arenas? To aid our friends and allies who may become—or already were—the victims of conventional aggressive and subversive action by the Asian communist states and their other-national proxies was "good," but were such promises of aid reliable in the face of ambiguous statements about decisions to be made according to *our* interests at the crucial time?

These and related questions arising from the Nixon-Kissinger Doctrine were being carefully examined in Asian capitals during the first half of the 1970s. Although the American leaders proclaimed repeatedly that the U.S. would "keep its commitments," a general uneasiness regarding U.S. credibility rippled through the capitals of friendly Asian states, many of them partners with the

---

[4]See Trager with Scully, *op. cit.*, pp. 204-05. I have been critical of the Nixon-Kissinger policies and "Doctrine" for a number of years. See my "Alternative Futures for Southeast Asia and U.S. Policy," *Orbis*, Vol. XV, No. 1, Spring 1971; and "The Nixon Doctrine and Asian Policy," *Southeast Asian Perspectives*, No. 6, June 1972.

U.S. in collective security treaties and agreements. For example, long-time Thai Foreign Minister Thanat Khoman, one of the most dependable supporters of SEATO, began after Nixon's Guam speech to question the organization's reliability. At least partially in connection with doubts regarding the future U.S. role in Asia, and taking into account the weakening of the Commonwealth Defense Agreement as a consequence of the virtual military withdrawal of the United Kingdom, Malaysia (led by the late Prime Minister Tun Abdul Razak) introduced a proposal in 1971 which would create in Southeast Asia a Zone of Peace, Freedom, and Neutrality (ZOPFAN). Japan, too, was "shocked" by the Nixon-Kissinger Doctrine and the Shanghai communique, a reaction which flowed less from the substance of these policies than from the manner in which the U.S. developed and then suddenly announced its proposals without consultation with its Asian friends and allies.

The advent of the Carter administration in 1976 added to the Asian feelings of political malaise and views of declining U.S. credibility. It was clear from the beginning of Carter's presidency that he and his major appointees would attempt, to the maximum extent possible, to distance themselves politically from the Nixon/Kissinger/Ford era. It was declared that there would be "no more Vietnams," "no more Watergates," no more "Metternichean" power ploys, and no more covert and clandestine "dirty tricks."

Nevertheless, however much Nixon's name (and, to a lesser extent, Kissinger's) was anathema to the Carter administration, the U.S. under Carter sought to carry out—even more vigorously than had Nixon, Kissinger, and Ford—the quintessential elements of the Nixon Doctrine, which the new administration reaffirmed in a series of speeches (e.g., Secretary of State Vance's Asia Society speech in June 1977 and Secretary of Defense Brown's Los Angeles World Affairs Council speech in February 1978). The Carter administration rejected as outdated the "belief that Soviet expansionism must be contained"—a stance, in Carter's view, which had flowed from an "inordinate fear of communism." Detente and arms control with the Soviet Union were pursued, along with plans for a cutback in the U.S. defense budget, and Carter sought to negotiate Nixon's SALT I into SALT II. Instead of designing its own provisions for dealing with the PRC, the Carter administration proceeded to fulfill the terms of Nixon's Shanghai communique regarding the normalization of relations with Peking, at the expense of continued diplomatic recognition of the Republic of China and the Mutual Defense Treaty with that nation. Even in view of Hanoi's continuing and multifaceted intransigence in Indochina, the Carter regime made overtures toward the normalization of relations with Vietnam in May 1977 and again in the Fall of 1978.

Evidence of the inadequacies of American foreign policy during the decade of the 1970s manifested itself in a number of ways. Toward the end of President Ford's term of office, some members of the government and some Congressional leaders began to worry about the growing size and expanding deployment of Soviet military power in the Warsaw Pact bloc and in the Indian and Pacific Oceans. Nuclear parity, an essential foundation for deterrence, seemed to be slipping away to Soviet advantage. Furthermore, it fell to the Ford and Carter administrations to witness the fulfillment of the much-scorned but not irrelevant Eisenhower-named "domino theory."

It is true that countries and people are not dominoes, susceptible to toppling by the first shove, and the "domino theory" may well be an inappropriate name for a theory of international relations. The meaning of the domino theory is quite simple, however, and retains its significance in today's international realm. Weakness in the power structures of various states invites power plays from stronger, aggressive, and/or unfriendly neighbors or adversaries. International politics is afflicted with a sort of contagion or infectiousness similar to that which affects the health of individuals living closely in society. These aspects of the domino theory are reflected in the course of recent developments in Indochina. Hanoi in succession invaded and took over South Vietnam in 1975 (in violation of the terms of the 1973 Paris Peace Treaty)[5]; established dominance over Laos in 1976-1977; invaded Kampuchea in late 1978, replacing the communist Pol Pot regime with Vietnam's own communist puppet government led by Heng Samrin; and in recent

---

[5] The unpublicized Nixon-Kissinger commitment to reintroduce American troops and to resupply the South Vietnamese in the event that Hanoi seriously violated the 1973 peace terms was not or could not be fulfilled.

months on at least one occasion has carried the armed conflict over the Thai border, ostensibly in "hot pursuit" of Pol Pot's Khmer Rouge forces which presumably were regrouping in Thai sanctuaries.

The 1970s also have witnessed an erosion of important segments of the institutional structure of collective security so carefully nurtured in earlier decades. Some treaties and agreements have been renewed (usually with amendments), but others have been formally abrogated or have withered on a contumelious vine. SEATO has been officially terminated, while CENTO—in a delayed death agony—retains Turkey as its sole "Asian" member.[6] From the beginning of the Carter presidency the 1954 Mutual Defense Treaty with the Republic of China came under constant attack by leading members of the administration. Uncritically accepting of the 1972 Shanghai communique, and apparently desirous of playing a so-called China Card in America's unresolved and continuing diplomatic contest with the USSR, Carter unilaterally denounced the ROC treaty to make way for the January 1, 1979 recognition of Peking—on the latter's terms. ANZUS also has suffered from neglect in Washington and from political opposition in Australia, especially during the preceding Labor government led by Prime Minister Whitlam. The successor Australian regime under Prime Minister Fraser, however, has been able to effect repairs with Washington, which seems belatedly to have recognized the importance of ANZUS.

Even those security arrangements which have been quite enduring have suffered some difficulties. The 1951 U.S.-Japan Security Treaty was renewed in 1960 for a ten-year period, and now continues on a year-to-year basis. In recent years an unprecedented series of Japanese White Papers on defense has emanated from both governmental and private sources.[7] While these White Papers cover many topics of concern, one recurring theme indi-

---

[6]Iraq, Iran, and Pakistan, the other three Asian members, had previously exited from CENTO.
[7]See "Defense of Japan, White Paper on Defense (Summary)," *Defense Bulletin* [Defense Agency, Tokyo], Vol. III, No. 2, October 1979; Jun Tsunoda, "Is Japan's Defense Posture Adequate?" [summary translation of *On National Defense—1977 Edition*], *Asian Affairs: An American Review*, Vol. V, No. 4, March/April 1978; and Research Institute for Peace and Security, *Asian Security 1979* (Tokyo: 1979). Also see "Japanese Establish Arms Policy Panel," *New York Times*, April 7, 1980.

cates that much unhappiness and dissatisfaction remain in Tokyo as a result of the "shocks"—e.g., the threatened withdrawal in 1977 of U.S. ground forces from the Republic of Korea and applications of the U.S. "Swing Strategy"[8]—perpetrated by the Nixon, Ford, and Carter administrations. In the view of the Japanese (and in the eyes of the South Koreans and other Asians as well), these apparent policy decisions seemed to signal a significant U.S. downgrading of, if not withdrawal from, its commitments to the defense of America's Asian allies. The Mutual Defense Treaty with the Philippines until recently was jeopardized by protracted disagreement on the issue of the important U.S. naval base at Subic Bay and air base at Clark Field. This dispute between Washington and Manila was settled for the time being on January 7, 1979 when the two governments signed an amendment to the 1947 Military Bases Agreement stipulating U.S. retention of the military installations, under revised non-sovereign conditions, until at least 1983, when the Agreement is scheduled for review.

V.

Many varieties of imperialism, both "eastern" and "western," have through the centuries impinged upon the peace, security, and territorial integrity of various Asian peoples. In the years after World War II, however, the Asian continent became home for many newly independent and sovereign nations which had determinedly thrown off the fetters of colonialism. Nevertheless, there exist today several states with imperialist designs which pose an actual or potential challenge to the continued well-being of the independent Asian nations.

The first of these states, the People's Republic of China, may be undergoing (at least to a certain extent) a change in its stance. The PRC, a country which has sought to export revolution on its own terms, is now being perceived in Asia as less of an ideological, subversive, and material threat than at any time since the Communist Party of China came to power in October 1949. Peking for decades has given propaganda and diminishing material assist-

---

[8]See Rear Admiral Robert Hanks (Ret.), "The Swinging Debate," *U.S. Naval Institute Proceedings*, June 1980; "U.S. Strategy Focus Shifting from Europe to Pacific," *New York Times*, May 25, 1980; and "U.S. Warily Expands Southeast Asian Security Role," *New York Times*, July 10, 1980.

ance to the communist insurgencies in Burma, Thailand, Malaysia, the Philippines, Indonesia, and Laos (until Hanoi came to dominate that country), and continues to support the communist Pol Pot regime in its war with Vietnam and Heng Samrin. However, since the termination of the Cultural Revolution, the death of Mao Tse-tung, the ousting of the "Gang of Four," and the restoration (for the second time) of Teng Hsiao-ping and his colleagues, the presumptive moderating influence of the most able Chinese communist of them all, the late Chou En-lai, has come to prevail in the PRC, at least for the time being. Under this influence, the PRC seems to seek not a "purist," highly ideological, almost Trotskyist "permanent revolution" (to use Mao's term), but rather some sort of populist, socialist revolution under the authority and control of the Communist Party. As long as this course is continued, it can be expected that the perception of the PRC as a threat to regional states will continue to diminish, if only slowly, cautiously, and tentatively.

A second source of imperialism is the Democratic Republic of Vietnam, supported in no small measure by the Soviet Union. Since the ill-fated Paris Peace Treaty of 1973, Hanoi has taken over South Vietnam (1975) and Laos (1976-1977); is now at war in Kampuchea; and has systematically proceeded to establish its de facto hegemony over the whole of the Indochinese peninsula. In addition to the general fears and anxieties generated in the region by Hanoi's successful aggressive behavior, Vietnam's actions may ultimately force upon its Asian neighbors the task of caring for some 500,000 to 600,000 Kampuchean refugees and Vietnamese inhabitants of Chinese extraction (the Vietnamese "boat people").

The third imperialistic force contributing to a pervasive atmosphere of political and military uncertainty in Asia is the Soviet Union. The USSR may be seen as an aggressive land and sea power whose borders are directly contiguous to three of the four major regional centers of Asia: 1) the oil-rich area of Southwest Asia; 2) South Asia (the world's second most populous region), with its fragile economies; and 3) East/Northeast Asia (the world's most populous region), with an industrial and technological capacity in Japan second only to that of the United States. With the aid of its present ally, Vietnam, the Soviet Union through its naval leapfrogging also has approached Southeast Asia, the fourth Asian subregion and one of the potentially richest resource areas in the world.

The Russian and later Soviet geopolitical penetration of the Asian land mass is an old story, but the ability of the Russian/Soviet bear to swim globally is a capability acquired mostly during the last quarter century, under the drive and leadership of Admiral S. G. Gorshkov. The growth of Soviet naval power is visibly in evidence in both the Indian and Pacific Oceans, and the Soviets now have access to base facilities in such disparate parts of the globe as Ethiopia, Yemen, Vietnam, and the maritime provinces of Siberia. With the emplacement of Soviet seapower athwart the sea lanes vital to the economies of all nations, the Soviets may be in a position to threaten the commercial routes in the area of Southeast Asia and through the Indian Ocean (as well as the Cape Route), at a time of growing Western and virtually absolute Japanese dependence on the oil, other minerals, and raw materials produced in non-Western lands. The ability of Soviet naval power to close off the vital chokepoints in the Persian Gulf and through the Malacca, Sohya, Tsugaru, Tsushima, and Taiwan Straits—waterways which are essential for the preservation of the fuel and food life lines of all trading Asian nations—poses a new challenge which must be seriously considered.

The 1978 Soviet-fomented coup and 1979 armed intervention in Afghanistan constitute the most recent and blatant examples of Soviet imperialistic behavior. A more longstanding situation is the continued Soviet occupation of the northern Japanese islands (Southern Sakhalin and the four lower Kuriles) which the USSR acquired as "booty" at the end of World War II. This acquisition enabled Stalin to boast of the "Soviet Sea of Okhotsk," rounding out Soviet predominance in that gateway from the Sea of Japan to the Pacific Ocean. It is not without some historic irony to note that the Japanese have built a beautiful commemorative shrine (and associated museum rooms) to honor Admiral Togo Heihachiro (1848-1934) for his great victory over the Russian fleet in the Battle of Tsushima Strait on May 27-28, 1905 (a victory which ended the Russo-Japanese war of 1904-1905). The Japanese now are keenly aware of the strength of the Soviet seapower deployed in and near their waters, and realize as well that Japan today could not withstand a Soviet attack without reliance on its sometimes troubled alliance with the United States.

Every other state on the expanding boundaries of Soviet power and influence in Asia is faced with similar worries. The obvious growth of Soviet strength in the period since World War II—despite the country's climatic problems and difficulties in the areas of agricultural and industrial production and marketing—is indeed impressive and potentially threatening. It is not unfair to conclude that Soviet land and seapower in Asia form a potential giant pincer which affects all peoples and regimes from the Black Sea "apex" to the Sea of Okhotsk and the Pacific Ocean on the northern land arm, and from that same apex mainly by sea over the Transcaucasus landbridge to the Persian Gulf, the Arabian Sea, and the Indian Ocean. To close the pincer, the Soviet Union must complete the ring through the strategically important waters of Southeast Asia—a difficult and as yet unaccomplished task, to be sure, but one toward which Soviet progress is being made.

VI.

A belated "political awakening" now seems to be taking place in Washington, but it is not the one which was suggested by the easy optimism of Jimmy Carter as he assumed the presidency in 1977. Such traumatic events and developments as the Soviet invasion of Afghanistan, the Vietnamese-perpetrated war in Indochina, the dangerous situation in the Caribbean Basin, and the tinder-box circumstances in the Middle East and the Persian Gulf at long last have shaken the complacency of Washington, particularly as it contemplates the deteriorating defense posture of the United States vis-a-vis its major—and aggressive—adversary, the Soviet Union. Prodded by its allies and friends, and warned repeatedly by well-informed international security analysts both public and private, Washington has begun to take stock of its foreign policy—Asian policy included—as the country squares away for yet another of its quadrennial presidential elections.

However America's approach to foreign affairs may become sloganized for the 1980s, it will be necessary—if sound policy is to eventuate—to make a return to fundamentals. In the case of the U.S.-Asian scene, what is required is the systematic re-examination of the mutually shared political, military, and economic data base. While Washington can and should make clear its own values and interests, the U.S. cannot successfully design an Asian policy (or any foreign policy) *unilaterally*. Because the U.S. can no longer "live alone and like it," if ever such a stance was possible, the U.S. must decide *with other international actors* what objectives and goals will jointly be sought to enhance mutual well-being and defend against the power and threats posed by adversaries.

It is here assumed that we will continue in the 1980s to live in a non-peaceful and (at least in some sense) confrontational world. Just as the so-called Cold War period was never "cold" in Asia, so it is likely that the coming decade will continue to exhibit small wars, insurgencies, other forms of armed conflict, competition for scarce resources, economic difficulties, unmet humanitarian needs, and other threats to peace and human progress.

In the search for mutually shared responses and approaches to these problems, the international actors involved in any particular understanding or common policy necessarily must be limited to those whose projected view of the future is based on roughly similar assumptions. In this sense, the interaction between the United States and other international actors is *not* global in orientation; it should instead take place in terms of the recognizable regions which in fact constitute the geopolitical context for rational international security policy. Mutually shared analysis eventually can issue into bilateral or multilateral agreements, treaties, alliances, or other formal and informal instruments of international discourse. These instruments necessarily will be characterized by two conditions: a) they will not be passive, but will be directed toward actively meeting and resolving the central issue(s) at stake; and b) they will be collective in nature, entailing for all involved parties mutual obligations, while taking into account differences in capacity.

There is little reason to doubt that a mutually shared political, military, and economic data base can be developed and set forth for Americans and Asians, and that from this base can be extracted a mutually shared set of values, interests, objectives, and goals. Such a step is fundamental to the process of designing mutually acceptable policies, and while it is not easy, it is the less difficult of the two tasks. In this analysis, values are regarded as the most basic principles upon which the social and political order and the physical existence of the state are based. Values often are abstract, ambiguous, and couched in the most general terms. Interests, on the other hand, are specific, particularized illustrations (in geopolitical or social psychological terms) of the values held by the state.

One list of major values and some related interests reads as follows:[9]

1) The preservation of national institutions and survival of the nation as a self-governing entity, as opposed to subjugation to an alien power.
2) The ensurance of territorial integrity, or the preservation or freely negotiated restoration or rectification of national boundaries.
3) The protection of the commonly accepted rights and privileges of all nationals at home, on the seas, and in foreign lands.
4) The maintenance or improvement of the national wealth, health, and welfare.
5) The maintenance of prestige and responsibility in all foreign undertakings.
6) The establishment of security, including the assured capability for meeting any threat to the foregoing.

Each such list produced by individual authors will of course show variations in language, but the essential terms of reference will not vary considerably. What is valued by each nation-state is its security, stability, and improvement in the conditions of living. In the pursuit of these values, each state seeks the maximum degree of support from its own people and the cooperation—because it is necessary, not merely desirable—of other nations and peoples.

The United States and its presumptive friends and allies in Asia must begin to find solutions to a number of policy puzzles—some urgent, some important, some uncertain—which flow from or are otherwise connected to such sets of values. Among the policy puzzles to be resolved are:

1) The existing distribution of power in the world and its possible consequences for states large and small.
2) The competing geopolitical views prevalent in today's international politics, and the line-up of states behind these respective views.
3) The choice of economic models and priorities for resource allocation in a world of speeded-up expectations.

---

[9]See Frank N. Trager and Frank L. Simonie, "An Introduction to the Study of National Security," in Frank N. Trager and Philip S. Kronenberg, eds., *National Security and American Society* (Lawrence: The University Press of Kansas, 1973), pp. 35-48.

4) The calculus of interests from among present trends and future stresses.

The security equation always must include the political and economic dimensions as well as the military component, and all three aspects have suffered from neglect and/or unwise or unpalatable U.S. decision-making in the last decade. In seeking solutions to the above-mentioned puzzles, it is necessary to yield the shopworn and procrustean concepts which too often have constricted the formulation of policy, and proceed to a re-examination of the current Asian data-base, taking into account the perceived and experienced realities of the recent past and the present. This data-base will certainly include a recognition of the roles played and the impacts exerted by the "super-powers" and the other "big powers" in the region. At the same time, however, full attention must be paid to the importance of the smaller regional powers, for at this juncture in history each of the states in the Asian/Pacific area has acquired some power to undergird its respective interests and is learning that shared interests can be mutually enhanced and protected.

While past decades cannot be negated—for, as mentioned earlier, there is no *tabula rasa* in international affairs—it is time for a curtain of sorts to be drawn on the past thirty years. As we enter the 1980s, the search for new policies will entail a number of complex considerations and challenges which must be taken carefully into account. For example, more than three decades' experience with a variety of failed or at least flawed security alliances involving the U.S. and various Asian/Pacific nations has created justifiable diplomatic anxiety in the region with respect to alliance systems in general. The U.S. should aim to reinvigorate the existing defense treaties with its remaining Asian and Pacific Basin allies (i.e., with the Republic of Korea, Japan, the Philippines, Thailand, Australia, and New Zealand). Washington should not attempt, however, to revive old alliance structures such as SEATO and CENTO, which once were useful but no longer can serve as strong and viable foundations for mutual security in the Asian/Pacific region. It furthermore seems to me that this is not the proper time to forge a grand new alliance of the sort formed during

World War II, for most of the presumptive members of such an alliance are not yet ready to join; their "houses" are not yet in order. An effort to forge a new triangular alliance with the PRC and Japan would also be unwise, for such an entente would cause worry among most of the other Asian powers and would certainly dispose the Soviet Union to accelerate whatever aggressive timetable it may have prepared as a contingency plan in response to this possible development.

There are signs that the United States may be proceeding toward sounder and more fully considered policies for the Asian/Pacific region. The U.S. has now begun to realize that it no longer can treat the defense of its interests in the Pacific as of secondary importance to the preservation of its interests in Europe. Washington is just beginning to acknowledge and recognize the importance of the fact that the volume of U.S. economic interaction with Asia has for the past several years been greater than that with Europe. The realization also is growing that the U.S. must divest itself of such ill-suited defense policies as maintaining a supposed capacity for fighting "two-and-a-half" wars (the stance during the 1960s) or "one-and-a-half" wars (the thinking of the 1970s). In the world of the 1980s, the U.S. must be prepared to defend its interests in the Asian/Pacific region (and in the Indian Ocean area) with whatever conventional and nuclear capabilities which may be required.

Other encouraging developments may be noted as well. The five member states of the Association of Southeast Asian Nations (ASEAN), for example, are steadily building their efforts in the areas of political, economic, and bilateral security cooperation. The ASEAN nations individually and ASEAN as an organization are looking outward and in various ways are encouraging the U.S. to demonstrate once again a genuine concern for the preservation and furtherance of mutual American and Asian interests.

The re-examination of U.S. policies and reassessment of the Asian data-base suggested herein, if carried out in conjunction with America's friends in the Asian/Pacific region, hopefully will lead to circumstances in the 1980s in which a book entitled *Found at Last: An Asian Policy* can justifiably be published. Whatever words or slogans may be used to describe such a policy, it must be a policy which reflects the recognition of the United States of the need to arrive at and carry out decisions *collectively* with the various nations in Asia and the Pacific Basin.

>Frank N. Trager
>*Director of Studies*
>*National Strategy Information Center, Inc.*
>and
>*Professor of International Relations*
>*New York University*

Chapter 1

POLITICAL/MILITARY DIMENSIONS OF SECURITY IN SOUTHEAST ASIA

Issues And Questions To Be Addressed: 1

The organizers of the Pattaya conference set forth the following paragraphs—which outlined some of the more specific problems to be addressed, both formally and informally, during the course of the conference—as a guide for conference participants. While conferees in their formal papers, discussion sessions, and committee reports were free to range over a wide range of subject matter and concerns, and not all the suggested questions were answered fully or directly, the "Issues and Questions to be Addressed" served to provide a framework and direction for the deliberations of the conference.

The Indochina Problem and the Soviets in Southeast Asia

The subregion of Southeast Asia constitutes a "strategic crossroad" between the Indian and Pacific Oceans, and between two continents, Asia and Australia, and straddles the vital sea lanes of communication from the Persian Gulf to Japan. Given the geopolitical and economic significance of this area, it is not surprising that the Soviet Union has sought to establish its influence in Southeast Asia, for such involvement might enable the Soviets, among other things, to exert political/military pressure on the surrounding region, threaten the transportation lifelines of the West, Australia,

New Zealand and Japan, and attempt to neutralize the influence and strength of the U.S. Seventh Fleet.

The growing military, political, and economic collaboration between the USSR and Vietnam was formalized in the twenty-five year Treaty of Friendship and Cooperation signed by the two nations in November 1978. Five months earlier Vietnam had joined COMECON, the Soviet-sponsored economic community. Fortified by these concrete manifestations of Moscow's support, Vietnam invaded neighboring Kampuchea in early 1979, installed a pro-Hanoi puppet regime, and continues to deploy occupation troops in both Laos and Kampuchea.

- What are the implications for the Southeast Asian nations, and for the region as a whole, of such developments as: Soviet construction of a long-range communications center at Cam Ranh Bay; regular visits to the base at Cam Ranh Bay by Soviet Bear aircraft, submarines, and surface vessels; construction by the Soviets of a semi-permanent facility at Da Nang, which is used by Soviet ships and aircraft; and the Soviet view—as expressed by a Soviet spokesman to the Japanese foreign ministry—that such Soviet military and naval rights in Vietnam flow inherently from the terms of the Soviet-Vietnamese friendship treaty?
- To what extent is Vietnam—in the manner of Cuba—becoming a surrogate to Soviet policy designs for Southeast Asia and a vehicle for the expansion of Soviet influence in the Asian/Pacific region?
- What are the dangers for Southeast Asian security and stability posed by the prospect of a Soviet-backed communist Indochinese Federation incorporating Laos and Kampuchea and centered on Hanoi?
- What is the impact on the region of the deterioration of Chinese-Vietnamese relations and the recent and possible future military and territorial conflicts between these two nations, including the danger that China's hardline approach toward Hanoi might cause Vietnam to align more closely with the USSR?
- How serious is the immediate and long-range threat to Thailand posed by the Vietnamese posture in Laos and Kampuchea, in view of such possibilities as: a) the danger that Vietnamese divisions in Laos could reach the outskirts of Bangkok very quickly in a Blitzkrieg across the flat Korat Plateau; b) the spillover into Thailand of Vietnamese operations against the remnants of the ousted Pol Pot regime; and c) increased Vietnamese-sponsored infiltration, subver-

Issues and Questions to be Addressed 5

sion, and guerrilla activity in parts of Thailand (and possibly in other Association of Southeast Asian Nations [ASEAN] countries as well)?
- In view of the dangerous, destabilizing events of 1979, how can and how should the inadequate military defenses of the ASEAN countries be bolstered, both individually and collectively?

The People's Republic of China and Southeast Asia: Force for Regional Stability or Instability?

The restructuring in recent years of Chinese policies toward Southeast Asia has eased tensions between the PRC and the ASEAN states, but nations in the subregion still have cause for concern with respect to their neighbor to the north. On the one hand, Peking has de-emphasized revolutionary confrontation and has embarked on the promotion of more cordial state-to-state relations with incumbent ASEAN governments. At the same time, the PRC insists on the retention of separate "state-to-state" and "party-to-party" ties; refuses to relinquish its ideological commitment to encourage and support Maoist revolutionary movements in the ASEAN states; continues to provide varying levels of actual assistance to insurgencies directed against the non-communist governments in Southeast Asia; and consistently demands that the Republic of China on Taiwan be integrated into the Communist Chinese state. Simply by virtue of its geographical size and large population the PRC can exert immense political influence and leverage in Southeast Asia and in the Asian/Pacific region as a whole.

- What are the implications for Southeast Asian security of China's increasingly pragmatic foreign policy approach of the post-Mao years, including such developments as: diplomatic, economic, and military openings to the U.S., Japan, India, and other non-communist states in Asia and the Pacific Basin; support for continued U.S. military presence in the region and for the proposed buildup of the Japanese Self-Defense Forces; formal renunciation of its past claims to be protector of the interests of the overseas Chinese in Southeast Asia; and Chinese support for ASEAN as a useful framework for regional stability?
- What are the current and potential Chinese strategic and theater force capabilities in the Asian/Pacific region?

- In view of China's strong desire to impede the expansion of Soviet influence around its periphery (what it has frequently called "Soviet encirclement"), should the PRC be viewed as a legitimate and valuable counterbalancing force to Soviet presence in the region?
- Given the fact that China's long-range intentions are at this point unclear and indefinite, how concerned should the Southeast Asian nations be about the changeable nature of Chinese foreign policy and the possibility that the current period of moderation in foreign affairs may be followed by a return to radicalism, as has occurred at times in the past?
- Is there cause for concern among the ASEAN states that Peking might deal with them in a manner similar to its "lesson" to Vietnam if they offend the PRC?

A Note on ASEAN

The Association of Southeast Asian Nations (ASEAN) is comprised of five member nations: Indonesia, Malaysia, the Philippines, Singapore, and Thailand. It was founded by the Foreign Ministers of the member states at Bangkok, Thailand on August 9, 1967.

ASEAN emerged from an ongoing effort during the 1960s to create a framework for regional cooperation among the non-communist states of Southeast Asia. Earlier attempts at regional cooperation included the Association of Southeast Asia (ASA), created in 1961 by Malaya, the Philippines, and Thailand; and the short-lived Maphilindo association, established in 1963 by Malaya, the Philippines, and Indonesia.

The ASEAN Ministerial Meeting, composed of the Foreign Ministers of the member states, ordinarily convenes once a year to establish the general policy and direction of the Association. The first summit meeting of the ASEAN heads of state was held in Indonesia in February 1976. Among the documents signed at that time was the Declaration of ASEAN Concord, which seeks to establish a foundation for expanded cooperation in the political, economic, social, and cultural fields and continues to guide the cooperative efforts of the ASEAN states.

THE CONTINUING STRUGGLE IN INDOCHINA:
Editor's Introduction

The tension and hostility between the respective communist parties and governments of Kampuchea and Vietnam—a multidimensioned conflict which reflects ethnic, historical, and political antagonisms between these two states, as well as the competing interests of the People's Republic of China (PRC) and the Soviet Union—erupted into overt warfare at the end of 1978, setting off a chain of developments which, many months later, continues to exert a destabilizing effect on international politics throughout the Southeast Asian subregion.

Earlier in 1978 Vietnam had strengthened and formalized its expanding ties with the Soviet Union by joining COMECON, the Soviet-sponsored economic community, and by signing a twenty-five year Treaty of Friendship and Cooperation with the USSR. During this same period, especially during the Fall of 1978, Vietnamese Prime Minister Pham Van Dong embarked on a campaign of friendly diplomacy throughout Southeast Asia, offering promises of non-intervention and non-interference in the internal affairs of regional states. Then, on December 25—backed by massive Soviet arms aid and Moscow's diplomatic support—Vietnam negated these assurances with a swift and decisive military intervention into neighboring Kampuchea.

On January 10, 1979 the Vietnamese ousted the Khmer Rouge government of Premier Pol Pot[1] and replaced it with a puppet government in Phnom Penh headed by Heng Samrin, a defector from the Pol Pot regime. The "People's Republic of Kampuchea," which was at its inception and remains almost totally dependent on Vietnamese material and political support, was accorded immediate recognition by the governments of Vietnam, the USSR, and a number of Soviet allies, but was unable to achieve a position of credibility from the vantage point of most of the international community.[2]

The growing collaboration between Hanoi and Moscow during 1978 had its counterpart in the increasing support of the People's Republic of China for the Khmer Rouge regime in Kampuchea. Relations between the PRC and Vietnam had been deteriorating for several years; relations worsened when Peking terminated its aid to Vietnam in mid-1978, and declined further with the signing of the Soviet-Vietnamese treaty in November. Now, at least partially in response to the ousting of its ally in Phnom Penh, the PRC on February 17, 1979 launched a punitive invasion at twenty-six points along the 480-mile border to "teach Vietnam a lesson" for its actions in Kampuchea and other aspects of Vietnamese intransigence.[3] The PRC waged a seventeen-day campaign, then announced a unilateral pull-out. The immediate outcome of the incursion was inconclusive: the Chinese, for a variety

---

[1] The Khmer Rouge communist regime, headed by Pol Pot and Khieu Sampan, was installed as the government of Kampuchea after the fall of the anti-communist Lon Nol government in April 1975.

[2] The United States, the PRC, the member nations of the Association of Southeast Asian Nations [ASEAN], and many other states continue to refuse to recognize the Heng Samrin regime.

[3] The Vietnamese military involvement in Kampuchea constituted only one part of Peking's annoyance with Hanoi. Other sources of animosity between the two states include disagreements regarding the division of territorial jurisdiction in the Gulf of Tonkin, disputes with respect to the status of overseas Chinese in Vietnam, and incessant armed provocations and hostile activities in the area of their common border.

of reasons, did not achieve the quick victory they evidently had hoped for, but did inflict extensive damage and significant casualties. In the long run, however, it can be seen that the PRC's punitive invasion did not seriously alter Vietnam's policies in Indochina, secure a withdrawal or even a reduction of Vietnamese forces in Kampuchea, nor significantly slow Hanoi's drive against the remnant Pol Pot forces.

While the Heng Samrin regime gradually established control over most of Kampuchea, Pol Pot and his Khmer Rouge followers retreated to mountain and jungle outposts to conduct a campaign of guerrilla warfare. While the Khmer Rouge have had little success in winning the support of the Kampuchean people, who suffered incalculable misery under Pol Pot's tyrannical rule, a series of Vietnamese-led offensives thus far has failed to completely crush the resistance.[4] Other anti-Vietnamese resistance groups, known collectively as the Khmer Serai ("Free Khmers"),[5] operate as disunited guerrilla bands seeking supporters among the refugees straddling both sides of the Thai/Kampuchean border. Additionally, from September 1979 onwards long-time ruler Prince Norodom Sihanouk has sought to form a new national front with himself as head.

There has been no major reconciliation, however, among Prince Sihanouk, the Khmer Rouge, and the Khmer Serai. Efforts (vigorously supported by the PRC) to form a united front against the Vietnamese-dominated government have been unsuccessful, and the much-discussed "third alternative" to both the Pol Pot/Khieu Sampan regime and the Heng Samrin government has also failed to emerge. The inability of the various forces opposing Heng Samrin and the Vietnamese to join in a common government has left the PRC and the ASEAN states in a position of continuing to support the despotic Pol Pot/Khieu Sampan regime as one of the only practical means of resisting complete Vietnamese dominance in Indochina.

---

[4]Largely under pressure from the PRC, an attempt was made in December 1979 to improve the Khmer Rouge image by shuffling the top positions of command. The premiership was assumed by the president of the ousted regime, Khieu Sampan, while the ill-reputed Pol Pot continued as commander of the armed forces of "Democratic Kampuchea."
[5]One important Khmer Serai group is the Khmer People's National Liberation Front, led by exiled Cambodian politician and former premier Son Sann. Other groups include the "National Movement for the Liberation of Kampuchea" and the "Serika National Liberation Movement."

In response to the events in Indochina, the ASEAN states have conducted an active diplomacy setting forth the position that a political solution—based on a total withdrawal of Vietnamese troops from Kampuchea and the establishment of a "truly independent and neutral" government—must be sought. On a number of occasions—beginning with a special conference of ASEAN's Foreign Ministers held in Bangkok in January 1979—ASEAN has "deplored the armed intervention" against the independence, sovereignty, and territorial integrity of Kampuchea and has reiterated its demand for "the immediate and total withdrawal of all foreign forces."[6]

ASEAN has led efforts in the United Nations to condemn the Vietnamese actions in Kampuchea. A resolution, similar to the ASEAN statement issued on January 13, 1979, was introduced in the Security Council by seven non-aligned nations, but was vetoed by the Soviet Union. In March 1979 the ASEAN governments, acting together, secured non-aligned sponsorship for a draft resolution before the Security Council calling for "the withdrawal of all foreign troops from the areas of conflict in Indochina." This too failed as the result of a Soviet veto.

At their annual meeting held in Bali in June 1979, the Foreign Ministers of the ASEAN states reaffirmed their earlier stance on the Kampuchean situation and also expressed serious concern with respect to the mass exodus of the Vietnamese "boat people," which had gained momentum during the late Spring months. The arrival on their shores of tens of thousands of illegal immigrants and displaced persons, approximately 85% of whom were ethnic Chinese Vietnamese, placed the ASEAN states and other recipient Asian nations under severe economic, social, and political pressures.[7] The mounting refugee crisis led in July to the convening of an international conference in Geneva. At this conference ex-

---

[6]It should be noted that ASEAN also registered disapproval of the Chinese punitive action into Vietnam, for this incursion seemed to confirm the fears of some member states with respect to possible PRC aggressive intentions in Southeast Asia.

[7]It has been estimated that between late 1978 and August 1979 some 293,000 refugees fled Vietnam by boat and reached other countries, but only after many thousands had died enroute. (John C. Donnell, "Vietnam 1979: Year of Calamity," *Asian Survey*, January 1980, Vol. XX, No. 1, p. 27). By the end of 1979, at least 140,000 "boat people" were still to be resettled from various camps in Hong Kong, Malaysia, and Indonesia. (Far Eastern Economic Review, *Asia Yearbook 1980*, Hong Kong, 1980, p. 115).

The Continuing Struggle in Indochina

panded provisions were made by participating countries for the eventual resettlement of the refugees, and Vietnam agreed to enforce a temporary moratorium on the boat departures so that nations providing resettlement could absorb the heavy backlog of refugees already crowding camps in Southeast Asia.

In August 1979 the ASEAN Foreign Ministers met again, this time in Kuala Lumpur, to facilitate adherence to a common set of policies before the convening of the annual session of the UN General Assembly. ASEAN, with support from the PRC, was at the forefront of the drive at the UN in late 1979 to resist Soviet and Vietnamese attempts to seat the Heng Samrin regime. The UN in general has seemed to follow the argument of the Khmer Rouge that the Vietnamese have acted in a colonialist fashion by establishing and sustaining in power a foreign-controlled puppet government in Phnom Penh. On September 21, 1979 the UN General Assembly voted decisively (71 to 35, with 34 abstentions and 12 absentees) to continue to recognize the Khmer Rouge phantom government of "Democratic Kampuchea" as the sole legitimate holder of Kampuchea's UN seat. Additionally, a resolution was passed calling for the withdrawal of "foreign forces" in Kampuchea, along with a ceasefire and the setting up of a democratic government. On November 14, 1979, by an even larger vote (91 to 21, with 29 abstentions), the UN General Assembly approved an ASEAN resolution again calling for the withdrawal of foreign forces.

The ASEAN states have been firm and consistent in their expression of solidarity with fellow member Thailand, which since the outbreak of the current round of conflict in Indochina has faced a direct and potentially serious security challenge on its eastern border with Kampuchea. Thailand has been confronted with the ongoing possibility that the fighting in western Kampuchea might spill over onto Thai territory [as in fact occurred in June 1980] as Vietnam continues its efforts to eradicate the remnants of the Pol Pot regime.[8] Many Khmer Rouge strongholds are situated close to the Thai border, the border has served as a major area of sanctuary and source of supplies for the Pol Pot forces, and the Khmer Rouge

---

[8] At the beginning of 1980, approximately 20,000 to 30,000 Khmer Rouge were still engaged in guerrilla warfare against the Vietnamese and the Heng Samrin regime.

on many occasions have crossed into Thailand (along with refugees from the fighting) so as to escape attacks by Vietnamese troops. Thailand also has encountered enormous difficulties arising from the burdensome presence of more than 300,000 Indochinese refugees on Thai soil.[9]

The devastation laid upon Kampuchea by the Pol Pot regime, the Vietnamese invasion, and the ensuing sustained guerrilla warfare have led to conditions throughout the country which are wretched almost beyond description. As a result of the destruction of the basic infrastructure, the disruption of the rice harvest, and the failure to plant new crops, the country has suffered widespread famine, and the eventual death of close to half of the Khmer people through war, starvation, and/or disease has become a genuine—if horrifying—possibility.[10]

Extensive efforts have been mounted by various international relief organizations to bring food, medical, and other aid to the Kampuchean people. The effectiveness of these programs has been greatly inhibited, however, by Hanoi's insistence that Vietnam and the Heng Samrin regime must control the distribution of relief and that aid must not reach the zones controlled by Pol Pot. Vietnam has repeatedly claimed that humanitarian efforts initiated by the West are a cover for supplying the Khmer Rouge insurgents, and it has seemed to many observers that the Vietnamese hope has been to put an end to the Khmer Rouge by starving out pockets of resistance. By the end of 1979 some aid was reaching the Kampucheans, either by land over the Thai border or through the willingness of some donors to deal directly with the Heng Samrin/Vietnamese authorities. However, the problems of absorption and distribution of the available supplies within Kampuchea have continued, and in the Summer of 1980 (as this book went to press) much of the population was still without sufficient rice, the staple of life in this part of the world.

---

[9]These are "land refugees" who have crossed over the border into Thailand from Laos and Kampuchea. See Far Eastern Economic Review, *Asia Yearbook 1980*, p. 115.

[10]Conditions in Kampuchea render impossible the task of accurately estimating population statistics. However, there is reasonable evidence that millions of Khmer people already have died. The population of Kampuchea in the early 1970s has been estimated at over seven million people; today, according to estimates offered by the Heng Samrin regime, it has dropped to four million. See *Ibid.*, p. 17.

The Continuing Struggle in Indochina

The early months of 1980 seemed to bring a somewhat more conciliatory posture from Hanoi toward its non-communist neighbors in Southeast Asia, and both ASEAN and Vietnam showed some interest with respect to the possible establishment of a "dialogue" on the Kampuchean question. Hanoi during these months offered repeated assurances that Vietnamese troops would not invade Thai territory and that the integrity of the Thai border would be respected. In blatant contradiction to these promises, however, on June 23, 1980 Vietnamese troops stationed in Kampuchea, backed by tanks and artillery, crossed the border for a quick strike into Thailand, mounting attacks on several villages in the Tap Prik subdistrict near the Thai border town of Aranyaprathet. The Vietnamese encountered rather strong resistance from the Thai army and withdrew quickly, but among the costs of this brief military action were a sharp decline in Hanoi's credibility[11] and regalvanized international censure of Vietnam's aggressive behavior in Southeast Asia.

The Vietnamese incursion into Thailand came barely a week after Thailand's initiation (with the cooperation of the UN High Commissioner for Refugees) of a scheme of voluntary repatriation for Khmer refugees in Thai holding centers who wished to return to Kampuchea. Fearing that the plan might facilitate the return to Kampuchea of Khmer Rouge (or Khmer Serai) sympathizers, Hanoi and the Heng Samrin regime lodged violent protests against the scheme, and some observers have theorized that the June 23 attack across the Thai border may have stemmed from a desire to stop the program.[12]

The thirteenth annual meeting of the ASEAN Foreign Ministers took place several days after the Vietnamese attack. At this meeting the ASEAN member states collectively condemned Hanoi for its intransigence in general and the border assault in particular, deplored that Vietnam had failed to respond constructively to calls for a political settlement of the Kampuchean conflict, and reiterated ASEAN's firm support and solidarity with the government and people of Thailand in the preservation of Thai independence, sovereignty, and territorial integrity.[13] The communique ex-

---

[11]The incursion certainly will constitute a setback to ASEAN efforts (carried forth especially by Malaysia and Indonesia) to seek a "dialogue" with Vietnam.
[12]Thailand did order what was referred to as a "temporary" stop to the repatriation.
[13]See *Far Eastern Economic Review*, July 4, 1980 and *Asiaweek*, July 11, 1980.

pressed ASEAN's determination to continue with efforts aimed at a durable political solution to the conflict in Kampuchea and the establishment of "an independent, neutral, and non-aligned Kampuchea, free from foreign interference."[14]

The sense of unity in the face of common adversity and the tough collective stance emanating from the June ASEAN meeting seemed to override suggestions that the Association's members were seriously split on how to achieve peace in Indochina.[15] It is the case that the political and diplomatic interests of the ASEAN states are not always in complete harmony, and the individual countries have at times taken somewhat divergent private positions with respect to issues relevant to the Indochina situation.[16] However, even in the face of certain private misgivings and ambivalences, the ASEAN governments to a remarkable extent have developed and adhered to a common diplomatic position and have showed a great deal of political solidarity and unity of purpose with respect to the issue of Kampuchea.

The extent to which international diplomatic pressure has restrained and will continue to influence Vietnamese actions in Indochina cannot be measured with any precision. What is apparent is that Vietnam thus far has taken no action with respect to the repeated demands from major portions of the international community that its troops be withdrawn from Kampuchea. Furthermore, Vietnam has proceeded systematically to attain a position of de facto dominance over all Indochina. Hanoi has consolidated its power through the presence of 50,000 Vietnamese military and 6,000 civilian officials and party cadres in Laos; at least 200,000 Vietnamese military and 8,000 officials in Kampuchea; and an influx of nonofficial Vietnamese through a kind of colonization and mass resettlement program.[17] Hanoi has initiated a network of

---

[14]*Ibid.*

[15]See *Asiaweek*, July 11, 1980.

[16]For geographical and other reasons, fears regarding Vietnamese expansionism have not been held with equal intensity by all ASEAN members. Thailand obviously has been the state most directly affected and threatened by Vietnam's actions in Kampuchea. While Thailand and Singapore have taken the general view that an expansionist Vietnam, backed by the Soviet Union, constitutes the most dangerous (and immediate) threat to Southeast Asia, many persons in Indonesia and Malaysia place more emphasis on the long-term dangers posed by the People's Republic of China, and it is felt by some that a strong Vietnam might impede the extension of Chinese influence in the Southeast Asia subregion.

[17]Justus M. van der Kroef, "The Indochina Tangle: The Elements of Conflict and Compromise," *Asian Survey*, May 1980, Vol. XX, No. 5, p. 479.

treaties which bind the three Indochinese countries in a triangular fashion under the aegis of Vietnam,[18] and the Hanoi media has referred repeatedly to the existence of a "unity bloc" among the three nations of Indochina. Vietnamese Foreign Minister Nguyen Co Thach in May 1980 openly declared in Bangkok that the solidarity of Vietnam, Laos, and Kampuchea is unbreakable.[19]

The extended fighting in Kampuchea, pressures flowing from the enmity of the PRC, and continuing production problems (especially in the realm of agriculture) have combined to render Vietnam ever more dependent on diplomatic, military, and economic aid from the Soviet Union, which in turn has increased Soviet influence in Indochina. Even fortified with this massive influx of Soviet assistance, however, the Vietnamese—after a costly and draining pacification campaign of many months' duration—have been unable to eliminate all pockets of Khmer Rouge (and limited Khmer Serai) resistance. Thus, while the resistance does not pose a major political or military threat to the Vietnamese-maintained government in Phnom Penh, the prospect for continued fighting and destruction in Kampuchea is high.

Reports in mid-1980 of an intensive buildup of Vietnamese and Vietnamese-led troops along the Thai border have caused concern with respect to the possibility of further Vietnamese incursions into Thailand and/or the outbreak of border clashes which may spill over onto Thai territory. In the face of continuing Sino-Vietnamese tension and animosity, the PRC has threatened occasionally to inflict a "second punishment" on Vietnam if Hanoi fails to "learn its lesson." In this connection, concern has been expressed about the possibility of a Soviet military response if the contingency of a second Sino-Vietnamese clash should occur. It can only be hoped that all parties directly and indirectly involved in the discord in Indochina will exercise restraint and avoid any actions and provocations which might lead to the further intensification and/or expansion of an already highly dangerous and extraordinarily costly conflict.

---

[18]Vietnam and Laos signed a "Friendship and Cooperation" Treaty in July 1977, Vietnam concluded a treaty of "Peace, Friendship, and Cooperation" in February 1979 with the newly-installed Heng Samrin government in Phnom Penh, and Laos signed a "Cooperation Agreement" with the Heng Samrin regime in March 1979.
[19]*Far Eastern Economic Review*, June 20, 1980.

Addresses

The Honorable Lt. General Ali Moertopo,
Minister of Information, Jakarta, Indonesia

His Excellency Dr. Upadit Pachariyangkun,
Minister of Foreign Affairs [at time of conference], Bangkok, Thailand

The Honorable Dr. Thanat Khoman,
former Minister of Foreign Affairs [appointed Deputy Prime Minister in March 1980], Bangkok, Thailand

INTERNATIONAL POLITICS IN ASIA AND THE PACIFIC: COMPLEXITIES AND UNCERTAINTIES

Ali Moertopo

An increasing complexity of forces is at work today in the Asian/Pacific region. With the possible exception of the situation on the Korean peninsula, where the military danger is readily apparent, security challenges in East Asia tend by nature to be more subtle and complex than is the case in the European theater. An examination of security issues in the Pacific Basin area must take into consideration social, cultural, and economic factors as well as geopolitical and military concerns.

The world's major individual powers—the U.S., the Soviet Union, the People's Republic of China (PRC), and Japan—are geographically located in the Pacific Basin region, and developments in East Asia are greatly influenced by the interactions among these powers. For this reason, over the past several years the focus of international politics in important respects increasingly has shifted toward this region. The four major powers are in the process of making gradual changes in their national and international outlooks, and of establishing their new positions in the altered international environment. In some instances, adjustments have been forced by the perception of new realities; in other cases, countries have made adjustments so as to make the best use of new opportunities created by the changing international climate.

International politics in this region currently is in a state of flux, and the nature of the interactions among the four powers—let alone their likely outcome—is not entirely clear. Although the ongoing developments might lead to new alliances which could help promote regional stability in the coming decade, the possibility cannot be eliminated that new or intensified antagonisms will develop, creating serious instability in the area. The greatest source of uncertainty in the Asian/Pacific region is the Sino-Soviet rivalry, which generates a multi-dimensioned threat to peace and stability in East Asia. There are no signs that this rivalry will be resolved in the immediate future.

World War II not only left unsettled many questions concerning the territorial borders of nation-states in the Pacific Basin area, but in fact added new sources of conflict to already existing territorial disputes. In Northeast Asia, disputes exist between the Soviet Union and Japan over the "Four Northern Islands" occupied by the USSR; between the Soviet Union and the PRC in connection with their long border; and over the territorial waters adjacent to Japan, Korea, the PRC, and the Republic of China on Taiwan. In Southeast Asia, the borderlines separating the Indochinese states constitute a continuous source of conflict. A large area of the South China Sea is comprised of waters involved in territorial disputes, and the Paracel and Spratley Islands are objects of contention. While concerns of sovereignty and security are the main motivating factors behind such struggles, conflicts in some instances have been intensified by the increasing economic interest in sea-bed resources. In one way or another, all these disputes involve one or more of the major powers. The major powers may become involved on their own accord, or at the invitation of the conflicting parties.

Economic growth in the Asian/Pacific region has maintained its momentum over the past ten years. Paradoxically, however, this degree of success has also produced new problems. In the developing countries of East Asia, internal instabilities may arise if political and social developments lag behind economic achievements. In the developed parts of the region, structural adjustments within the industrialized economies and new directions in economic management will be required so as to mitigate tensions arising from economic interactions among the nations in the area. The growing economic interdependence among countries in the region involves a number of forces; some bring these nations closer together, while others tend to create conflicts between or among them.

The recent conflict in Indochina illustrates the complexity of forces underlying the developments in the Pacific Basin region. The invasion of Vietnam into Kampuchea was a concrete manifestation of what many had predicted: increased polarization in Southeast Asia, with the Association of Southeast Asian Nations (ASEAN) on one side and Vietnam/Laos/Kampuchea on the other. ASEAN's responses to the Indochina conflict are best understood as an effort to contain the possible expansion of the Sino-Soviet rivalry further into Southeast Asia. Because observers tended to expect ASEAN to take a clear-cut stand, the Association's initial signals were not well understood, and its neutrality was puzzling to many. It should be recognized that ASEAN sent signals to both the PRC and Vietnam, a fact which Hanoi did not seem to appreciate. Implicit in ASEAN's attitude was a lack of encouragement for increased Chinese involvement in Southeast Asia, for the PRC is still an unpredictable factor in regional international politics.

The Indochina conflict points to the dangers which exist in the present power structure, and an end to the dispute is not yet in sight. These facts should constitute a powerful rationale and stimulus for nations in the region to take a more active and positive role in the re-establishment and maintenance of regional stability.

The United States in a variety of ways can contribute to the creation of a political/strategic configuration more stable than the currently prevailing situation. It is necessary that the U.S. watch very carefully the moves of the Soviet Union in the Asian/Pacific region. At the same time, the U.S. should use its influence with Peking as a rein on the PRC's actions in the area. The "China Card" as played by the U.S. is not without its possible pitfalls, especially in view of the various constraints which now characterize the American military role and posture in the region. Because of these constraints, the U.S., for example, may find it difficult or impossible to directly influence the course of events in Indochina.

Whether this is a gap which Japan can fill is a question which naturally arises. While the Western world seems bent on virtually isolating Vietnam, Japan has attempted to keep open its channels to Hanoi. The possibility that Japan might use these channels effectively and constructively provides a testing ground for Tokyo in taking a more active political role internationally, and the world will be watching closely Japan's handling of this situation. Japan's experiences in mastering this new role may at times prove cumbersome.

In this uncertain environment, there exist opportunities for the medium-sized powers in the region to assume a more active part in and greater responsibility for the nurturing and strengthening of regional stability. ASEAN in important respects has already become an effective force in dealing with the changing international climate. Along with the ASEAN states, the Republic of Korea, Canada, and other nations cannot ignore the challenge. Closer cooperation among these nations will constitute a vital building block toward the establishment of new foundations for security and prosperity in the Pacific Basin region.

THE STRATEGIC OUTLOOK FOR THAILAND IN THE 1980s

Upadit Pachariyangkun

Any discussion of the strategic outlook for Thailand in the 1980s must proceed from an identification of both the internal and international security interests of the nation and an attempt to perceive likely future trends.

I. Internal Security Interests

In the next decade, the internal security interests of Thailand will remain focused on fostering the unity of the Thai people, enhancing the stability of Thailand's government, and promoting the economic and social development of the country. We are determined to preserve our national institutions, which for centuries have successfully helped maintain Thailand's national independence and unity. Differences of opinion with respect to both political and economic problems have been openly discussed and peacefully resolved through democratic means. The Thai government also has dedicated itself to the task of promoting social justice and ensuring a fairer and more equitable distribution of wealth among the Thai people.

All the above factors have played a major role in contributing to the current political stability in Thailand. They also demonstrate the collective national will of the Thai to meet the new challenges of the next decade as a sovereign and independent nation and to build a strong economy based on the free enterprise system. Despite the country's existing economic problems—most of which were caused by events beyond its control—we have reason to believe that Thailand will be able to maintain a steady pace of economic growth and social and industrial development in the next decade. There exists much confidence that the exploitation of natural gas which will begin in 1981 in the Gulf of Thailand and the completion of various economic development projects will markedly contribute to the improvement of Thailand's economy and consequently to the living conditions of the Thai people in the 1980s.

Another aspect of internal security which is of great importance is the threat of subversion and terrorism posed by the various communist party factions operating in Thailand. Thailand has managed to cope with the communist activities for the last decade and will continue its ability to do so in the future. In the southern part of the nation Thailand has successfully cooperated with Malaysia in suppressing communist subversive and terrorist activities. Subversion and terrorism elsewhere in the nation are on the decline, a result of the Thai government's sustained economic and social development programs which have brought improved living conditions and social justice to an increasingly wide segment of the Thai population and have enabled the government to deal with the problem from a position of strength.

II. International Security Interests

Although it is true that events throughout the Asian/Pacific region and in the world at large in one way or another will have repercussions on Thailand's strategic situation in the 1980s, the country will be most directly and strongly affected by occurrences and changing conditions in the Southeast Asian subregion. A number of the factors likely to have a significant bearing on questions of peace and stability in Southeast Asia in the next decade are outlined in the following sections.

The Situation in Kampuchea

It is the tendency of many observers to view the current situation in Kampuchea as a problem of lesser magnitude than was the lengthy war in Vietnam which preceded it. While this may in fact be the case, one should not overlook the likely significant long-term repercussions of the Kampuchean conflict on the future strategic outlooks of and relations among the Southeast Asian nations.

By violating the cardinal principles of non-interference and respect for the sovereignty and territorial integrity of other nations, armed Vietnamese intervention in Kampuchea has created a dangerous precedent in Southeast Asia. The precarious regional political balance which seemed within reach before these events took place once again has been undermined, creating a situation in which it is even more difficult to find a new equilibrium which will be acceptable to all concerned. Moreover, the rivalry and differences among the socialist states themselves have created another hotbed of tension which is fraught with danger and could engulf other states in the region in a larger conflagration. Hundreds of thousands of Kampuchean people, particularly a whole generation of children, have already perished as a result of famine and starvation caused by the continued fighting in their country.

Furthermore, the events in Kampuchea may have serious consequences for the global strategic environment. The increasing military presence of the two superpowers already constitutes a problem for the Asian/Pacific region. The fact that one of these two superpowers, the Soviet Union, has now gained a firmer foothold over (if not complete control of) some of the naval bases in Indochina has heightened the strategic tensions in the area. For this reason, and others cited above, the outcome of the Kampuchean situation will have a far-reaching impact on the future security of Asia and the Pacific Basin as a whole. This fact takes on even more significance when one considers the importance of Southeast Asia, by virtue of its unique geopolitical location, as a vital strategic and trade link between East and West Asia.

Thailand has been the country most directly affected by the events in Kampuchea, finding itself faced with a massive influx of Kampuchean refugees and the possibility of a spill-over of the fighting into Thai territory. Despite this reality, Thailand to date has adhered firmly to a policy of restraint and non-involvement while attempting to find just and peaceful means to bring about the cessation of hostilities in Kampuchea. Thailand's effort in concert with the other Association of Southeast Asian Nations (ASEAN) members at the United Nations General Assembly can be seen as an important part of this process.

Through the U.N. General Assembly resolution on Kampuchea, the five ASEAN nations have called for the cessation of all hostilities in Kampuchea, the withdrawal of all foreign forces from that country, and an opportunity for the Kampuchean people to choose democratically their own government, without outside interference, subversion, and coercion. Many obstacles remain and the problem is far from being resolved. It is hoped, however, that ASEAN's initiative at the U.N. has placed the Kampuchean problem into its proper perspective and context so as to pave the way for an eventual peaceful settlement of the conflict. The United Nations has expressed its desire for such a solution. It now remains the responsibility of the parties directly involved to bring about the realization of a settlement.

The Sino-Soviet Conflict

The Sino-Soviet conflict is a factor which will continue to figure significantly in the shaping of events in Southeast Asia in the next decade. The conflicting interests of the two major communist countries have found testing grounds in many areas of the world, particularly in Kampuchea and Indochina as a whole. The Vietnamese invasion of Kampuchea and the ensuing Chinese military action against Vietnam have plunged the Southeast Asian region deeper into a gravely dangerous situation, the final consequences of which are not yet known.

In its attempt to keep the Chinese off-balance, the Soviet Union has found its closest friend in Vietnam. The price for the Soviet Union is the continued provision of massive aid to Hanoi. As a result of these developments, Vietnam and Laos seem to have

The Strategic Outlook for Thailand

been drawn more deeply into the Soviet sphere of influence, a circumstance which may one day prove to be in conflict with the fiercely independent nature of the Vietnamese, a characteristic previously demonstrated during the Vietnam war. The events in Kampuchea have driven the PRC even further apart from Vietnam and Laos and intensified the tensions along its borders with these countries. The Chinese must also find it costly to give their support to the dissident group in Kampuchea.

With these developments in mind, the ASEAN nations in their U.N. resolution have called upon all states to refrain from acts or threats of aggression and all forms of interference in the internal affairs of states in Southeast Asia. In other words, while further attempts should be made to persuade Vietnam to accept some form of a political settlement of the Kampuchean problem, the ASEAN nations believe that a parallel effort should also be undertaken to protect the sovereignty and security of all Southeast Asian states, both communist and non-communist.

Indochinese Refugees and Displaced Persons

Refugees and displaced persons from the Indochinese states will remain a problem for other countries in the region for a considerable period of time. Although the mass exodus of these unfortunate people may subside in the near future, the problems incurred by the countries of first refuge will become more acute during the coming decade. Thailand has had experiences in the past with Indochinese refugees, particularly during the period of French colonial rule, and is well aware of the economic, social, political, and security burdens that the problem has entailed. Unless close international cooperation continues into the 1980s, the problem of the Indochinese refugees and displaced persons will become a major source of destabilization in the region as well as a source of political friction between the states of Indochina and the ASEAN nations.

An entire generation of Kampuchean young people already may have died in the fighting or from starvation and disease, and it is estimated that at least one-fourth of the total Kampuchean population will eventually find their way to Thailand to seek food, medicine, and shelter. The people of Kampuchea are now threatened with extinction. The burden for Thailand and the international community in general will become far too great if the situation in Kampuchea continues unabated. Therefore it is necessary that the international community as a top priority should work toward the cessation of hostilities in Kampuchea so that most, if not all, Kampucheans will be able to return to their homeland to begin a new life.

It has been the objective of Thailand to make useful contributions toward the cessation of hostilities, the defusion of tensions, and the search for political and humanitarian solutions for the situation in Kampuchea, and Thailand will continue to devote its energies to this end. Since the Kampuchean problem is a common challenge not only for the Southeast Asian states but for all humanity, the Thai government is convinced that individual and collective efforts at the United Nations provide the best possible avenue toward lasting peace and stability in the region. For this reason, a U.N. fact-finding mission has been asked to come to Thailand to evaluate the potentially explosive situation resulting from the continuing massive influx of Kampuchean refugees and the possibility of a spillover of the fighting into Thai territory along the eastern border.

This was only one of many steps undertaken which hopefully will lead eventually to the restoration of peace and stability in the region. Long-range planning and sustained efforts to focus the world's attention on the problem are necessary. The U.N. not only should maintain but in fact should intensify its active role, both with respect to monitoring the peace along the Thai-Kampuchean border and channelling effective relief to the masses of suffering Kampucheans in the border area. For these purposes, it may be necessary to establish a permanent U.N. observation unit in the area of the border.

Military Strategy

Thailand will enter the 1980s with a greater degree of confidence, and with better preparation for its self-defense and for the preservation of the country's sovereignty, territorial integrity, and chosen way of life. Thailand has no intention to attempt to turn ASEAN into a military alliance. Nevertheless, bilateral military cooperation between ASEAN member states has already been a

The Strategic Outlook for Thailand

reality for some time, and the future course and possible intensification of such cooperative efforts will depend on the further development of conditions and requirements in the Southeast Asian region.

The Role of the United States and Japan

Japan within the last few years has begun to play a more active and constructive role in regional and world politics. It has become more conscious of its ability to influence events in the region, and has appeared to become more responsible as an economic power. The Thai leadership welcomes Japan's new attitude and foresees an even greater Japanese role in Southeast Asia and the world arena in the 1980s. Leaders in Thailand are also encouraged by assurances that the U.S. is and will remain an Asian and Pacific power, and also by the fact that the U.S. has begun to revive its active interest in the affairs of the region, particularly in connection with the events in Kampuchea and the problem of the Indochinese refugees and displaced persons.

Closer relations and understanding between the U.S. and Japan will serve as constructive and stabilizing factors in world politics. In view of the manner in which events are unfolding in various parts of the world, particularly in the Middle East, the U.S. and Japan in the 1980s may be more active in international politics than was the case in the years after 1975. As a great power with global interests, the U.S. cannot afford to be overly selective in its reactions and responses to problems affecting the peace and stability of the world at large. While it may be unrealistic to expect the U.S. to reassume the once extensive responsibilities which it undertook during the 1950s and 1960s, a stronger and more decisive U.S. in the 1980s will be welcomed by the international community. Japan, with its ever increasing economic power, also will be compelled by circumstances to play a more meaningful role in world politics.

The Increasing Importance of ASEAN

The ASEAN countries in the 1980s increasingly will become a constructive stabilizing factor for the Southeast Asian subregion and the world at large. ASEAN's efforts in the areas of economic and social cooperation will begin to yield fruitful and tangible results for the peoples in its area, and even closer cooperation in the fields of common interest among the ASEAN states can be expected. ASEAN cooperation with other countries will continue to expand worldwide. The ASEAN countries will continue to promote closer economic cooperation and good relations with the other states in the region. Above all, the ASEAN nations will continue to attempt to avoid a confrontation with the communist states of Indochina.

Although in the immediate future it can be expected that relations between ASEAN and the Indochinese states will continue to be characterized by suspicion and distrust, all the ASEAN states still maintain regular contacts with Vietnam. It is also within the realm of possibility that once a satisfactory solution to the Kampuchean problem is found, all the states in the region might dedicate themselves to the task of establishing a Zone of Peace, Freedom, and Neutrality in Southeast Asia which will allow each nation to preserve its chosen way of life and to co-exist with other states, free from external interference and coercion.

CONFLICT AND COOPERATION IN SOUTHEAST ASIA: THE NEW CHAPTER

Thanat Khoman

The current chapter in the security situation prevailing in the Asian/Pacific area began in 1969 with former President Richard M. Nixon's enunciation at Guam of his doctrine of U.S. disengagement from mainland Southeast Asia. The changed situation was confirmed by the decision of the United States to extricate itself from the Vietnam war by concluding the Paris ceasefire agreement with North Vietnam. This separate peace accord opened the way for the conquest of South Vietnam by the North and the overthrow of the Lon Nol regime in Kampuchea. The power vacuum which resulted from these developments was extended to the wider Asian/Pacific region by President Jimmy Carter's announced intention to withdraw U.S. troops from the Republic of Korea, a course of action which was subsequently postponed.

The policy shift on the part of the U.S. and the communist successes in Vietnam and Kampuchea upset the balance of power and created uncertainties in the entire region. These developments also heralded new expansionist moves by the victorious belligerents in Southeast Asia and an increased Soviet military presence on land and sea in both Northeast and Southeast Asia.

The Vietnamese leaders in Hanoi turned almost immediately to the task of implementing the cherished national project envisioned and left in legacy by Ho Chi Min. First, without difficulty they brought into their orbit the poorly organized Laotians, whose new communist leaders have many affinities and ethnic or family ties with the Hanoi leadership. When the Vietnamese moved on to Kampuchea, however, a number of obstacles began to emerge. In contrast to the situation in Laos, the Kampuchean leaders did not share personal ties with the leaders in Hanoi. Even more importantly, the Kampuchean leadership was not isolated, but was in fact receiving the support and assistance of the People's Republic of China (PRC), which shares with the Kampucheans an abhorrence for the prospect of Vietnamese hegemonistic dominance over all Indochina.

Vietnam, hoping to cow the Chinese into indifference, entered into partnership with the East European economic grouping of COMECON and then signed a twenty-five year Treaty of Friendship with the Soviet Union. Hanoi by these actions made it clear that Vietnam had chosen sides in the Sino-Soviet dispute, with the implied possibility of Vietnamese support and assistance for Soviet efforts to encircle the PRC. These developments undoubtedly reinforced the conviction of the Chinese that Vietnam is now a lost cause and should be viewed as an adversary rather than as a brother Marxist state. This recognition in turn led Peking to offer stronger support to the Pol Pot regime in Kampuchea.

Vietnam also launched sustained military operations in Kampuchea, which led to the ousting of the Pol Pot regime and its replacement with Hanoi's own protege, Heng Samrin.* With logistic and financial assistance from the Soviets, Vietnam then took actions designed to eliminate any resistance to its control. Such measures occasioned widespread disturbances in that embattled land, forcing its suffering inhabitants to flee from the fighting

---

* See this Chapter's "The Continuing Struggle in Indochina: Editor's Introduction," pp. 9 to 17, for a brief chronological account of the Vietnamese actions in Kampuchea and the conflict between Vietnam and the PRC.

which endangered their lives and the acute shortage of food which resulted from the conflict. In the belief that people in the rural areas support the ousted Pol Pot regime, a supposition which is far from substantiated, the new Kampuchean leaders and their patrons used the threat of famine and starvation to compel their compatriots to leave their homeland, thus in theory cutting off support to the rival group.

As a result of this machiavellian policy, Thailand is now being flooded with refugees in search of shelter and survival. Additionally, some fifteen divisions of Vietnamese forces have closed in near the Thai border, occasionally making incursions and engaging in the hot pursuit of Pol Pot guerrillas into Thai territory, committing depredation and destruction along the way.

The growing tensions between the PRC and Vietnam erupted when Hanoi began to expel Vietnamese people of Chinese origin. The Chinese then initiated a military conflict which was intended—according to Peking—to teach Hanoi a "lesson" in response to the unbecoming Vietnamese behavior in Kampuchea and toward the PRC. To counter the Chinese actions, Vietnam entered even more deeply into cooperation with the USSR, allowing its new ally to use military facilities on Vietnamese territory, particularly at the American-built air base at Danang and naval base at Cam Ranh Bay.

The foregoing account demonstrates that the security situation now prevailing in Southeast Asia is fairly complex, with local, regional, and global components. The communist regime in Vietnam, in nurturing its hegemonistic ambitions, seeks to serve as a substitute for the erstwhile colonial rule of France by placing the former French colonies and protectorates under its dominance in a Vietnamese-led Indochina Federation. The first step toward this goal, the absorption of Laos, was accomplished without bloodshed. The subsequent moves to take over Kampuchea, however, have raised many dimensions of conflict which show no sign of early resolution and which have significant regional and perhaps even global ramifications.

The Chinese military intervention in February 1979 expanded the warfare in Indochina from a local to a regional conflict. If Vietnam should fail to complete its undertaking in a fairly short period of time, other complications are likely to result. On the other hand, if Vietnam becomes overly impatient and attempts to overcome resistance to its hegemonic rule in Indochina by spilling over the fighting into areas beyond the Kampuchean border, Hanoi may touch off other interventions which may prove even more costly than the Chinese actions.

The fact that hostile major powers are now backing antagonistic clients in Southeast Asia does not make the prospects for stability and security in the area very encouraging. However, while a deterioration of the situation into one of direct confrontation or conflict cannot be ruled out entirely, such a development does not seem probable.

It should be noted that, in recent times, varying sorts of security challenges have come into play. While military power, both nuclear and conventional, remains of utmost importance, the security of a nation or a group of states can be affected gravely by many different elements. Terrorism, or threats to oil supplies, or a combination of the two, for example, may render an awesome arsenal of the most destructive weapons ineffectual or useless. In such unpredictable contingencies, even the most powerful nations may find themselves shackled by their own might and held in a situation of blackmail by mere fanatic weaklings.

While the seizure of the hostages at the American Embassy in Teheran probably represents an isolated case, it is difficult to deny that this development is related psychologically to the post-Vietnam posture adopted by the United States. Washington's sometimes loud proclamations of policies of withdrawal and disengagement have given the impression, painful to its friends around the world, that the U.S. wishes to back away from its role as a global power and maintain itself modestly as "Fortress America."

In this connection, [former] Israeli Defense Minister Ezer Weizman remarked to [former] Secretary of State Cyrus Vance that the U.S. may be losing its power throughout the world, and America's mighty aircraft carriers and other impressive weapons will have little meaning if the U.S. is unable or unwilling to use them. (This statement prompted a strong reaction from the U.S. government, which termed the comment "unfriendly.") A similar opinion was voiced by columnist William Pfaff in the European *Herald Tribune*: ". . . A great power, by traditional definition, is one whose security is not contingent. By that definition, the U.S. is not today a great power. The reason is not military weakness. . . ." U.S. presidential candidate Ronald Reagan has wryly observed that the Iranian terrorists would not dare do to the Soviet Embassy what they have done to the Americans in Teheran. It seems to be the case that great powers today feel compelled to observe considerable restraint in their conduct of international affairs. Even the Soviet Union shows some sign of restraint, for if it did not, Moscow might seek to gain advantages for itself everywhere, as it has in Angola, Mozambique, Afghanistan, and Vietnam.

These recent events and developments suggest that the notion of security is in need of revision, particularly for those nations which still believe in the concepts of international law and civilized international practices. However, for the world in general, and for the Asian/Pacific region and the subregion of Southeast Asia in particular, the concept of cooperation among interested parties still retains a great deal of validity, as has been demonstrated by the ASEAN countries. Rather than relying on outside powers whose interests may be divergent, nations sharing similar concerns and goals can join together in a cooperative grouping to strengthen and sharpen their effectiveness in protecting themselves against external interferences. The validity of this contention has been tested and proven in recent years by the ASEAN nations, which have been left to themselves to fend off the threats coming from militant and aggressively hostile neighbors.

Now that the first dangers have been warded off, a system of security should be evolving in Southeast Asia which will take a pragmatic approach toward the establishment of a de facto balance of power favorable to stability. Such an approach cannot guarantee absolutely the preservation of peace; but in this unsettled region where so many divergent forces are at work, it may prevent those forces from heading toward a collision course. As matters now stand, reliance must be placed not on a single world policeman, but rather on the stabilizing forces which emerge from the mutually neutralizing balance of opposing sides.

Conference Papers

Mr. Lim Joo-Jock,
Member of Research Staff, Institute of Southeast Asian Studies, Singapore

Mr. Jusuf Wanandi,
Head of Department of Public Affairs, Center for Strategic and International Studies, Jakarta, Indonesia

THE INDOCHINA SITUATION AND THE SUPERPOWERS IN SOUTHEAST ASIA

Lim Joo-Jock

This paper is an analysis of the situation in Indochina, the role of the major powers in Southeast Asia, and the impact of the growing Soviet naval presence on the strategic environment of the Southeast Asian subregion at the end of the 1970s and the beginning of the 1980s.

Some Features of the Indochina Situation

The present Indochina[1] situation reflects the recurrence of historical patterns and the reassertion of geography as factors of extreme importance in contemporary Southeast Asian affairs. From one point of view, the conflict in Indochina can be seen as a replay of old ethnic and cultural animosities, with the new ideologies sub-

---
[1] The term "Indochina" is used here for sake of convenience and denotes the area which was once French Indochina and is presently comprised of Vietnam, Laos, and Kampuchea. The use of the term in this manner should not in any way imply that Indochina is seen as a single *political* entity.

merged (at least for the time being). With respect to geography, the geographical interpenetration of land and sea in Southeast Asia provides a filter between two oceans, the Indian and the Pacific. If the subregion as a whole were to develop a stance hostile to Japan and the West, direct access between these two important if not vital oceanic basins might be barred.

There is no need here to recapitulate the details of the recent events in Indochina; an overview will suffice. The main components include the conflict between Vietnam and the People's Republic of China (soon after Hanoi's victory in South Vietnam) over their border and the Paracel and Spratley Islands, Vietnam's insistence on independent policies[2], the signing by the Soviet Union and Vietnam in November 1978 of a twenty-five year Treaty of Friendship and Cooperation, the quarrel between Vietnam and the PRC with respect to the ethnic Chinese in Vietnam, the movement of sea-borne and land refugees and the ensuing repercussions, and the development of the wars in Kampuchea and on the Sino-Vietnamese border. These events and developments have led to many political and strategic consequences with an impact reaching far beyond Indochina itself.

In its Kampuchean campaign of early 1979 Vietnam once again demonstrated its high skill in the art of war. Vietnam (like Sparta) can outfight most if not all other states in its region, with a military capability sharply honed in wars fought in varying terrain and against such diverse foes as the world's most technologically advanced power (the United States), determined guerrillas, and the massive PRC People's Liberation Army. Well-armed and confident, Vietnam carries out expansionist policies backed by the most skillful diplomacy, as did Prussia in times past. The Vietnamese not only have perfected the techniques of mounting a people's guerrilla war; in addition, they appear to be more effective than were the Americans in suppressing guerrilla outbreaks which are against their interests. In Kampuchea the Vietnamese also have demonstrated their mastery of Soviet-style mechanized war, including (with Soviet technical and material help and the use of U.S.-trained personnel and -manufactured equipment, such as

---

[2] After its victory in South Vietnam Hanoi at first tried to follow a policy of equidistance between Moscow and Peking. It soon became clear, however, that Hanoi had rejected the Chinese model of development. The Hanoi government continued to insist on maintenance of an independent foreign policy, especially toward Kampuchea.

The Indochina Situation

the Hercules C-130 transport) the supply of forward columns by air and the rapid multiple crossing of rivers by large columns of troops with heavy equipment.

The type of thoroughness—or ruthlessness, if you like—shown by the Vietnamese was not characteristic of the anti-guerrilla sweeps conducted by the U.S. in Vietnam. The thoroughness executed by the Vietnamese in Kampuchea has not excluded massacres, nor the strategic use of mass starvation to kill off a population suspected of supporting a guerrilla force, so as to drain off, in Mao's phrase, the water in which the (guerrilla) fish swim. French and American sources separately have alleged that Vietnam is siphoning off even the meager international food aid reaching Kampuchea and that rice-fields have been mined to prevent the Kampucheans from ploughing for the next season.

If the Vietnamese invasion of Kampuchea and the accompanying famine and disease ultimately result, among other things, in the extinction of the Kampuchean people and culture, the Vietnamese then will carry the distinction of having obliterated two ancient indigenous civilizations of Southeast Asia in their march south from the Tonkin delta. After a prolonged struggle, the southward-moving Vietnamese exterminated the Malay kingdom of Champa by the close of the fifteenth century and took over the kingdom's rice fields; now, the same fate may befall Kampuchea, another historical arch-rival. Wars in Southeast Asia traditionally have been fought with a savagery, with the hand-to-hand combat between elephant-riding Burmese and Thai kings and princes constituting the only sign of chivalry. The Burmese, Thais, and Khmers, however, did not exterminate whole nations; by contrast, the victors viewed the men and women, farmers and artisans as a valuable resource and brought back prisoners to strengthen the population of their own countries. To cite another example, the Tang movement into south China resulted in the Sinicization of indigenous peoples. It appears that the habit of killing off rather than assimilating is a trait peculiar to Vietnamese expansionism.

Factors Aiding the Anti-Vietnamese Kampuchean Resistance

Even with their military successes—and in spite of Soviet aid estimated to reach about U.S. $2 million per day—the Vietnamese have not managed to break the back of the organized Kampuchean resistance. The situation once again reflects the continuing influence of topography, the seasons, and patterns of vegetation on the course of conflict. The Kampuchean resistance still is lodged in the mountains and forests and, judging from Pol Pot broadcasts, along the swamps fringing the Mekong River and its tributaries.[3] As was always the case in past wars in continental Southeast Asia, action is stilled during the rainy seasons, according the anti-Vietnamese forces an opportunity to regroup and gather strength.

Insurgencies and movements of resistance have a better chance of success if they can be supplied by sea or through a friendly rear-area, and the Kampuchean resistance may have access to both land and sea resupply lines. The Vietnamese communists during the Vietnam war had both advantages: overland, by the Ho Chi Minh Trail from North to South Vietnam and by rail from the PRC to North Vietnam; and by sea, from Soviet convoys to Haiphong. When Yugoslavia ceased aiding the Greek communist revolt in the 1950s, the insurgency collapsed. The same occurred in the case of the Kurdish revolt in Iraq when Iran stopped granting sanctuary.

Supplies for the Kampuchean resistance may have been infiltrated across the difficult-to-police Thai/Kampuchean border, but they may also have come by sea. As it has thoughout history, the sea provides an avenue for succor and revictualization for all protagonists; as such it ultimately may be a major factor in determining the outcome of the situation in Indochina.

During the Vietnam war the very best of U.S. naval and air surveillance techniques and a large force were required to throttle off the coast-hugging Vietnamese movement by small boats of supplies from North to South. Vietnam's small navy now is stretched from the Gulf of Tonkin to the Gulf of Thailand and in patrols and logistics is extended to its limits in the Spratley archipelago. Under these circumstances, it can be questioned whether Vietnam's navy can expect to cut off all supplies being infiltrated by fishing boats, or even larger vessels, onto the Kampuchean coast. It is not difficult to visualize the PRC sending such

---

[3] It must be noted, however, that the three Cardamom ranges in south and southwest Kampuchea are not entirely rugged. Though there exist many ravines, steep cliffs, and limestone outcrops, there also are considerable tracts of relatively gentle gradient where tanks can operate.

supplies, escorting its boat convoys with units from China's very large force of conventionally-powered submarines. In the absence of this possibility, it would be difficult to understand why the Soviet Union has given to Vietnam two Petya-class anti-submarine frigates equipped with the most modern detection devices and anti-submarine undersea missiles (which have been used by the Indian navy with deadly effect against Pakistani submarines). It would seem that missile gunboats and supply vessels would be more urgently needed and more competently used by the Vietnamese at this stage.

About 200,000 Vietnamese troops are entangled in Kampuchea and up to 60,000 Vietnamese troops are engaged in garrison duties in Laos. The troops in Laos soon may have to face a renewed Meo, or Hmong*, and Lao rightest rebellion fanned by the Chinese, who reportedly are recruiting up to 20,000 mountain fighters from Meo refugee camps in Thailand. Additionally, a pool of an estimated seven million Meo people reside in southern China, many of whom have kinship ties with the fiercely anti-Vietnamese Hmong of northern Laos.

It may be that the Chinese demonstration of force on Vietnam's northern frontier, which tied down probably as many as a half-million men (including the crack Hanoi garrison), will render Vietnam unlikely in the immediate future to play the role in Southeast Asia of an adventuresome "Cuba" for the Soviet Union. Furthermore, Hanoi's political policies and ideology so far have been fiercely independent. In the medium-term future, however, Soviet military weight in the region, potential disunity in the Association of Southeast Asian Nations (ASEAN), and U.S. disinterest in the area may give Moscow and Hanoi an opportunity to replay the well-tried technique of weaving entanglements with other regional states by offering twenty-five year treaties of "friendship and cooperation." They also may find it possible to extend their joint influence by setting up more Heng Samrins in the region, albeit through protracted Laos-type infiltration rather

---

* *Editor's note:* The Meo, or Hmong, are a tribal group prevalent in northern Laos. A majority of the Meos were sympathetic to the American side during the U.S. involvement in Indochina. Thousands of anti-communist Meos fled to Thailand after the communist Pathet Lao victory, but many remained and, in the midst of harsh treatment, have resisted Laotian attempts to put an end to their autonomous existence.

than through direct assault, which might trigger off a united ASEAN response.

The Growth of Soviet Naval Power in Southeast Asia

This paper will not dwell on the numbers of ship-days and ship-types and the movement of Soviet vessels in Southeast Asia. First of all, this data is extremely difficult to obtain with any degree of accuracy. It is complicated further by the presence of numerous Soviet trawlers and other unarmed ancillary units, which in the Soviet naval philosophy perform functions for the Soviet navy as important as those carried out by its armed vessels. In this analysis two working assumptions will be employed: 1) the growth of Soviet naval power in the Asian/Pacific region has accelerated since the appearance of the first outward signs of strong Vietnamese-PRC disagreement, and has grown most dramatically—in terms of visibility and strength—in the period since the Vietnamese-PRC war in early 1979; and 2) the USSR will not be persuaded easily to withdraw its naval units from the region, and the units can be expected to remain into the medium-term future, at the very least.

Since the Cuban missile crisis the navy of the Soviet Union has been expanded in size and improved in weaponry and techniques. Even more importantly, it has been given a clear doctrine under the leadership of strategist and thinker Admiral S. Gorshkov, whose writings reveal a clear appreciation of British, French, Japanese, and American naval history and who has added refinements to the classic Western naval doctrines represented by Alfred Thayer Mahan.

A considerable segment of Soviet military expenditure is spent on the navy. The Soviets in fact have engaged in a mobilization of total Russian sea capacity—naval, commercial, fishing, and exploratory. The Soviet navy possesses technology of the highest caliber, enabling it to achieve a capability for global surveillance, and has developed such weapons as long-range ship-to-ship missiles which compensate for its weakness in naval air power and the preponderance of the United States in aircraft carriers. Over the years the Soviet navy has developed the techniques of mid-sea bunkering and even repairs (buoy-marked anchorages are used regularly by Soviet naval units for this purpose). The Macclesfield

Shoal in the South China Sea, claimed by the PRC, has been used by Soviet ships—naval and "commercial"—for rendezvous, anchorage, and bunkering at sea.

The Soviet lack of base facilities has been obviated by the procurement of a string of facilities to which the Soviet navy has access, stretching from Angola to Mauritius and now apparently eastward to Haiphong and Cam Ranh Bay (with its modern American-built equipment and facilities). Additionally, there is evidence that the Soviet Union has built a long-range communications center in the Danang area to link its global network. Rapid responses to the data gathered by such centers often have tipped the scales of battles or wars. Facilities for Soviet ships and aircraft also have been constructed at Danang, and these facilities already have been utilized by long-range electronic surveillance aircraft flying in from bases near Vladivostok over Japanese territorial waters.

The Soviet Entry into Southeast Asia

It is the sea which provides for the Soviet Union the opportunity to be involved directly in the Indochina situation. Such involvement serves the Soviet objectives of mounting an encircling confrontation with its archrival, the PRC, and gaining for the first time a means of entry into the Southeast Asian subregion.

The Soviet entry into the subregion has come at a time which is best described as a telescoping of historical periods, with Vietnam reverting to its traditional patterns of southward and westward expansion and the PRC showing signs that it may utilize its resources and geostrategic advantages to become eventually an important if not dominant force with respect to continental Southeast Asia. Seldom, if ever, have these two thrusts come together simultaneously. Other factors currently in operation include the partnership between the PRC and the Khmer Rouge forces of Kampuchea and signs of tacit Sino-Thai cooperation.

In important respects, as has been acknowledged by many observers, the present situation is less a matter of ideology and struggle between communist and non-communist elements than a set of circumstances resembling the entry of the colonial powers into Asia. Well-known political figures in the region have remarked that the old imperialism now has been replaced by a new imperialism, involving an aggressive white nation with global naval power and ambitions (i.e., the Soviet Union) and perpetuated by the Soviet-Vietnamese combination. This new imperialism utilizes the most potent tool of the old Western imperialism, naval power, and repeats the traditional pattern of colonial thrusts from the open oceans into the narrow seas of Southeast Asia.

The Soviet movement thus can be interpreted as a new form of sea-borne colonial intrusion which uses as proxies local states with regional "hegemonistic" ambitions. When the invading colonial powers overwhelmed Southeast Asia in the past, they invariably possessed a powerful fleet but only a small sea-borne army, sometimes numbering only a few hundred men. The colonizing power, however, was able to manipulate local rivalries and fan local conflicts in order to improve its position in the region. In the current case, the Soviet Union now has gained a foothold and has reached a stage of influence beyond that of mere manipulation. Given the growing presence of the Soviet Pacific fleet and Moscow's special relationship with Vietnam, the USSR now is in a position to influence firmly the main trend of regional events.

The growth of Soviet influence in Southeast Asia also can be viewed as representing the first time in history that communist expansion perpetrated from Europe—what Admiral Gorshkov has called "the building up of world communism"—has had the firm and reliable backing of missile-backed warship diplomacy, now reinforced by an entente with an ambitious and militarily competent regional power. With the exception of Sukarno's Indonesia, where the challenge was more broadly based, previous communist challenges to the national governments of the states which now comprise ASEAN have sprung from groups of dedicated but often ill-armed insurgents and have been matters entirely of internal security.

Although the United States objected in many ways to the domestic policies of the Pol Pot regime in Kampuchea, with respect to relations between and among states the status quo situation in the period after 1975 and before the Vietnamese invasion of Kampuchea—a period characterized by at least a relative degree of regional interstate stability—seemed acceptable to the U.S. and the

The Indochina Situation

PRC but apparently was unacceptable to Vietnam and, by extension, the Soviet Union. During these years of relative stability, the Soviet Union had little success in extending its influence in the subregion, but Moscow has fared better since. The Soviet Union seems quite adept at gaining advantage in conditions of instability. In this connection, the provision of arms to proxies in unstable regions has been the consistent *modus operandi* of the USSR throughout the world.

The Soviet navy by its presence in the waters of the Asian/Pacific region is the direct military instrument which gives power to Moscow's policy of linkage with its proxy, Vietnam. Soviet naval power and a battle-tried Vietnam, living a Spartan-like existence, constitute a lethal duo. Through the bolstering of Vietnamese policies, the Soviet fleet poses a potential threat to the member nations of ASEAN. If allowed by the occasion, the Soviet fleet can be used to intimidate ASEAN militarily and to weaken any coordinated ASEAN policy toward Vietnam. It is unlikely that the Soviet Pacific fleet will engage ASEAN forces in direct battle, for such actions would constitute the crudest form of gunboat diplomacy. However, the more subtle aspects of gunboat policy—such as those embodied in the visible maritime parade of potentially applicable force—are being utilized to demonstrate the Soviet policy of support for its chosen ally. It is this mobile and flexible projection of Soviet military power into the region which partly underlies Vietnamese strategic boldness.

The Soviet experience in sending transports to Haiphong during the Vietnam war demonstrated the ability of the Soviet Union to link up strategically with Vietnam. Of even more significance, this experience proved that when superpowers fight through proxies, even the supply ships of the superpower weaker in naval strength [the USSR] can enjoy freedom of movement and immunity from attack or even blockade. In other words, the sea is neutral for superpowers engaged in proxy wars.

The Soviet capability for further extension of power and influence in the region should not be underestimated. In Southeast Asia it it is the American aircraft carrier which bears the main responsibility for protecting U.S. interests. Admiral Gorshkov in his writings has stressed that a prime objective of the Soviet navy is the neutralization of U.S. carriers, the backbone of American naval power, through appropriate deployment and training. Furthermore, some U.S. naval authorities regard the constricted Southeast Asian waters as "hazardous seas," especially for carriers. With these considerations in mind, it is not difficult to imagine that Moscow might have the capability to assemble squadrons able to effectively counter any morale-boosting movements in the area which might be mounted by the U.S. navy.

The Role of the People's Republic of China

The present and long-term policies and capabilities of the People's Republic of China constitute a factor with important strategic implications for the security of ASEAN and the Asian/Pacific region in general.

There is a current debate in the ASEAN countries, especially in Indonesia, with respect to whether the PRC or Vietnam constitutes the main threat to Southeast Asia, and whether Vietnam, as Hanoi claims, in in fact a buffer against the PRC's southward expansionism. Despite past warnings from the West—warnings which seem curiously echoed by the current propaganda emanating from Moscow on the "Yellow Peril" and by charges from Moscow and Hanoi regarding the existence of a "Fifth Column" among "overseas Chinese"—the ASEAN states for the most part appear to see the PRC as a land-based power with a short reach which would be most unlikely to indulge in the costly luxury of sending massed armies marching across the region.

By comparison to those of the U.S. and the Soviet Union, the naval capabilities of the PRC are limited, and it appears that they will remain so into the medium-term future, at the very least. An effective PRC blue-water capability may be a factor of the future, but not of the present. Although in terms of numbers of ships and sailors the PRC navy is said to be the world's third largest, the navy's role is confined mainly to the realm of coastal defense, with the exception of part of the PRC's fleet of diesel-powered submarines and a small but growing flotilla of Luta-class missile-armed destroyers, described by some U.S. naval sources as "good ships." These submarines and early generation missiles, however, can be countered effectively by current Soviet anti-submarine and electronic anti-missile techniques.

The Indochina Situation

The PRC has labelled Vietnam "the Cuba of the Orient" and perceives Hanoi as posing an expansionistic threat to the ASEAN states. The Chinese efforts to contain Vietnam, however, to a large extent have been effectively offset or negated by the presence of Soviet ships (up to missile-cruiser type), first in the Bashi Channel in early 1979 when the Sino-Vietnamese armed conflict seemed imminent, then reportedly off the central Vietnamese coast and in the Gulf of Tonkin, and now in Cam Ranh Bay and possibly Haiphong.

The kind of operation necessary to counteract Vietnamese expansionism would include such components as the supplying of arms to Khmer forces and the constant posing of the threat of a sea-borne landing on the Vietnamese coast opposite Hainan Island. These measures would result in an extension of Vietnamese resources, thereby alleviating the Vietnamese pressure in Kampuchea and, by extension, on Thailand. The PRC would have the capability to carry out these actions only if the Soviet Pacific fleet did not intervene. It must be remembered, however, that one major aim of the Soviet naval intrusion into Southeast Asia is to "encircle" what it perceives to be its major global enemy—i.e., the PRC. In its actions to attempt to contain Vietnamese ambitions—and, by extension, Soviet objectives in Southeast Asia—the PRC has demonstrated that it has the will but not the seapower. The United States, on the other hand, has the seapower but not the will or the inclination.

The Continuing Relevance of the "Domino Theory"

After its initial acceptance, the "domino theory" espoused by many American politicians and scholars came to be decried during the years of the Vietnam war's unpopularity in the United States. In fact, however, events now indicate that the validity and usefulness of the theory should be re-examined, for it appears to have much relevance to the current security problems faced by the ASEAN states. For example, if and when the PRC is rendered impotent by Soviet buildups and pressure on its northern frontier and intimidated by the demonstration of force by the Soviet navy in the East and South China seas, Thailand may falter under such pressuring circumstances. In such an event, would the domino sequence be entirely irrelevant?

Vietnam may not behave exactly like a second Cuba. However, in combination with the Soviet Union—and protected and assisted by the twenty-five year "friendship and cooperation" treaty—Vietnam can act very efficiently as the spearhead to reactivate the domino process. This can be achieved by combining diplomacy with armed intervention, assassinations, subversion, inflammation of local racial and religious animosities, and extension of treaties of "friendship and cooperation" beyond the western borders of Kampuchea. Soviet arms in the hands of Russians in the region are not likely to be used as effectively as Soviet arms and military technology in the hands of the Vietnamese, given their knowledge of regional conditions and superb "feel" for terrain and the tactical use of vegetation cover. In this symbiotic relationship, Soviet gunboat diplomacy is sharpened and rendered more effective as a political and strategic instrument by having a reliable and efficient proxy in the region.

The Vietnamese—schooled in warfare to be conducted in the minds of people as well as in the field—make a point of searching for contradictions in capitalist systems. Vo Nguyen Giap, for example, perceptively pointed out some contradictions extant in a Western democratic society like France when he predicted that internal political schisms would bring France to its knees in any protracted war with the Viet Minh. The Vietnamese may prove to be equally adept at exploiting contradictions arising from the ethnic and cultural diversity which marks the whole of Southeast Asia. As the refugee situation has shown, Vietnam already has been able to manipulate ethnic issues to its own advantage. Vietnamese adeptness in feeling out the cleavages combined with Soviet power may prove to be a new combination lethal to the ASEAN states, individually and/or collectively. What makes this scenario possible is the backing of Soviet power through its Pacific fleet.

The communist schizophrenia exacerbated by the conflict between the PRC and the Soviet/Vietnamese alliance may lead to a decline in the internal threat of ideologically-fed insurgency. However, various forms of cultural, ethnic, and religious dissent remain powder kegs. For example, the consequences stemming from the exploitation of latent racial cleavages in Malaysia at the very least would drive away much-needed foreign investment and might lead even to widespread bloodshed and, more horrendously, civil war. If Vietnam, with a fallen or compliant Thailand, were to decide to strike at the very roots of Malaysian stability, Hanoi—with the aid of the Soviet Union—would have the capacity to do so. (As the Vietnamese boat people well know, the east coast of peninsular Malaysia is only a short boat ride [about 200 miles] from the Mekong delta.) As a further consideration, if Malaysia were to face both internal strife and a hostile external naval presence, how would Singapore fare? Then, if the whole Malay peninsula were to be used as a conduit for fuelling dissent, insurgency, and regional irredentism in Indonesia, could Jakarta's armed forces hold down the sprawling Indonesian archipelago, open as it is to sea-borne infiltration?

It may be protested that the above chain of developments contains features which many observers may see as constituting the unlikely "worst possible scenario." However, the worst possible outcome already has come to pass at least three times in Southeast Asia since 1950—with respect to the fate of the French at Dien Bien Phu, the non-communist forces in South Vietnam, and now in Democratic Kampuchea.

The Importance of the U.S. Naval Presence

Whether or not the non-communist nations of Southeast Asia wish to acknowledge it publicly, their security in the currently evolving situation—in which internal revolt, although still important, now is subordinated to the historical pattern of nation-against-nation conflict in a sea-penetrated environment—depends to a considerable extent on the U.S. navy. Can the U.S. navy outnumber, outmaneuver, and—if necessary—outfight the aggressive and rapidly growing Soviet navy, not only in Southeast Asia but globally as well? Does the U.S. leadership, and do the U.S. people, desire to continue the traditional American policy of attainment and maintenance of global parity in numbers and technology? Finally, will there exist sufficient U.S. determination—in the face of the post-Vietnam war trend of domestic revulsion against intervention—to continue the historic use of America's navy, backed now by its air force, in coordination with and in support of avowed U.S. foreign policy objectives?

As the leader of one of the ASEAN nations has stated, the only answer to a Soviet ship is an American ship. The mutual Soviet and U.S. naval presences need not lead to battle, but can result in a mutual stand-off posture which would help prevent any further deterioration in the international situation from the point of view of ASEAN. A Mediterranean-type naval balance (in which all hostile forces mutually cancel out one another) would deprive Vietnam of one strategic advantage. However, if the U.S. Congress decides that Southeast Asian seas are of low priority to the U.S., then a situation will develop offering advantages to Vietnam.

The argument here is that U.S. naval power, with its supporting air arm, underpins the status quo and security of Southeast Asia. In the parlance of gunboat diplomacy, the mere presence of U.S. naval forces will serve as a projection of power which will help deter efforts to unduly destabilize the area. Such a presence will provide a check against the emergence of a state of Soviet-Vietnamese preponderance in the Southeast Asian subregion—a check which the PRC, for its part, presently can provide only on the landward fringes of Southeast Asia.

The command of the South China Sea and its environs is beyond the capacity of the Soviet Union and its allies now and in the foreseeable future, and in fact is not necessary for the accomplishment of their purposes. Denial of the sea to the potential adversaries of Vietnam and protection of the Soviet Union's supply routes to Haiphong and Cam Ranh Bay in themselves would constitute strategic gains. Finally, temporary and localized Soviet naval superiority—or, in Soviet terms, "sea control"—can be quite effective if applied with speed and acumen, especially when a situation elsewhere serves to distract U.S. attention. By presenting ASEAN with a rapidly achieved fait accompli, such naval superiority—even if limited both in time and space—might be the deciding factor which would tip the regional balance inexorably in favor of the Soviet-Vietnamese axis.

To prevent such a denouement, the unwavering display of will by the United States can play the role of a crucial balancing factor. For example, any ASEAN aid to Thailand in the final analysis must depend on firm American backing, especially in the form of strong and guaranteed naval support. Demonstration of American determination to react sharply is well within the ambit of

U.S. security policies. Prior notice that the U.S. can and will employ its mobile fleets to deliver a sharp riposte to any move unsettling to ASEAN's collective security would serve as a timely warning to any state or combination of states seeking to set off yet another chain of heightened instability. Here again, however, the problem ultimately devolves onto ASEAN's own solidarity of purpose.

The Challenges Facing ASEAN

The quarrels between the PRC and Vietnam and the Vietnamese-Kampuchean conflict have given the ASEAN states time to strengthen their economic and political structures so as to better withstand their ever-present internal threats. However, with the so-far invincible Vietnamese army close to the Thai border (bringing attendant dangers of accidental conflagration) and Hanoi's totally unyielding posture regarding ASEAN and U.N. pleas concerning Kampuchea, the breathing spell may be ending.

Important questions remain unanswered with respect to the possibility of direct ASEAN participation in the defense of Thailand. Indonesia already has earmarked sixty elite battalions for long-range "raiding operations" and thirty-eight of these are reported to have reached an excellent standard of competence. Malaysia has stated that it will come to the aid of Thailand if faced with circumstances in which its own security is threatened. There remains much uncertainty, however, regarding the outcome of political decisions connected with ASEAN military help to Thailand. Additionally, it must be recognized that the armies of the ASEAN states are designed primarily, if not entirely, for dealing with matters of internal security and for the suppression of relatively small groups of insurgents. The heavy equipment, air support, logistics, experience, training, and possibly generalship needed for conventional war on the scale at which Vietnam can wage it do not appear to be readily available in the Southeast Asian subregion (outside Vietnam and the southern portion of the PRC).

Amid the instability prevailing around ASEAN, suggestions often have been made with respect to formal ASEAN security cooperation and the possibility of an ASEAN military "alliance." It is difficult, however, for an observer to reach any conclusion regarding the likely outcome of these issues. The contradictory positions taken by separate ministries and different interest groups within and among the ASEAN states are evident in the many statements emanating from various sources within ASEAN. It might be noted that this sort of globally audible discordance further emboldens Vietnam in probing for additional contradictions within ASEAN.

The differences of view prevalent within ASEAN stem partly from differing perceptions with respect to Vietnamese expansionism. The level of apprehension naturally is highest in Thailand, which now is no longer buffeted by an independent Kampuchea, and perhaps lowest in Indonesia and the Philippines, which are relatively distant and protected by expanses of seas. Faced by pressing problems of economic development and the proclaimed commitment to eradicate social and economic disparities, all ASEAN governments find themselves placed on the horns of a dilemma: should priority be placed on internal development or on preparations to meet a worsening of the situation on Thailand's doorstep?

A student of regional affairs may perceive the dimensions of the problem but find it difficult to shed further light on the impellents and constraints which will underlie any ASEAN attempt to break-out, security-wise, from ASEAN's self-imposed inclination to limit formal cooperation to the economic and cultural realms. In any case it is vital that the ASEAN nations should display a firm consistency of collective purpose in the security field, as they have done in the political arena with respect to the question of Vietnamese withdrawal from Kampuchea.

Preparedness in terms of political, economic, and social efforts to alleviate internal discontent and to ensure national unity, together with military alertness to meet external threats, are the challenges facing the ASEAN nations. What can safely be said is that the leaderships of friendly powers which might decide to assist ASEAN first must be convinced that ASEAN is willing and determined to help itself in the face of emergent difficulties and threats.

THE INTERNAL AND EXTERNAL DIMENSIONS OF SOUTHEAST ASIAN SECURITY

Jusuf Wanandi

I. Introduction

To fully comprehend the issues and problems associated with Southeast Asian security, one must examine not only the internal and external dimensions of security but also the interconnections which exist between these components. The basic premise in the ensuing analysis is that the interdependence between these dimensions becomes more manifest and increases in strength as the individual and collective resilience of the Southeast Asian nations deteriorates. Stated somewhat differently, it is herein argued that the greater the threats to security which originate from within the nation, the greater will be the external threats faced by the country. Security therefore cannot be perceived merely as a military matter, as is usually the case, but must include other noteworthy elements,

---

This essay, which was first presented at the Pattaya conference, also appeared (in slightly variant form) in *The Indonesian Quarterly*, Vol. VIII, No. 1, January 1980.

such as political, economic, social, ideological, and even cultural factors.

Over the next three to five years the most immediate security problems to be faced by the Southeast Asian states are likely to originate from within the individual nations themselves. The nature and intensity of these internal threats will depend, to a great extent, on the success of the respective governments in meeting the challenges arising from the increasing demands and expectations of their populaces. An adequate response naturally implies the successful implementation of a balanced developmental program, which encompasses all aspects of national life and takes into consideration the elements of national stability and social justice. Obviously the challenges facing the respective governments cannot be met easily. The tasks become all the more difficult when external threats—whether or not they are of a deliberate nature—create an environment which necessitates the diversion of the attention and resources of the respective governments from the internal considerations at hand.

While external threats to the security of the Southeast Asian nations cannot be discounted, such threats are likely, however, to be of a secondary nature, for externally-fomented and/or supported infiltration and subversion become effective only in circumstances characterized by the existence of local communist organizations or other rebellious groups. External threats become more direct and challenging when the national stability and resilience of the various states deteriorate as a result of the failures of the respective governments to deal effectively with the above-mentioned domestic challenges.

In view of the fact that the main potential threats to the security of Southeast Asia originate from within the individual countries, the following section of this paper will examine the internal security dimensions of the various Association of Southeast Asian Nations (ASEAN) member states. The third section will deal with the external dimensions of security, including an analysis of the role played by and the power configurations among the four major external states impacting on Southeast Asia—i.e., the United States, the Soviet Union, the People's Republic of China (PRC), and Japan. The essay ends with a brief section of concluding remarks.

II. The Internal Dimensions

In view of the fact that each of the ASEAN states has its own history, cultural values, national character, and patterns of and conditions for development, to attempt a summary analysis of the domestic problems of these countries is certainly no simple task. The difficulties involved are evident when one tries to compare Indonesia (with a population of over 140 million) with Singapore (with a population of some 2.5 million) and when one considers the variations in the colonial heritages of the ASEAN nations (Malaysia and Singapore formerly were British colonies, the Philippines experienced both Spanish and American rule, and Indonesia was under Dutch control). In this paper a rough sketch will be presented of the internal challenges faced by the ASEAN nations. While this presentation does not pretend to analyze all the problems of these states, it does attempt to examine those major aspects which have a direct bearing on the security of the individual nations.

While the many differences existent among the various ASEAN countries must be recognized, certain similarities exist as well, especially in the realm of difficulties which are common to all. These common problems include:

1. The problematical side effects of national development, such as changes in the nation's cultural values and the unequal distribution of the gains of development;
2. The ongoing struggle for the establishment and maintenance of the unity of the nation and the state;
3. The need for increased national participation through the development of political institutions in conformity with the schedule of improvements in economic development, as well as steady improvements in the adherence to the rule of law and the protection of human rights; and
4. The problem of succession, which still presents a serious challenge to the stability and continuity of the nation and the state.

National Development and its Side Effects

A major problem which arises in connection with any developmental program is the sufficient securing and insuring of that effort so that it can be sustained, thus enabling the respective government to fulfill its promises to the nation. It is through achievements in this regard that governments of developing states can maintain their legitimacy.

During the last ten years the ASEAN nations have been able to achieve high economic growth rates of between five and ten percent annually. Recent developments and uncertainties in the international economic order, however, may affect the future performances of these nations, making the sustenance of high growth rates more difficult. At the same time, it is likely that short-term measures can help to overcome these difficulties. Continuing increases in the price of energy resources have placed significant pressures upon Thailand and the Philippines, for example. Given the abundance of natural resources, however, the situation over the longer term may not be as critical as it now appears. The Philippines, in particular, should give special attention to the management of its financial resources. Similarly, Indonesia may need to adopt certain measures to deal with inflation, particularly in view of the currency devaluation of 1978. Such measures may be of particular importance given the fact that prolonged high rates of inflation directly affect the fixed income earners, primarily the civil servants who are the main supporters of the government.

In an overall sense, however, the sustenance of high economic growth rates may prove to be less difficult than dealing with the side effects which result from the very successes of economic development itself. The changes in cultural values which accompany economic development necessitate a search for a new national identity. This search ideally will seek to incorporate both viable traditional qualities and new values adopted from abroad. As can be expected, it often takes a good deal of time to find the proper balance between traditional values and modern perspectives. Reforms in the educational system may facilitate this process. At present, however, not a single ASEAN country has accomplished this process of acculturation. During this transitional period, it can be expected that insecurity and instability will be widespread among sectors of the populace in these nations. When the historical record in Southeast Asia is taken into account, however, one can be optimistic that this problem will be resolved; already several cultures—Hindu/Buddhist, Sinitic, and Islamic—

The Internal and External Dimensions of Security

have been not only absorbed but also assimilated in Southeast Asia.

Other problems flowing from the developmental process include the explosion of demands, luxurious consumption patterns, and inequalities in the distribution of income. To some extent these elements are inherent in strategies of development, especially where open economies rely upon the market mechanism. The governments of the ASEAN states have initiated a number of programs to correct these problems. For example, advertising on television and in other components of the mass media, as well as other methods of marketing, are being controlled in order to suppress demonstrative consumption patterns, fight corruption, and enhance national solidarity. Other efforts also have been made to eradicate forms of blatant corruption, especially among the ruling elite. Progressive tax systems are being adopted, and other social policies—such as increases in public education, public health, and public housing, especially for the poor—are being undertaken. Thus even if the disadvantaged group for the time being cannot participate directly in economic development, its members nevertheless can enjoy the fruits of development.

The Struggle for National Unity

The existence of religious and ethnic diversities continues to have widespread socio-political implications in each of the ASEAN nations. The Philippines presently faces difficulties with Moslem minorities in the South, and Malaysia has not resolved the problem of ethnic segregation between the Malays (45 percent of the population) and the Chinese (35 percent). Singapore is still struggling to build a Singaporean nation. Thailand and Indonesia likewise have many minorities and ethnic groups and must deal with the associated problems.

Nation-building thus becomes a necessary task for each of the respective ASEAN governments. It is hoped that through these efforts the various minority groups—ethnic and religious—will be integrated fully into the national society. The historical record shows that minorities are among the groups most easily exploited by external forces. Such exploitation is intended to create unrest and instability leading ultimately to the overthrow of the existing national regime.

Religious fanaticism is another potentially disruptive and disintegrative force. The Islamic revolution of the Ayatollah Khomeini in Iran initially served as an inspiration for some Moslems in Southeast Asia. However, as the uncertainty of the consequences of the Iranian revolution has become more evident, its influence has declined. The majority of the subregion's Moslem leaders acknowledge that the overall situation in Southeast Asia is quite unlike the situation in Iran and that the practice of Islam in Southeast Asia differs significantly from Iranian practices. Even more importantly, these leaders realize that any alternative governments in Southeast Asia cannot be based on religious principles and elements alone.

The crucial factors determining whether a government can maintain the support of the population are the degree to which the demands of the populace can be fulfilled and the scope of opportunities available for the population's participation in all aspects of development. The socio-political implications of religious fanaticism can magnify and complicate the problems faced by a government, but religious fanaticism alone is not the determining factor in replacing a government. This was shown particularly in the case of Darul Islam (a rebellious theocratic movement) in Indonesia.

The governments in some Southeast Asian nations—notably Malaysia and Indonesia, where the majority of the population is Moslem—are sensitive to the role that Islam can play in both the formulation and implementation of national policies. In point of fact, however, a distinction is always made in these nations between state and religious affairs; in the absence of such a distinction, Islam could become a disintegrative factor for the pluralistic societies existing in these countries.

National Participation

One of the significant aspects of political development is that it gives the populace a greater sense of participation and involvement in the policy-making process. Such participation and involvement contribute meaningfully to national developmental programs.

Each success achieved in a developmental program creates

more diversified demands and greater expectations, so that economic gains are not sufficient. Such demands and expectations go beyond the need for material well-being and call for the establishment of a genuine rule of law, opportunities for political participation, and assertion of a wide spectrum of human and civil rights. It should be noted, however, that in developing countries it is important to create a proper balance between individual and communal rights. This balance depends upon achievements in economic development, political stability, and the degree of national unity. Western models and values cannot be adopted indiscriminately; such indiscriminate adoption not only would create new demands which, given the prevailing scarcities and constraints, cannot be satisfied yet, but also would create a climate of instability which could nullify the achievements already made.

However, it is never too early to embark upon the process of establishing the political institutions which could provide appropriate mechanisms for the absorption of the problematical side effects of economic development. In addition to national parties, various other socio-political organizations have important functions as well, e.g., labor unions, farm unions, youth groups, women's organizations, etc. Special attention also should be given to intellectuals, students, and persons involved in the mass media, as they constitute the most vocal groups within these societies.

The military is an important factor in the ASEAN states but alone it is not sufficient to deal with the complexities of national development. The military forces have a crucial role to play in the security and defense of each country, particularly with respect to the potential threats posed by rebellious and extremist groups operating within the state. Ultimately, however, these problems too require political solutions.

The government, together with social leaders, must design and properly implement a long-term development plan. In sum, a sound political program carried out in conjunction with the various stages of economic development can help to overcome the negative implications of development mentioned above.

The Problem of Succession

Democracy functions best when the transfer of power proceeds smoothly and constitutionally. The existence of established and viable socio-political institutions can help guarantee the continuation of the process of development, thus ensuring that the fate of the nation is not dependent upon a single individual. In other words, political development has the capacity to eliminate gradually the problem of succession.

During the 1980s all the ASEAN nations will be confronted with problems of succession. Notwithstanding their various shortcomings, the present governments of the ASEAN states—under strong leadership and with a broad base of popular support—have been able to further the development of their respective countries. Uncertainties with respect to the process of succession arise from the fact that the existing political institutions, which ultimately will have to manage the transfer of power, thus far have not been tested in this regard. For this reason, in recent times in Southeast Asia the importance of political institution-building has been widely acknowledged by political parties, other political organizations, and top leaders themselves. However, it may be necessary to accelerate this process in the Philippines.

Internal Dimensions of Security: The Role of ASEAN's Friends and Allies

In view of the manifold challenges faced by the Southeast Asian states, it is hoped that in the future ASEAN's friends and allies, especially the United States, will show a greater perception and understanding of the values, history, traditions, and patterns of economic and political development which characterize the individual ASEAN countries. The attainment of a higher level of perception and understanding can help to avoid any reinforcement of the difficulties which already prevail and over the long term will assist the ASEAN governments in their quests for development gains.

The conduct of U.S. foreign policy in the recent past has been much too shortsighted. Despite the noble principles involved, considerations in the realm of human rights cannot be applied indiscriminately and should be viewed within the broader context of relationships among nations. The United States cannot and should not impose its values upon other nations but instead should promote the furthering and protection of human rights through intensive consultations with individual governments.

Even if from a Western perspective certain authoritarian tendencies can be found in the management of Southeast Asian countries, any evaluation of the human rights situation must take into consideration the relative well-being of the population *as a whole*. In the absence of progress in this regard, it is unlikely that leaderships in the ASEAN states could have remained in power for more than a decade, as has been the case in Indonesia, the Philippines, and Singapore. Strong leadership has been accepted as a necessity in the ASEAN nations, especially in the earlier stages of development. Now such leadership must be balanced by visible results and the more equal distribution of the gains of development.

It may be that foreign governments by now have gained a larger measure of understanding with respect to the real dilemmas faced by the various governments in Southeast Asia. However, public opinion also constitutes an important factor in the relationships among countries. A sustainable relationship requires the participation of and support from large segments of the population within the respective interacting nations. Unfortunately, the situation obtaining within one country, sometimes an ASEAN member, at times is exploited for the purposes of internal politics in another state. Visits to other nations by heads of state often are accompanied by political statements designed solely for domestic consumption back home. These statements, however, may have a negative impact within the host ASEAN country in several respects: a) they may encourage certain opposition forces to raise their voices, and b) they may cause irritation to the government, in turn complicating the internal situation.

While several of the ASEAN nations still require some foreign aid, trade and investment will play a greater role in the future. With respect to aid assistance, Western governments should recognize that emphasis on funding for basic human needs projects should be somewhat curtailed, since these projects are more easily financed by domestic resources. With regard to investment, new formulae must be found which will facilitate an accommodation between the profit orientation of the multinational corporations and the national objectives of the host governments, primarily in the realm of a more equitable distribution of the gains of development.

III. The External Dimensions

The Vietnamese Threat to Thai Security

Because of the effects its military involvement in Kampuchea has had upon neighboring Thailand, Vietnam today is considered by the ASEAN states to pose the most immediate threat to the peace and security of Southeast Asia. While an open invasion of Thailand by Vietnam is not likely to occur in the immediate future, there nevertheless exist certain threats to Thai security which may manifest themselves in several ways. For example, pressures along the Thai border could result either from a Vietnamese hot pursuit action against Pol Pot's soldiers or from some form of support to rebellious groups within Thailand. Additionally, in the long run the possibility of a Vietnamese invasion of Thailand cannot be discounted.

It remains unclear whether Vietnam's ambitions extend beyond Indochina, and whether Hanoi in fact will actively pursue the expansion of the Vietnamese sphere of influence to the whole of continental Southeast Asia, an ultimate aim which has been stated officially by the Lao Dong party. In the assessment of many observers, Vietnam in the short term will be incapable of implementing such a plan due to the great internal difficulties which it already faces. Vietnam presently is experiencing dramatic reverses in its economic development and is encountering difficulties in the absorption and integration of the South into one national identity with the North. The burden of Vietnam's military involvement in Kampuchea is becoming greater as time passes and may deem any further adventures into Thailand unfeasible. Furthermore, apart from the problem of securing the long logistic lines necessary for the success of such an operation into Thai territory, Vietnam would find no support from within Thailand itself, largely because the orientation of the Communist Party of Thailand is toward the PRC. Pro-Vietnamese factions within Thailand remain insignificant today and do not pose the prospect of a serious threat.

Even given these possible restrictions on Vietnamese actions, several situations may arise which could threaten significantly the stability of Thailand. Vietnamese forces in a hot pursuit action may come into contact with and overrun Thai forces in the border areas, or Vietnam may occupy certain portions of Thailand, a danger which applies primarily to the thirteen provinces which historically have been an area of dispute among Thailand, Vietnam, and Kampuchea. Such developments, singly or in concert, would increase visibly the political pressures upon the Thai government, greatly increasing the complexity of Thailand's internal situation and leading possibly to conditions of instability.*

Soviet and Chinese Involvement

The threats posed by Vietnam are complicated further by the Treaty of Friendship and Cooperation which Vietnam signed with the Soviet Union in November 1978. Involved in this treaty are logistical support, intelligence gathering, political and economic aid, as well as an increased Soviet military presence in Southeast Asia, particularly at the Vietnamese military facilities at Danang and Cam Ranh Bay. The Vietnamese threat also takes on added significance by virtue of its emergence as an integral part of the Sino-Soviet conflict. Both the Soviet Union and the PRC can be expected to try continually to increase their spheres of influence in Southeast Asia through the utilization of allies and "proxies," as is the case with the Soviet Union and Vietnam.

The involvement of the People's Republic of China in the Indochina conflict has had two contrasting effects upon developments in the region. Firstly, by demonstrating its willingness to apply physical pressure upon Vietnam the PRC has relieved some of the pressures exerted by Vietnam upon the ASEAN states. Secondly, however, it is possible that PRC actions might have the effect of magnifying the Sino-Vietnamese conflict to such an extent as to necessitate greater involvement by the Soviet Union, the United States, and the ASEAN states. Under such circumstances, the area of conflict well might be expanded to include the whole Southeast Asian subregion. Furthermore, while the immediate threat to the ASEAN nations flows from Vietnam and the Soviet presence which looms behind it, the PRC—despite the existence of some convergence of interests between Peking and the ASEAN countries and the PRC's possible role in helping to maintain a power balance in the region—still is considered a potential threat to ASEAN, though of a more remote nature.

---

* *Editor's Note:* Vietnamese-led troops made a quick strike into Thai territory on June 23, 1980 and then withdrew. See this Chapter's "The Continuing Struggle in Indochina: Editor's Introduction," p. 15.

The convergence of interests between ASEAN and the PRC, the more moderate attitude in the PRC's domestic politics and foreign outlook, the tendency of the PRC political leadership to place greater emphasis on government-to-government rather than party-to-party relations, and Peking's recognition of the need to support the efforts of the ASEAN states to resolve their problems with their overseas Chinese populations may well have an effect on Indonesia's attitude toward the restoration of diplomatic relations with the PRC. It has been argued that ASEAN will be able to initiate certain diplomatic moves—with the aim of influencing the situation in Indochina—only after Indonesia has re-established its relations with the PRC. At the same time it is argued that ASEAN should improve its relations with Hanoi. The adoption by ASEAN of a more active and balanced relationship with both the PRC and Vietnam would better serve and help to guarantee stability in Southeast Asia.

The Need for Diplomatic and Political Initiatives

ASEAN's diplomatic initiatives vis-a-vis Vietnam should focus on two major objectives. Firstly, ASEAN should attempt to convince Vietnam that in order to further its economic development it cannot rely solely upon help from the Soviet Union and COMECON. The fact should be stressed that assistance from the international community will require Vietnamese adherence to peaceful means in its foreign policy and a genuinely cooperative attitude toward ASEAN.

Secondly, Vietnam also should be persuaded that achievement of a political solution to the Kampuchea question is desirable, since a military solution cannot be obtained in the next one to two years. Apart from the burden which would be placed upon the Vietnamese economy, a prolonged military involvement by Vietnam in Kampuchea would provide legitimate reasons for the PRC to continue and increase its pressures upon Indochina and Southeast Asia as a whole. Moreover, such a venture would result in further deterioration in Vietnam's relations with ASEAN, destroy the Khmer nation, and ultimately isolate Vietnam totally from the international community. The attitude of the international community (as has been seen in the United Nations) toward Vietnam's recent actions in Kampuchea should have taught Vietnam this lesson. ASEAN also should direct diplomatic initiatives toward the PRC and the Soviet Union with the objective of involving these states in the achievement of an immediate political solution in Kampuchea. Additionally, a more flexible attitude toward Vietnam on the part of the U.S. could influence Hanoi to adopt a more compromising attitude.

A political solution in Kampuchea ideally would require a withdrawal of Vietnamese troops from that country; the conduct of a referendum among the Khmer people, supervised by the United Nations; and the establishment of a truly neutral government. Two scenarios seem possible in the near future. If Vietnam is able to destroy the forces of Pol Pot, a political solution in Kampuchea might take form with the country under the suzerainty of Vietnam and a pro-Vietnamese regime, not necessarily headed by Heng Samrin, in power. However, if Vietnam is unable to eliminate the Pol Pot forces, it may have to compromise and accept a neutral government in Kampuchea along the lines laid down in the United Nations resolution. Each scenario possibly could lead to a withdrawal of Vietnamese forces, thereby lessening the pressures on Thailand and the other ASEAN nations.

A matter of great urgency lies in the need for increased humanitarian aid to the Khmer people, who as a result of the Vietnamese invasion and the harsh conditions prevalent under the earlier Pol Pot regime are greatly in need of food and medication. The United States and Japan play a crucial role in this regard.

ASEAN's Military Capabilities

Apart from diplomatic initiatives, as a last resort ASEAN also should be prepared to respond militarily. The military capabilities of the ASEAN states gradually should be enhanced to the level required to meet external threats. Cooperation among the ASEAN countries toward the achievement of this goal is likely to be strengthened, but the emergence of a military pact is not likely to occur. The ASEAN nations are aware that a military pact is not the proper response to the immediate (i.e., internal) threats they now face. With respect to meeting these immediate threats, it is expected that the ASEAN states will continue to cooperate on a *bilateral* basis, a mode of cooperation which also is regarded as a sufficient means of dealing with external threats likely to arise in the near future. If Thailand were to face a real threat along its borders, the other four ASEAN states independently could provide the necessary assistance—e.g., by contributing supplies of such strategic materials as oil and food.

The ASEAN countries will enhance their military capabilities gradually so as to avoid placing a great burden upon their individual processes of economic and social development. It therefore is expected that in the short-and-medium-terms the ASEAN states will confine their military enhancement programs to the strengthening of their capabilities to deal with increased subversion and infiltration. In the long-term, namely five to ten years, these programs of military improvement can be augmented and intensified to face potential threats of a more conventional nature. The United States can assist the ASEAN nations in this regard through guarantees of orderly sales of military goods, in a manner similar to the recent arrangements reached between the U.S. and Thailand.

The Economic Realm

In addition to the political-diplomatic and military-security efforts discussed above, ASEAN must continue its efforts in the realm of economic development and cooperative economic ventures. Cooperation among the ASEAN states in the economic sector seems to have lost momentum due to the recent events in Indochina. A strong and broad base of economic cooperation in the long-term could guarantee the viability of ASEAN. Furthermore, an enlarged structure of economic cooperation in the Asian/Pacific region could reinforce ASEAN economic cooperation by facilitating increased economic interaction between ASEAN and the region's industrialized nations, which are the main trading partners of and sources of capital and technology for the ASEAN states.

Looking Toward the Future: ASEAN and the Four Major Powers

To support the political, military, and economic efforts mentioned herein, ASEAN must attempt to preserve an international environment characterized by a balanced presence in Southeast Asia among the four major outside powers—i.e., the United States, Japan, the People's Republic of China, and the Soviet Union. Such a balanced presence will serve to enhance the stability of the Southeast Asian subregion. To achieve this objective, a structure of relationships must be established between ASEAN and each of the major powers. In the following paragraphs a number of suggestions are made with respect to the sorts of policies which might contribute to the security and the continued economic and political development of the ASEAN states and the Pacific Basin region as a whole.

The United States. The U.S. now seems to have reversed the trend of disengagement from the Asian/Pacific region which followed the Vietnam debacle. However, it is not to be expected in the near future that the American presence in the region will be increased from the current minimal level.

1. Public opinion in the United States now reflects an increased interest in Southeast Asia. A concerted effort must be made to strengthen this interest as a support for a continued U.S. presence in the subregion. A closer relationship is also needed between ASEAN leaders and the U.S. Congress.
2. As a minimal stance the U.S. should maintain its current military presence in Southeast Asia (at Clark Field and Subic Bay) and a presence in the Indian Ocean.
3. In support of the military security of the ASEAN states the U.S. should arrange for guaranteed and orderly sales of military hardware to these nations.
4. In support of ASEAN's efforts to obtain a political solution in Kampuchea and to solve the refugee problem the U.S. could:
    a. use its leverage vis-a-vis the Soviet Union and the PRC so as to prevent these states from further expanding the Sino-Soviet conflict into the rest of Southeast Asia;
    b. lessen the dependence of Vietnam on the Soviet Union by taking a more flexible attitude toward Hanoi; and
    c. provide economic assistance to ASEAN in the form of Official Development Assistance and private investment, and facilitate for ASEAN-manufactured products greater access to the U.S. market.
5. The U.S. should intensify its consultations with ASEAN as a collective grouping and with the individual ASEAN states.

Japan. Japan is and will continue to be ASEAN's major economic partner. Additionally, Japan's political and security roles may increase in the future.

1. Japan can assist ASEAN mainly in the economic sector through trade combined with investment in the areas of capital and technology.
2. Japan gradually should increase its political role in the Asian/Pacific region. For example, Japan could serve more strongly as a mediator in the North-South dialogue and support ASEAN's diplomatic moves toward a peaceful resolution of the problems in Indochina. In view of these opportunities and possibilities, Japan should intensify its consultations with the various ASEAN states.
3. With respect to Japan's possible military role in the Asian/Pacific region, Japan should discuss the matter openly in consultation with the ASEAN states. Openness in this regard is of great importance so as to avoid misinterpretations and possible opposition from other countries in the region. Japan ultimately will find it necessary to take on a greater military role, but this should be accomplished gradually. Japan initially must defend more fully its own homeland and waters; at a later stage, however, Japan must assist in the securing of the vital sea lanes in the area. The ASEAN states will not necessarily oppose such a development if Japan proceeds in a gradual manner, in consultation with the U.S. and other countries in the Asian/Pacific region.
4. Japan's role in the cultural field should also be increased. Although Japan recently has increased its activities in this sector, such efforts still lag in comparison with Japan's economic initiatives.

The People's Republic of China. The PRC can become a balancing factor for Vietnam and the Soviet Union in the Southeast Asian subregion, thus contributing to the maintenance of stability in the area. Additionally, it can be expected to play an increasingly significant economic role in the Asian/Pacific region.

1. The PRC can become an alternative market for ASEAN products.
2. To enhance its credibility vis-a-vis the ASEAN states, the PRC should prove that it is a trustworthy partner by placing greater reliance on government-to-government relations than on party-to-party relations. Additionally, the PRC should adopt an unambiguous policy toward the overseas Chinese living in Southeast Asia.

Peking also should refrain from fueling further the conflict in Indochina.
3. As a basis for participation in multilateral efforts to maintain stability in the Asian/Pacific region, the PRC should demonstrate that it is genuinely willing to adopt and adhere to the established rules of the game accepted by the larger international community.

The Soviet Union. The Soviet presence in Southeast Asia is a reality. It still remains, however, for the Soviet Union to prove itself to be a trustworthy partner. The USSR only recently reversed its previously hostile attitude toward ASEAN, and it is possible that this change constitutes only a tactical move.

1. The Soviet Union can contribute to the stability of Southeast Asia by restraining Vietnam from attacking Thailand.
2. Moscow should do what it can to create an international atmosphere in which Vietnam can co-exist with the ASEAN states.
3. It is of crucial importance that the Soviet Union demonstrate self-restraint with respect to the Sino-Soviet conflict. An expansion of this conflict in Southeast Asia would be most undesirable for the ASEAN states. (In view of this reality, ASEAN must continue to take a neutral stance with regard to this dispute.)

IV. Concluding Remarks

The ASEAN states value highly a stable and peaceful Southeast Asia, for the maintenance of peace and stability is a prerequisite for further economic and political development.

The discussion in the second section of this paper illustrates the internal challenges faced by the ASEAN states and the threats these challenges pose to the security of the ASEAN nations. Correcting the troublesome side-effects of economic development involves a wide range of factors and is not an easy task, especially when the unity of the state and the nation is at stake. While the endeavor of political institution-building necessarily involves an ongoing process and cannot be accomplished overnight, it does constitute a crucial element in securing the continuity and sustained stability of the state. A specific and extremely important contribution of political institution-building lies in the elimination of great uncertainties surrounding the problem of succession in the ASEAN nations.

Although the prospects for the solution of internal problems are not as pessimistic as some observers have asserted, the challenges ahead remain great. The necessary tasks are rendered even more complicated when the external environment is not conducive to supporting the internal efforts of the respective governments. In view of this reality, a balanced presence in Southeast Asia of the four major powers is a requirement for regional security. The pursuit of domination by any one power likely would invite another power to increase its activities in the region so as to offset the former's gain. Illegitimate means more often than not are used to achieve such augmentation of power.

While the current degree of American presence in the Southeast Asian subregion is considered minimal, it is of a sounder form than in previous years. The nature of American relations with the ASEAN states today is more in the spirit of consultation among equals and has transcended the "superpower-client" relationship which was most evident in the past.

Despite some occasional dissatisfactions, Japan's economic presence in the area generally is accepted and encouraged by the ASEAN states. It appears that Japan also should be encouraged to take on a greater political role in the Asian/Pacific region, but it should be noted that Japan will need some time to formulate more concrete guidelines for performance of this role. Additionally, while a military role for Japan may be inevitable in the most distant future, it must be developed in consultation with the other countries of the Pacific Basin region.

The sort of role which the PRC can play in the region and which will be acceptable to the ASEAN states will depend to a large extent on the attitudes and behavioral patterns of the present leadership in Peking, the PRC's internal policies, and the country's foreign policy stance and outlook, especially with respect to party-to-party relations and the problem of the overseas Chinese. For its part, the role of the Soviet Union in Southeast Asia currently is perceived as an ambiguous one and will be watched closely by the ASEAN nations. Most important in this regard will be the policies of the USSR with respect to a resolution of the Indochina conflict.

REPORT OF COMMITTEE #1

The members of Committee #1 considered and made recommendations with respect to the broad range of issues falling under the general heading of "Political/Military Dimensions of Southeast Asian Security."

Co-chairmen:
Professor Chandran Jeshurun,
*Department of History, University of Malaya,
Kuala Lumpur, Malaysia*

Dr. Peter Polomka,
*Office of National Assessments,
Canberra, Australia*

I. Introduction

A. Recent developments have led to growing concern about the prospects for peace and stability in the Southeast Asian subregion. Principally these developments are:

1. Vietnam's invasion of Kampuchea (following Hanoi's failure to resolve its conflict with the Pol Pot regime by diplomatic means);
2. The growing Soviet naval presence, particularly the Soviet Union's (so far limited) access to naval, air, and communications facilities in Vietnam; and
3. The widespread perception of shrinking U.S. "will" to counter security threats in the region (e.g., as manifested by the Guam Doctrine and proposals to withdraw U.S. land forces from the Republic of Korea).

B. The concerns of the ASEAN states, particularly Thailand, arise foremostly from the threat a Soviet-backed Vietnam may pose to their territorial integrity and their continued economic growth and progress toward the development of viable and stable political institutions. There is also apprehensiveness about the major, long-term refugee problem being created by Vietnamese policies and activities. The ASEAN states to varying degrees are concerned about the expansion of Soviet naval power and the emergence of a Soviet/Vietnamese military nexus, especially with respect to the possibility that the Soviet navy may gain permanent military facilities in the Southeast Asian subregion.
C. States external to the subregion—the United States, Japan, Australia, and New Zealand—are concerned about the growth of Soviet influence in the subregion. The expansion of Soviet naval power and the threat this poses to the security of the sea lanes in the subregion—particularly through the strategic foothold the USSR has gained in Vietnam—have caused these nations considerable concern.

II. Summary of Discussion

National Resilience

1. It is likely that internal security concerns will continue to be of paramount importance for the ASEAN states.
2. The lesson which the ASEAN states learned from the Vietnam war was that their long-term defense relations could not be based on the certain assumption that the U.S. would come to their aid in time of need.
3. There was general agreement among the committee members from the ASEAN states on the importance of developing their individual and collective capacities for self-reliance. It was recognized that there are dangers inherent in certain forms of U.S. assistance which could destroy the confidence of those countries it seeks to help. The committee also recognized that the U.S. would respond to events or circumstances which constitute a major threat to the regional balance of power.
4. The ASEAN states will continue to pursue their long-term objective of the establishment of a Zone of Peace, Freedom, and Neutrality

Report of Committee #1

(ZOPFAN), the minimum price of which would be a gradual easing out of all external military presence.
5. The long-term security interests of the subregion would be served best by the conscious development of the national resilience of the Southeast Asian states. National resilience is defined as the ability to be self-reliant in every respect, including the social, economic, political, and military spheres. The emergence of such national resilience would help generate regional resilience, which in turn would enhance and help to preserve peace and stability in Asia and the Pacific Basin. The achievement of regional resilience among subgroupings in Northeast Asia, Southeast Asia, and the South Pacific would lead to the emergence of a broad spectrum of stable and independent states in the Asian/Pacific region.

Threat Perception

1. Many but not all committee members felt that although it cannot be ruled out, an overt Vietnamese invasion of Thailand is unlikely to occur in the foreseeable future. Vietnam will be constrained in part by economic difficulties and by its attempts to consolidate its position in Kampuchea. With respect to any aims Vietnam might have to undermine Thailand, Hanoi is more likely to pursue a longer-term strategy of insurgency and the development of united front tactics than to engage in a Kampuchean-type invasion.
2. There is no unanimous view among the ASEAN states with respect to the degree of danger to regional security posed by a Hanoi-dominated Indochina. In general, the more distant the state from Indochina, the lower the "level of apprehension" this prospect raises and will continue to engender—provided Hanoi's behavior is such that Vietnam is perceived as an independent regional power and not a Soviet proxy.
3. The most immediate threat arises from the presence of Vietnamese military forces in Kampuchea on the Thai border. The ASEAN states seek as a political aim the complete withdrawal of Vietnamese forces from Kampuchea. As a minimal immediate objective, the withdrawal of Vietnamese forces from western Kampuchea will help to allay Thai fears and reduce tensions on the border.
4. The People's Republic of China (PRC) could prove to be a positive force in the development of regional security. However, the ASEAN states perceive the PRC to be a long-term threat and do not wish to "run from one threat to another" or to "escape the tiger to meet the crocodile."

5. The committee in general felt that Vietnamese policy in Kampuchea constitutes primarily a long-term threat to Thailand and the rest of Southeast Asia. Several persons in the committee, but not the committee as a whole, expressed concern about another possible scenario and course of events. In this view, there is a real danger that in the face of concerted international criticism of and opposition to Vietnamese policy, Hanoi might make a tactical move by provoking border incidents with Thailand, thus heightening the tensions in Thai-Vietnamese relations. Such a move might serve to direct world attention away from the Kampuchean situation and give Vietnam relief from unfavorable pressure, for Vietnam then would appear to be engaged in a communist versus non-communist struggle. This in turn would earn sympathy for Hanoi and consolidate communist and non-aligned support for Vietnam. The possibility that such a shifting of focus might occur has been evident in Vietnam's insistence that its involvement in Kampuchea is an internal matter. Thus, argued some committee members, the danger of such a tactical ploy should constantly be borne in mind.

Relations with Indochina

1. With respect to the development by the ASEAN countries of relations with the communist states of Southeast Asia, relations with Vietnam are regarded as pivotal. The inherent and latent differences among the members of the Vietnamese ruling elite in their leanings toward the PRC or the USSR hold some promise of offering a certain scope for maneuverability in ASEAN's conduct of relations with the communist states. These conflicting tendencies in Vietnamese attitudes toward the major communist powers should be utilized to the advantage of the non-communist nations in their relations with Vietnam, Laos, and Kampuchea.

Relations between ASEAN and Vietnam

1. The committee was of the view that the current channels and modes of communication which have been established between ASEAN and Vietnam should be further developed and strengthened. Joint efforts in the taking up of initiatives with Vietnam and the adoption of a common stand with respect to issues between ASEAN and Vietnam should be encouraged. An ASEAN-Vietnam dialogue on a wide range of subjects of mutual interest should be maintained. Some committee members felt that as far as possible, ASEAN

should adopt a conciliatory approach and encourage moves toward the peaceful settlement of disputes, but it should be noted that not all committee members were comfortable with this language.

Relations between Vietnam and the Soviet Union

1. While the Treaty of Friendship and Cooperation between the Soviet Union and the Socialist Republic of Vietnam formalized the growing military, political, and economic collaboration between the two countries, the acquisition by the Soviet Union of access to Vietnamese military facilities followed the attack on Vietnam by the PRC, suggesting an earlier reluctance by Vietnam to compromise its independence. That the nature of Soviet access to Vietnamese military facilities thus far has been limited may also suggest that Vietnam will not further compromise its independence lightly.
2. Present Vietnamese defense relations with the Soviet Union seem largely related to the parallel interests of Hanoi and Moscow in opposing the PRC, rather than to any Soviet/Vietnamese aims in Southeast Asia. It is the side-effects of this relationship—e.g., the situation in Kampuchea—and the relationship's potential to threaten ASEAN interests which cause concern. In the medium-term, the USSR is likely to use a "carrot-and-stick" approach to gaining greater acceptance as a power in the Southeast Asian subregion. With respect to U.S. and Soviet naval power in the area, a "Mediterranean-type" situation can be expected to develop over time.
3. An issue of immediate importance concerns the psychological impact of Soviet gains in the region and how this impact can and should be countered.
4. A need exists for an active response from the United States to the growing Soviet activities and influence in the region.
5. Pressure from the PRC is likely to determine largely the extent to which Vietnam becomes a surrogate for the pursuit of Soviet aims in the region.

Communist Indochina or an Indochinese Federation?

1. With respect to the likely future character of relations among Vietnam, Laos, and Kampuchea, two clearly opposed points of view emerged from the committee sessions. Individuals holding the first viewpoint felt that in the long-term an Indochinese Federation characterized by predominant Vietnamese influence is inevitable. In

a variant form of this outlook, some felt that the three would continue to exist as independent and sovereign nations, but that Vietnam would play the most significant role in the relations among these states. As a corollary to this assessment, committee members holding this view felt that the non-communist states of Southeast Asia should tolerate the emergence of either of these two forms of the future Indochina and try to cultivate normal relations with whichever one emerges. Those holding the second point of view, however, were strongly opposed to either prospect described above and asserted that every effort should be made to ensure that each of the three communist states would be genuinely independent and sovereign. This scenario was considered by these persons to be the most desirable one for the future security of Southeast Asia.

Security Cooperation

1. The committee concluded that the sort of contribution individual Southeast Asian states could make toward regional security would be mainly diplomatic in nature. The Philippines has made an important specific gesture—i.e., by affording the United States the utilization of military facilities at Subic Bay Naval Base and Clark Air Base. In view of the absence of any immediate threat of a direct Vietnamese attack against any of the ASEAN states and the obvious limitations in the military capabilities of these nations, the committee saw no real need for cooperative military efforts other than those already in operation on a bilateral basis between individual Southeast Asian countries.

Refugees

1. The Committee perceived the possible influx of some 600,000 Kampuchean refugees into Thai territory as an immediate threat to Thailand and, by extension, to the subregion as a whole. It was anticipated that this problem would arise as one of the major consequences of the likely large-scale Vietnamese assault against the remnants of the Pol Pot regime. The position of these refugees may eventually result in the creation of a situation akin to that of the Sudeten Germans in 1938 and the Palestinians in the late 1960s.

III. Policy Proposals

1. To recognize and build upon the economic and other gains made by the ASEAN states in the past two decades toward development of

their individual and collective capacities to resist internal and external threats to their security.
2. To counter Soviet policies in Indochina and to seek in the medium-term a balance of military forces in the Asian/Pacific region.
3. To neutralize the effects of Sino-Soviet rivalry and to minimize the impact of the military nexus between Hanoi and Moscow.
4. To avoid or at least minimize direct confrontation between ASEAN and Vietnam, and to cultivate and improve the understanding which had begun to develop between ASEAN and Vietnam in 1977-1978.
5. To maintain the neutrality and self-reliance of ASEAN vis-a-vis the conflict among the communist states in the Asian/Pacific region and, in particular, avoid heightening Sino-Soviet rivalry in the area.
6. To seek from the United States an adequate response to the growing influence and activities of the Soviet Union in Southeast Asia.
7. To continue to develop consultations and schedule activities with respect to security matters between and among the individual ASEAN states and with other states in the wider Asian/Pacific region.
8. To continue to work toward the long-term ASEAN aim of creating a Zone of Peace, Freedom, and Neutrality in Southeast Asia.

Chapter 2

POLITICAL/MILITARY DIMENSIONS OF SECURITY IN NORTHEAST ASIA

Issues And Questions To Be Addressed: 2

The organizers of the Pattaya conference set forth the following paragraphs—which outlined some of the more specific problems to be addressed, both formally and informally, during the course of the conference—as a guide for conference participants. While conferees in their formal papers, discussion sessions, and committee reports were free to range over a wide range of subject matter and concerns, and not all the suggested questions were answered fully or directly, the "Issues and Questions to be Addressed" served to provide a framework and direction for the deliberations of the conference.

The Japanese Defense Posture and the Soviet Challenge

The Soviet Union in recent years has engaged in a military buildup of significant dimensions in the subregion of Northeast Asia. The Soviets have deployed 44 divisions along or near the Sino-Soviet border, with more than 32 of these situated east of Lake Baikal. These forces have recently received large numbers of new weapons. The Soviets have increased their air defenses and stationed approximately 800 fighter aircraft in the area. The greatly modernized and expanded Soviet Pacific Fleet, based in Vladivostok, is now second in size only to the Soviet Northern Fleet and has recently been strengthened by the addition of the aircraft carrier *Minsk* and two escorts.

Of particular concern to the countries of Northeast Asia is the increasing activity of Soviet ships and aircraft in the sea and air around Japan. The Soviets, for example, have constructed a large military base on the island of Etorofu, one of the four Japanese islands in the Kurile group occupied in 1945 and still retained by the Soviet Union; and have increased their naval and air activities in the other Kurile Islands adjacent to Japan, with particular emphasis on amphibious and air-borne capabilities.

A growing number of observers, both Japanese and foreign, have noted the widening disparity between Japan's constitutionally restricted defense measures and the increasing threats to Japanese security posed by the strengthening of Soviet military power in the Pacific area. The sea lanes of communication in the region—upon which Japan is dependent for the import of food and raw materials and the export of manufactured goods—are highly vulnerable to harassment, embargo, or attack. As one British analyst has asked, is it viable and realistic for Japan to "continue indefinitely to rely on the United States for protection, and for the maintenance of the balance of power, security, and stability in the Pacific Basin area, without adopting political and military policies commensurate with its economic power and influence, separate from but allied to those of the United States"?

- What are the requirements for an effective and viable system of territorial defense for the Japanese homeland?
- What are the major weaknesses in Japan's general defense capability, and to what extent should Japan be prepared to augment quantitatively and qualitatively its armed forces? What are the possibilities of increased defense spending, and what can and should such expenditures buy?
- What are the implications for the countries of Northeast Asia of such developments as: the appearance of Soviet Backfire bombers on the Kamchatka peninsula; the deployment of the new Russian SS-20 mobile missiles in East Asia; and evidence that Najin in the extreme northeast of North Korea is being developed as a potential Soviet warm water base?

Issues and Questions to be Addressed

- What are the requirements for the maintenance and strengthening of the U.S.-Japan security system?
- What are the potential security implications of the Japanese rapprochement with the PRC?
- How can Japan contribute to the development of a cooperative system for the protection of maritime transportation?
- By what means can Japan become more actively involved in the 1980s in defending its own security interests, and make a meaningful contribution to the defense of Northeast Asia and the Asian/Pacific area in general?

The Tensions on the Korean Peninsula

Recent Western and Asian intelligence reports have presented strong evidence of substantial increases in North Korea's warmaking capacity, indicating, for example, that: North Korean ground forces have increased from 440,000 to between 550,000 and 600,000 (compared to 520,000 for the Republic of Korea [ROK]); the number of North Korean brigades has increased from 29 to 37; the number of tanks has increased by 35%; and artillery tubes and armored personnel carriers have increased by about 20%. Commentators point to the danger of a possible North Korean concentration of its forces in a surprise, Blitzkrieg-style drive to capture or threaten Seoul, especially in view of recent studies which indicate a sharply reduced estimate of the warning time which would be available to defenders in South Korea. There is also cause for concern that, in the absence of clearly articulated American commitments to South Korean security, Pyongyang might calculate that an invasion of the South could be carried out successfully due to the lessened credibility of the American presence and American guarantees.

- What are the improvements required of the South Korean armed forces so as to provide for an effective and viable system of territorial defense for the Republic of Korea?
- What are the implications for South Korean policy of the imbalance between the respective defense efforts of North and South Korea, in view of reports that the North now allocates close to 25% of its Gross National Product for defense spending?
- What are the implications for South Korean and regional security of

the PRC's support for Pyongyang's policies and North Korea's heavy dependence on the Soviet Union for political support, economic aid, and sophisticated weaponry?
- What is the outlook for a political settlement between the two Koreas?
- What are the political and military consequences of the now-modified Carter Administration decision in 1977 to withdraw American ground forces from South Korea?
- Given the new intelligence findings regarding North Korean military strength, what should be the continued role of the U.S. Second Division as a deterrent and stabilizing force, and how important is the Division's warfighting capacity as an ingredient of the military balance?
- What are the American and South Korean military and political policies most likely to increase the prospects for peace and stability on the Korean peninsula in both the short- and long-term?
- What relationship is there, or should there be, between the defense of the ROK and the defense of Japan?
- By what means can South Korea make a meaningful contribution to the defense of Northeast Asia and the Asian/Pacific area in general?

JAPAN AND THE SECURITY OF NORTHEAST ASIA:
Editor's Introduction

Japan maintains a military establishment and defense posture of remarkably low profile for a country of such immense economic and political importance, both regionally and globally. Japan thus far has determined, first of all, that it will adhere to the "Three Non-Nuclear Principles" of "no possession, no manufacturing, and no introduction of nuclear weapons in Japan." Additionally, the Japanese government holds to the view that the nation's defense capabilities must be "exclusively self-defensive," and the possession of "offensive" weaponry is prohibited under any circumstances. As stated in the 1979 Defense Agency White Paper, and as the Japanese Diet has resolved, ". . . the dispatch abroad of armed personnel, with a mission to engage in military action, is not permitted under the terms of the Constitution."[1]

---
[1] Defense Agency, Japan, *Defense of Japan (1979)*, translated into English by the Mainichi Daily News.

These restrictions flow from Japan's World War II experiences and its unusual post-war history. Japan, at the time of surrender, was ordered to abolish its armed forces. This step was accomplished and was codified in Article 9 of Japan's 1947 "Peace Constitution," adopted under the guidance of the American occupation authorities, which states that the "Japanese people forever renounce war as the sovereign right of the nation. . . . Land, sea, and air forces, as well as war potential, will never be maintained." In practice, however, the need for some Japanese defense capability was soon recognized. In 1950, when Japan was still under American occupation, General Douglas MacArthur formed a 75,000-man "National Police Reserve" to fill the gap left by occupation troops which had departed for Korea, thus in effect ambiguously "sidestepping" the constitutional ban on armed forces which he himself had urged upon the Japanese. The Treaty of Peace with Japan signed by forty-eight nations in September 1951 recognized Japan's inherent right to self-defense. In the U.S.-Japan Mutual Security Treaty which was signed immediately thereafter, the Japanese pledged "that Japan will itself increasingly assume responsibility for its own defense against direct and indirect aggression." By 1954 the Police Reserve had metamorphosed into the Japanese Self-Defense Forces (SDF), composed of all-volunteer air, maritime, and ground forces.

While the formal constitutional ban on war potential has not been rescinded, in effect the Japanese government has rationalized the legality of the SDF on the basis of the nation's inherent right of self-defense. As the 1979 White Paper spells out, "It is clearly recognized . . . that no objection is raised by the Constitution to the right of Japan as a sovereign nation to defend itself against foreign invasion. . . . [T]he Japanese government holds the view there is no Constitutional prohibition on the maintenance of a minimum defensive force able to protect Japan's territory and people."

Within the context of this constitutional interpretation, Japan has followed a defense policy which rests on two primary foundations: adherence to the U.S.-Japan security system and gradual buildup of a Japanese self-defense capability. The terms of Article 9 cited above impose great limitations on the SDF with respect to troop strength and equipment, however, and while Japan has implemented a series of defense buildup plans covering three- to five-year periods, these plans have aimed at developing a defense capacity "able to effectively meet the type of aggression on a scale no greater than localized conflict with conventional weapons."[2]

Japan relies for its ultimate defense guarantee on the "nuclear umbrella" provided by the United States. Under the terms of the Security Treaty, the U.S. is obligated to defend Japan in the case of an armed attack against the Japanese homeland, and Japan is protected by the U.S. Seventh Fleet, the Fifth Air Force, and a Marine division in Okinawa. In the event of war, the SDF will conduct defensive operations in Japanese territory and its surrounding waters and air space, relying on the U.S. to supplement Japan's domestic defense capabilities in dealing with nuclear threats or large-scale conventional aggression.

For a number of reasons, which will be set forth extensively in this chapter's essay by Admiral Kitamura and Professor Tsunoda, a significant number of Japanese have begun in recent years to question, albeit cautiously, the adequacy of their country's security posture. There is now more open and public discussion of defense-related issues in Japan, and such discussion raises fewer and less intense political storms than in times past. While public opinion still strongly opposes actual revision of the constitution, a great majority of the Japanese people now have come to support the existence of the SDF. Of Japan's opposition political parties, only the Communist Party continues to take a clear official stand against the SDF and the U.S.-Japan Security Treaty.[3]

A national debate seems to have opened on several crucial defense issues, including such matters as: a) how much, if at all, Japan should expand its military establishment; b) whether it is possible and/or prudent for Japan to remain so overwhelmingly dependent on the U.S. for its security and defense; and c) what contribution, if any, Japan can and should make to East Asian regional security. Considerable attention has been focused on the

---

[2] Ibid.
[3] Evidence emerged during the first half of 1980 indicating that the Socialist Party was abandoning its long-held hostility toward the U.S. and shelving its longstanding opposition to the Security Treaty and the existence of the SDF. See Henry Scott Stokes, "Socialist-Communist Split Alters the Political Scene in Japan," *New York Times*, June 19, 1980.

issue of the possibility of increased defense spending, which up to the present has been limited by political (not constitutional) barriers to not more than 1% of Japan's Gross National Product.[4]

Political opposition to closer security cooperation between the United States and Japan seems to have lessened. A Joint Committee on Defense Cooperation, with subcommittees on operations, intelligence, and rear-support, was formed in 1976, and the "Guidelines for Japan-U.S. Defense Cooperation" drafted by this group were approved in November 1978. Among other provisions, the Guidelines called for the SDF and U.S. forces to engage in studies on joint defense planning; conduct necessary joint exercises and training; and carry out a joint study of combined operations for the defense of Japan.

Some of the Guidelines have been acted upon, and there was evidence at the end of the 1970s and the beginning of the 1980s that support now exists in Japan for a more serious and substantial security effort, within the context of the U.S.-Japan security system. The studies of combined operations have been undertaken (but are not yet completed), and combined naval and air force exercises have increased in number. The Maritime SDF will continue its exercises in anti-submarine warfare with the aircraft carriers of the U.S. Seventh Fleet, and in early 1980 Japan participated in joint maneuvers off Hawaii with the navies of the U.S., Canada, Australia, and New Zealand.[5] The first specific plans for joint

---

[4] There are several ways of viewing the dynamics of Japanese defense spending. During 1979 Japan's GNP exceeded that of the Soviet Union, making Japan the world's second-largest national economic unit (after the U.S.). Thus, even the comparatively low percentage of GNP devoted to defense results in a not inconsequential monetary amount, and Japan's military budget is now eighth largest in the world. Japanese defense spending has risen at an annual rate of 8% for the past decade, compared with an annual 2% decline in real U.S. defense expenditures over the same period (*Wall Street Journal*, March 28, 1980). It also has been pointed out that Japanese defense spending, when computed on the same basis as is used by the North Atlantic Treaty Organization, is actually equivalent to approximately 1.5% of GNP (*New York Times*, March 20, 1980). A somewhat different light may be cast on these figures, however, when it is remembered that credible estimates of Soviet defense expenditures lie in the range of 11 to 15% of the USSR's similarly enormous GNP.

[5] In February and March 1980 Japan's Maritime SDF participated in Operation RIMPAC, a joint training exercise held in the Central Pacific off Hawaii. Other participating nations were the U.S., Canada, Australia, and New Zealand. The exercise included some 40 warships, 200 aircraft, and 20,000 men, with Japan contributing 2 destroyers, 8 anti-submarine patrol craft, and 700 seamen. While Japan has conducted military training with the U.S. since 1956, this was the country's first participation in a multinational exercise.

ground maneuvers, to be held in Okinawa in 1980, have now been made. Exchanges of visits by the most senior Japanese and American defense officials took place in 1979, and the Japanese are now bearing a larger portion of the costs of stationing U.S. forces in Japan.

Japan is moving toward gradual augmentation of the capabilities of the Self-Defense Forces. According to the 1979 Defense Agency White Paper, efforts will be made to modernize equipment, improve operational postures, and strengthen the logistics support structure. Recent plans have been made to improve capacities in the areas of anti-submarine warfare and air defense, including the purchase of 100 F-15 fighters, 8 E2-C early warning aircraft, and 45 P3-C anti-submarine aircraft.

Much resistance and many obstacles remain along the path toward a stronger Japanese defense posture. Varying ideas with respect to the proper interpretation of Japan's "Peace Constitution" in the context of East Asia's changing international environment will result in much political controversy, and major policy changes are likely to come slowly. However, it is clear that Japan is paying more and closer attention to security issues, with a heightened awareness of the implications for an adequate defense and security posture which flow from the country's growing economic and political involvement in the Western Pacific region and the world at large.

While Japan's participation in RIMPAC touched off some demonstrations and protests at home, the level of protest was relatively mild in comparison to past displays of anti-military sentiment. See William Chapman, "Japan Joins 5-Nation Naval Games," *Washington Post*, February 27, 1980; and Henry Scott Stokes, "6,000 Protest Japan Participation in Naval Exercise," *New York Times*, February 26, 1980.

Address

General Masao Horie (Ret.)
Councillor, Japanese Diet, Tokyo, Japan

NORTHEAST ASIAN SECURITY: THE JAPANESE ROLE

Masao Horie

The basic principles of the Japanese Constitution include the maintenance of a liberal democratic political system, striving for international cooperation, and the solidification of peace. On the basis of these principles, it has been Japan's consistent policy to make a contribution to the development of a free and peaceful international community. As far as can be foreseen, there will be no basic change in this orientation.

In line with the "Basic Policies for National Defense" adopted by the Cabinet in 1957, the successive governments formed by the Liberal Democratic Party have followed policies of: 1) the establishment and maintenance of domestic stability, always an essential foundation of any security policy; 2) the gradual buildup of effective Self-Defense Forces (SDF), to operate within the confines of the boundaries of self-defense; and 3) the maintenance of the U.S.-Japan security system as the basis for all Japan's defense efforts.

We are aware of the criticism being voiced that Japan has been using its constitution—and the restrictions on the Japanese defense posture contained therein—as a sort of shelter to avoid facing squarely the issue of security. It is a fact, however, that for all countries a constitution is the moral code of the nation, and Japan cannot afford to benignly neglect its constitution. A nation may, of course, choose to fundamentally revise its constitution, but such a move is not possible given the present domestic political alignment and situation in Japan.

The need to respond to the recent military developments taking place in Northeast Asia, however, does constitute an urgent problem for Japan. The recent Soviet military buildup in the region of Northeast Asia should be understood as one aspect of the offensive global strategy of the Soviet Union, which aims, among other things, to establish a posture of superiority to the U.S., exert military pressure on both Japan and the People's Republic of China (PRC), and thrust further into the Southeast Asian and Indian Ocean regions. Other factors serving to heighten the tensions in East Asia include the relative decline of American military presence in the area, Chinese military policy with respect to Indochina, and the military buildup in North Korea. Particularly threatening to Japan is the recent Soviet military activity in and around the four northern Japanese islands occupied by the USSR since 1945. Although the Japanese have kept calm and avoided psychological panic, the Soviet moves have caused grave concern and apprehension and have brought a new level of awareness to issues of national defense.

The immediate task before Japan is to increase its defense effort, improve substantially its capabilities, and thereby demonstrate the nation's true resolve to withstand threats to the countries of the Pacific Basin. Japanese national consciousness with respect to defense matters has been growing, as has support for the SDF. In a recent public opinion poll, when persons were asked the question, "Should Japan have Self-Defense Forces," 86% answered affirmatively, including many supporters of the Socialist and Communist Parties.[1] (Ten years ago the figure was around 75%). When asked about SDF force levels, a large number

---

[1] The figures for the Socialist and Communist Parties were 81% and 61% respectively.

of Japanese responded that the current size is appropriate,[2] but the number in favor of an increased military buildup went up by a few percentage points.[3]

In the current program for the buildup of the SDF, emphasis is placed on the modernization of weapons and materials and on the cultivation of war-sustaining power—for example, through the improvement of logistics. Maritime and air defense capabilities will be improved by the purchase of 100 F-15 fighters, 8 E2-C early warning aircraft, and 45 P3-C maritime surveillance aircraft; and by the introduction of ship-borne missiles. Efforts will be made to enhance Japan's ability to protect the three straits choking the Sea of Japan and the sea lanes of communication around the Japanese islands. Japan and the U.S. are currently engaged in drawing up specific plans for the practical implementation of security cooperation between the two countries, and the Japanese government has approved the participation of the Maritime SDF in the RIMPAC exercise to be held in the Spring of 1980, around the core of the U.S. Pacific Fleet.[4]

Japan's total defense-related expenditure in year fiscal 1979 was $9.52 billion (up 10.2% from the preceding year), which constituted 5.4% of Japan's total government budget and 0.9% of its Gross National Product. Spending for the improvements in the SDF noted above would necessitate an annual increase of about $1 billion. Japan has also increased its share of the financial burden of stationing American troops in Japan.[5] Although the Japanese government has in recent times faced a tight fiscal situation—financing about 40% of its budget through governmental bonds and possibly finding it necessary to reduce spending in such fields as social security and education—the need for increased defense spending is an issue of extraordinary importance and should be evaluated separately on its own merits.

---

[2] 53% of the respondents felt that the ground force is of appropriate size; the corresponding figures for the maritime force and the air force were 49% and 48% respectively.
[3] 22% of the respondents felt that the ground force should be enlarged; the corresponding figure for the maritime force and the air force was 23% in each case. This represented an increase of 8% with respect to the number favoring a larger air force; the increase with respect to the ground force and the maritime force was 5% in each case.
[4] See footnote 5, p. 92.
[5] Japan now contributes approximately $7 billion, as compared with $5.7 billion in the previous fiscal year.

In the hope that such activity will contribute to the development of a peaceful regional environment, Japan will in the future play an even more active role in providing economic assistance to countries in East Asia. Japan's recent provision of non-military credit to the PRC was carried forth only after understanding had been secured from other Asian countries. Japan in fact has no intention of helping China improve its military strength, and the same holds true with respect to the terms of the Soviet-Japanese economic relationship.

In summary, Japan will endeavor to strengthen its defense forces for the sake of Japan's own security and as a contribution to the security of Northeast Asia and the Pacific Basin region as a whole. At the same time, Japan will work to increase the credibility of the Japanese-American treaty system and help the U.S. maintain its military presence in the region, which is so crucial to the stability of the area.

Conference Papers and Commentary

Admiral Kenichi Kitamura (Ret.),
Former Chief of Naval Operations, Tokyo, Japan

Professor Jun Tsunoda,
Department of International Relations, Asyama-Gakuin University, Tokyo, Japan

Ambassador Hogan Yoon,
Consul General of the Republic of Korea, New York, N.Y., USA

The Honorable Dr. Frederick F. Chien,
Vice Minister of Foreign Affairs, Taipei, Republic of China

THE JAPANESE DEFENSE POSTURE AND THE SOVIET CHALLENGE IN NORTHEAST ASIA

Kenichi Kitamura and Jun Tsunoda

1. The Soviet Challenge in Northeast Asia

The Growth of Soviet Military Power

Reliable reports indicate that the U.S.-Soviet strategic nuclear balance, which now stands at rough parity, may tip in favor of the Soviet Union in the mid-1980s. Such a development would throw into question the ability of U.S. strategic nuclear power to deter a Soviet attack outside the boundaries of the American homeland. Thus, it cannot be assumed that the U.S.-Soviet mutual deterrent relationship will in the future effectively deter all conventional warfare. The theater-nuclear and conventional power balances in the various regions around the world are therefore of great importance with respect to the continued deterrence of Soviet aggression. It is in this light that the altering military balance in East Asia takes on tremendous significance, especially in view of the reported Soviet deployment of SS-20 medium-range ballistic missiles and Backfire bombers in the region.

The Soviet Union in recent years has strengthened its military power and presence both quantitatively and qualitatively in the Asian/Pacific Basin region. Approximately one-quarter of the total Soviet ground forces (i.e., 400,000 men in 44 divisions) are deployed along or near the Sino-Soviet border; 32 of these divisions are deployed in areas east of Lake Baikal. About 2,000 combat aircraft (including Backfire bombers), comprising one-quarter of the total Soviet air force, are deployed in the Far East. Approximately 30% of the total Soviet strategic missile force of Intercontinental Ballistic Missiles (ICBMs) and Submarine-Launched Ballistic Missiles (SLBMs) are deployed in the region, in inland areas and with the Soviet Pacific Fleet. Additionally, as noted above, it is now reported that the Soviets have added SS-20 missiles to their capabilities in the Far East.

Shifts in the East Asian Naval Balance

That the Soviets have built from their former coastal defense fleet an ocean-going navy is a development of great political and military significance. The Soviet Pacific Fleet—which is based in Vladivostok and operates in seas ranging from the Pacific to the Indian Oceans—has been tremendously strengthened in recent years, with expanded activity throughout its area of operations. While the Soviet navy's lack of sea-based tactical air units was in times past one of its weakest points, this weakness has now been modified by the Soviet development of modern aircraft carriers, and the Pacific Fleet since Summer 1979 has been supplemented by the latest model Kiev-class carrier, the *Minsk*.

The steady growth of Soviet power in the Western Pacific region has had an impact on the U.S.-Soviet military (particularly naval) balance in the area. Approximately 770 ships (1,380,000 tons total), comprising one-third of the total Soviet naval forces, are assigned to the Pacific Fleet; the U.S. Seventh Fleet, on the other hand, is composed of about 55 ships (600,000 tons total), including two aircraft carriers. In estimating the relative strengths of the U.S. and Soviet navies, however, a number of things must be taken into account, including differing force structures, strategies, weapons systems, national policies, and geopolitical conditions. A comparison conducted merely in numerical terms is meaningless and may lead to serious misevaluation. The Soviet Fleet includes many ships and units unavailable for modern operations on the ocean, such as coastal defense units, ships under repair, and old or obsolete vessels. On the other hand, the U.S. Seventh Fleet is a mobile striking force manned by sophisticated, ocean-going combatants, is ready for operations at any moment, and can be augmented by the Third Fleet as may be required.

In a large-scale military conflict involving the U.S. and the USSR, the activities of the Soviet units based along the coast of the Sea of Japan would be quite restricted due to geographical conditions. Furthermore, if the U.S. aircraft carriers were to remain in the Western Pacific, the Soviet military bases and units in and outside the Sea of Japan area might be destroyed. For the Soviets, the U.S. carriers would be the most important targets of destruction. In view of the notable development of Soviet military technology, much debate has recently arisen with respect to the possible vulnerability of U.S. carriers which may approach the USSR's well-defended territories. While much confidence is still placed in the survivability of these ships, their invulnerability cannot safely be assumed, and the allies of the United States in Northeast Asia should endeavor to contribute to increasing the safety of the American carriers.

Dangers of the U.S. "Swing Strategy"

U.S. political/military presence in and commitment to the Asian/Pacific Basin region are essential to the security of the area. It seems, however, that the first priority of the U.S. is toward NATO and the European theater. Recently it was revealed that the U.S. includes in its military plans a "Swing Strategy," in which a considerable portion of the U.S. forces under the Pacific Command would be redeployed to Europe in case of a conflict involving NATO. Japan and other free-world Asian nations—which had just begun to regain confidence in the U.S. commitment to Pacific Asia—were shocked to learn of this strategy and have expressed serious concern with respect to its possible consequences.

If war involving the U.S. and the USSR were to occur in the NATO area or the Middle East, it is likely that the conflict would quickly widen to include the Pacific region, at least as far as the sea lanes of communication are concerned. As reported in the *Washington Post* on October 8, 1979, the U.S. Commander-in-Chief, Pacific, in discussing the implications of the "Swing Strategy," noted that if half his fleet were sent to Europe, "He would have to turn his back on U.S. alliance commitments and become totally defensive in order to survive in the Pacific." On the other hand, geography would not allow the USSR to shift its Pacific Fleet activities to the European theater; thus, the Soviet Far Eastern navy would remain concentrated in the Pacific, but without the counterforce of a strong Seventh Fleet.

The *Minsk* and the newest Soviet cruisers possess combat capabilities inferior to those of comparable U.S. ships, and as long as the American carriers remain in the Western Pacific, the presence of the *Minsk* will not present a serious problem. Application of the "Swing Strategy," however, would drastically alter the strategic situation in the Pacific region, resulting in Soviet air and marine supremacy in Asia. In this situation, with U.S. carriers shifted to another area, the *Minsk* could no longer be ignored.

Beyond the obvious military consequences, the "Swing Strategy"—if it were to be carried out—would have political and psychological ramifications which would weaken the Asian/Pacific Basin defense structure. The fact that it is impossible to anticipate the probable response of the People's Republic of China (PRC) to a war contingency involving the Soviet Union only adds to the uncertainty. In the worst case, the USSR and the PRC might come to some accommodation whereby Moscow could shift its armed forces from the Sino-Soviet border to Europe. For all these reasons, the "Swing Strategy" has severe negative implications for the security of the Asian/Pacific region, and may be inappropriate for the defense of NATO as well.*

---

* *Editor's Note:* It has been reported that President Jimmy Carter in April 1980 decided that the U.S. would no longer adhere to the decades-old "Swing Strategy," in view of the requirements of the increased American naval presence in the Indian Ocean and the growth of Soviet ground and naval forces in East Asia. According to government officials, the policy shift will increase flexibility by enabling the U.S. to keep its forces in the Pacific, move them into the Indian Ocean, or send them to Europe as circumstances require. See Richard Burt, "U.S. Strategy Focus Shifting from Europe to Pacific," *New York Times,* May 25, 1980.

Increased Soviet Military Activity Around Japan

Soviet warships and aircraft have been more assertive recently in the sea and air around Japan. Japan's territorial dispute continues with the USSR over the four islands in the South Kuriles (near Hokkaido) occupied by Russian troops at the end of World War II. The Soviet Union, which refuses to return these islands, has strengthened its military facilities on this territory, including the positioning there of a considerable number of troops, and has recently begun conducting military maneuvers in and around the islands. Soviet objectives in undertaking this military buildup are not clear. The Soviets may aim to establish advanced bases in the Kurile Islands so as to strengthen their defensive and/or offensive position in the region. Another goal may be the imposition of political and psychological pressure on Japan so that Tokyo will abandon its claim to the islands. In any case, close attention should be paid to future developments in the South Kuriles.

Soviet Use of Military Power as a Means of International Politics

In attempting to expand its influence around the world, the USSR takes advantage of every available opportunity. The Soviet Union appears to a large extent to follow a strategy which focuses on the achievement of political objectives through the indirect utilization of its military power. By displaying its powerful warships before the people of the developing nations, the Soviet Union hopes to gain the awe and/or respect of these countries, for Soviet leaders recognize the political effect which can be imposed by a strong military presence. Additionally, utilizing another set of tactics, Moscow supports anti-government forces engaged in "liberation" campaigns in various Third World countries, air- and sea-lifting military goods to these forces and sometimes involving Soviet satellites as its proxies.

It is of great political significance that the Soviet Union is now able to project tactical air units and ground forces to many distant overseas areas, especially in view of the self-imposed American restraint in recent years with respect to U.S. willingness and capability to intervene abroad. In this connection, the numerical superiority of the Soviet navy takes on greater significance, for larger numbers of ships can provide more opportunities for naval presence. Correlatively, if the United States continues to reduce the quantitative level of its naval forces, the resulting reduction of American naval presence around the world may entail a loss of political influence, despite the continued qualitative superiority of U.S. carriers and amphibious units.

With these considerations in mind, more attention should be paid to the political and psychological pressure which can be exerted in peacetime on Asian nations by the presence of the *Minsk* in Far Eastern waters.

The Importance of the Sea Lanes in the Event of War

In the case of a world-wide armed conflict, assuring the security of the sea lanes of communication running to-and-from North America, Australasia, Southeast Asia, and the Persian Gulf area would be of vital importance for the survival of the non-communist nations in the Asian/Pacific Basin region and essential for the conduct of war by the United States and its allies. A sustained disruption of normal activities in the sea lanes would create social, economic, and military shocks to all countries in the area, including Japan, which is dependent upon these transportation routes for its imports of food, oil, and other raw materials. Furthermore, the U.S. and its allies should not too easily assume that a possible future war will be short-lived and that supplies of oil and raw materials required during that period can be met with stockpiling. It may well be necessary to endure a protracted conflict lasting longer than the time-frame now expected by many analysts.

Even if the communist bases in Asia were to be destroyed in the early phases of war, the security of the Pacific sea lanes would continue to be jeopardized by the presence of Soviet submarines and Backfire bombers. The USSR has established the largest submarine fleet in history, and deploys in the Far East about 125 submarines, approximately one-third of its total fleet. Many are either SLBM-submarines comprising a component of Soviet strategic nuclear power or missile-equipped or attack-type submarines, which likely would be assigned to carry out attacks on the U.S. carriers. The remaining vessels would be assigned to attack the sea lanes during the early period of a conflict. Although most of these submarines would be of conventional type, including not a few of rather old vintage, the submarines available for such a sea lane interdiction mission do constitute a considerable number, with much power at their disposal. It is possible that present older conventional submarines may be replaced by nuclear-powered vessels in the future.

In any case, it is clear that close attention must be paid to the likelihood of sea lane attack during a conflict involving the USSR, since the Soviets are surely aware that the sea lanes are vital to the Western allies, Japan, and other nations in the Asian/Pacific region.

Future Soviet Foreign Policy in Asia

The most likely future Soviet courses of action in East Asia include the following:

Increased pressure on the PRC. There are no indications at this time suggesting that the PRC will move to restore relations with the Soviet Union. It is possible, however, that the Soviets might make efforts at least to ease the existing Sino-Soviet confrontation. In the absence of such moves—or if such efforts fail—the USSR will desire to contain the PRC. While the Soviets will employ both hard and soft tactics, they will certainly continue to exert and may increase their political and military pressure on China by maintaining a powerful military force along the Sino-Soviet border. The Soviets can also be expected to attempt to increase their influence on North Korea and in Southeast Asia, especially Indochina, thus effecting an encirclement of the PRC.

Neutralization of Japan. One of the most important Soviet political achievements in East Asia would be the neutralization of Japan and the accomplishment of Japanese-Soviet cooperation for the economic development of Siberia. As with the PRC, the USSR in its relations with Japan will employ both hard and soft tactics. The USSR can be expected to continue to exert military and political pressure on Tokyo by demonstrating more frequently and impudently its naval and air power in the areas around Japan and by pushing for more strict control over Japanese fishing in the northern seas. The possible Soviet establishment of more favorable strategic positions in the Korean peninsula and Southeast Asia will contribute to the achievement of these goals.

Expansion of Soviet influence over the Korean peninsula and in Southeast Asia. These are subregions of great geopolitical importance. As noted above, increased Soviet influence in these areas will facilitate Moscow's foreign policy aims with respect to the PRC, Japan, and the Asian/Pacific region as a whole.

The Soviet Union has already made gains in these subregions. It appears that North Korea now leans more toward the USSR than toward the PRC, and it is reported that the North Korean armed forces recently have been reinforced with substantial military assistance provided by the Soviets. Soviet ships and aircraft now have access to, and have been visiting with increasing frequency, naval and air facilities in Vietnam, and the USSR and Vietnam have signed a twenty-five year Treaty of Friendship and Cooperation.

North Korea's substantial strengthening of its armed forces and Vietnam's emergence as the strongest military power in Southeast Asia are made more significant by the possibility that the Soviet Union might use either or both of these "client states" as proxies to instigate conflicts with neighboring states without direct Soviet military involvement. Certainly it is evident that Soviet military forces in these areas could be mobilized quickly to support insurgencies in various Southeast Asian nations and/or to challenge the influence or presence of the U.S. Seventh Fleet.

For all the reasons noted above, increased Soviet control over either of these subregions would result in tremendous pressure on Japan.

To Sum Up

While the Soviet Union may not appear to have any fixed, long-range program for achieving its ultimate objective of world domination, Moscow does avail itself of every opportunity to pursue its aim. It is difficult to draw a clear distinction between the political and military threats posed by the USSR. What can be recognized is that both dimensions of the challenge stem in large part from the existence of the immense military power of the Soviet Union. Soviet seapower is of particular importance, since without seapower the Soviets would lack the ability to approach target areas in Asia and elsewhere which do not border the Russian heartland. The increase of Soviet naval power and the possible future shifts in the U.S.-Soviet naval balance therefore should be most serious concerns not only for Japan and the other Northeast Asian nations but for all the non-communist nations of the Asian/Pacific region.

2. The Present and Future Japanese Defense Posture

Need for a Reappraisal of the Japanese Defense Posture

As indicated by the foregoing analysis, a number of significant changes have occurred in the international environment which call for a reappraisal of the existing Japanese defense posture and Japan's role in ensuring the security of the Asian/Pacific region. These developments include the shifts in the U.S.-Soviet military balance noted above; the possibility of an altered role for the PRC in the international configuration of power; progress in economic development in various parts of the world and the consequent changes in the international economic structure, particularly with respect to economic relations between Japan and the U.S.; and the development of an energy crisis of a seemingly fundamental and permanent nature.

The Japanese are beginning to realize that the security of Japan and of the Asian/Pacific Basin cannot be separated. It is also increasingly recognized that greater attention must be given to defense matters, closer cooperation with other nations must be promoted, and more careful and extensive efforts must be made to ensure the continued effectiveness of the Japan-U.S. security system.

Japan's Basic Concept of Defense

Up to this point in time, official Japanese defense thinking has been confined almost exclusively to the defense of Japan's four major islands within the framework of the U.S.-Japan security system. Japan has adhered to a policy of building up a moderate self-defense capability while eschewing offensive weapons of any sort. Deriving their stance from the constitution, the Japanese Diet has resolved that Japan may sustain a self-defense force but should not send troops abroad for the defense of other regions.

Japan's basic concept of defense has been based on the premise that tasks beyond the capabilities of the Japanese SDF could and would be covered wholly by the U.S. armed forces. Although it was only logical for Japan to conclude that the American enforcement of the "Peace Constitution" implied the assumption by the U.S. of a moral obligation to wholly defend a demilitarized Japan, the U.S. government has never officially made such a commitment. This basic disarray in the American-Japanese defense relationship has been obscured in the past due to the overwhelming superiority of U.S. military power vis-a-vis that of the Soviet Union, a now-eroded condition which served effectively to deter any Soviet attempt to invade or mount aggression against Japan.

In limiting its policy only to the defense of Japanese territory and the immediately surrounding seas, Japan has felt no need to pay attention to contributing to the maintenance of regional or global security. The U.S., confident of its utter superiority in the Pacific, for long took the stand that Japan should remain an American protégé with no independent defense posture and policy of its own. Japan also has been extremely sensitive to the danger that the U.S. and the Southeast Asian nations might regard any strengthening of Japan's defense forces as a return to "militarism." Many persons in Japan have been apprehensive that other Asian/Pacific nations would be resistant to the idea of a direct Japanese military role in cooperative regional security endeavors.

All these factors serve to significantly restrain the degree to which Japan under present circumstances can make a contribution to or take direct action for the security or defense of areas outside the Japanese homeland.

Strengthening the U.S.-Japan Defense System

Japan can contribute *indirectly* to Asian/Pacific security in an extremely important way by enhancing its own capacity to defend the Japanese islands and surrounding seas. Geopolitically, a secure and stable Japan is indispensable to the security of Northeast Asia and, indeed, the whole Western Pacific. In view of this fact, it is Japan's duty as a member of the region to prepare and maintain a fully-equipped and-manned national defense structure, within the framework of the U.S.-Japan security system and the concept of self-defense.

It may be the case that—in the absence of a large-scale military conflict between the U.S. and the USSR—no nation will attempt aggression against Japan as long as the "umbrella" of the U.S.-Japan security system is maintained. However, it should not simply be assumed that the security pact will always function automatically, requiring a minimum of effort from Japan. In fact, from a military point of view, the credible and effective functioning of the system may be in doubt unless some improvements are made.

The first requirement is that Japan and the U.S. should reach agreement as soon as possible on the particulars of combined operations for the defense of Japan, as called for in the November 1978 "Guidelines for Japan-U.S. Defense Cooperation." At present, the respective defense departments of the two countries are in the midst of discussing how to implement practically this cooperative agreement. Upon conclusion of the joint study now being conducted by military officials, the two governments should agree upon the responsibilities to be assigned to Japan, and Japan should make the improvements in its defense capabilities necessary to carry out these responsibilities. To maintain and bolster the viability of the Japan-U.S. security system, it will be necessary to strengthen the capabilities of the three components of the SDF, both quantitatively and qualitatively.

Japan's Role in the Event of War

In the event of a large-scale war involving the U.S. and the Soviet Union and reaching into the Pacific Basin, U.S. allies and friends in the region will continue to rely on the nuclear "umbrella" and mobile striking forces of the United States. It is possible and advisable, however, for these countries to make contributions in the defensive sphere—according to each nation's military capability—by assuming greater responsibility for local ground, air, and naval defense and for guarding the sea lanes of communication, thus lightening the burdens of the U.S. in these areas.

If war occurs, Japan's role will include ground defense of the homeland territories; air defense of the homeland as far as Okinawa and Ogasawara; and defense of the Sohya, Tsugaru, and Tsushima straits, including the conduct of anti-submarine warfare. Japanese ability to prevent or impede Soviet naval forces from passing through these straits which surround Japan would be of vital importance, for such actions would serve to limit Soviet air and naval entry into the Pacific from Soviet bases in the Japan Sea, thus squeezing or even severing links vital to the Soviet effort. If Soviet bases in other areas were to be destroyed, by guarding the straits Japan to a large extent could prevent Soviet submarines from returning to bases in the Japan Sea. Additionally, constant surveillance of the straits would yield critical information about the movements of Soviet submarine traffic—information pertinent to the assessment of Soviet strategy in related activities on the high seas.

Japanese efforts would also be essential to protect (in coordination with the U.S.) the maritime transportation lines not only in the vicinity of the Japanese islands but also in the Western Pacific. By conducting defensive anti-submarine activities, Japan could enhance the relative security of these vital sea lanes, thus enabling Japan and other Western Pacific states to sustain their defensive capabilities through the continued flow of supplies from the U.S. and other friendly nations. Furthermore, with Soviet naval activity curtailed, Vietnam would lose its essential supply line from the USSR, and would thus be constrained from military attacks on other nations.

Japan must also consider making a contribution toward the protection of U.S. carrier task forces operating near Japan. These forces are of tremendous importance in deterring the threat of enemy invasion of the Japanese homeland, and would play a crucial role in the event of an outbreak of war. However, quantitative and qualitative improvements in the Soviet submarine fleet and naval air squadron based in the Pacific area now pose a growing threat to the U.S. carrier task forces in the region. Japanese ability to curtail Soviet submarine activities at the three major straits, bolstered by improvements in Japan's air defense and anti-submarine warfare capabilities, can contribute to increasing the safety of the task forces and the freedom of the carriers to move about the region as necessary in the event of war.

The deployment of Soviet SS-20 missiles and Backfire bombers in East Asia has greatly complicated defense matters for Japan. The Japanese must rely on U.S. carriers and bombers to deter the possible Soviet use of its SS-20s. In view of this reality, Tokyo at some point in the future might be forced to reappraise one of its "Three Non-Nuclear Principles" (i.e., that there will be "no introduction of nuclear weapons in Japan"), for although heated political debates will result, approval of a visit to a Japanese port of a U.S. warship with nuclear weapons aboard might prove necessary. The Soviet Backfires pose a serious challenge to the safety of the U.S. carriers and the Japanese sea lanes, and require that Japan devote greater attention to air defense measures and defending the waters around the Japanese islands.

Required Improvements in Japan's Defense Capabilities

The primary tasks of the Japanese Self-Defense Forces are air defense, anti-submarine warfare, defense of the major straits, control of the sea around Japan, and ground defense of the homeland territories. Japan would be well advised to make the following improvements in its defense posture:

1. *Air defense:* Fighters and anti-air missile units should be increased quantitatively, with an emphasis on expanding the share of missile units in the total air defense system. Base facilities must also be improved, so as to reduce the overall vulnerability of the air defense system. Japan can contribute to the safety of the U.S. carrier task forces by improving the air defense capabilities established on the Japanese mainland and on Okinawa and Bonin Islands.
2. *Anti-submarine warfare:* The P3-C patrol plane has now been introduced. Urgent priorities should be the improvement of submarines for the ASW mission and an increase in ASW surface units, which possibly should be doubled in size. The anti-Backfire defense system on surface units should be improved, possibly to include anti-air Verticle and Short Take-off and Landing (V/STOL) aircraft. ASW cruisers with ASW helicopters and anti-air V/STOLs aboard could be constructed to the extent possible; and it might be possible to effectively organize a future ASW surface unit around a core of an ASW cruiser, accompanied by several frigates.
3. *Defense of the major straits:* Mine-laying capabilities should be improved, as should the system of defense against bombing, missile-attack, and commando raids on defense facilities.

4. *Control of the sea around Japan:* Improvement of anti-surface attack weapons is an urgent necessity, and introduction of Harpoon anti-surface missiles has begun. Also imperative is the improvement of tactical air units.
5. *Ground defense of the mainland territories:* Ground forces must be qualitatively and quantitatively improved.

Obstacles to Improvements in Japan's Defense Posture

The necessary reappraisal of Japan's present basic defense posture and development of an appropriate program for the new buildup of the defense forces will require considerable time. It is time for the Japanese to shift their thinking and attitudes toward a broader and deeper appreciation of Japan's interdependence with the region as a whole and Japan's concomitant responsibilities. There are, however, several obstacles and forms of resistance to the implementation of the defense and security measures outlined above.

Japan's presently unsound financial conditions will make it difficult to increase defense expenditures in the immediate future, for the government must focus on other financial concerns as well. Increases in defense spending are also restricted by the fact that the Japan-U.S. joint military study on defense cooperation has not yet been completed. Japan's share of the joint defense responsibilities, and the appropriate function and size of each self-defense force required for carrying out Japan's tasks, have not yet been established.

As indicated earlier in this paper, there are also serious problems in connection with the present interpretation of the Japanese Constitution, and the restrictions on defense contained therein. A particularly troublesome issue concerns the interpretation of the right of collective self-defense.

Cooperation for Defense of the Sea Lanes

There is one area in which Japan, within its constitutional limits, conceivably can contribute *directly* to the security of areas outside the Japanese homeland: maintenance of the safety of the sea lanes of communication on the open seas, and participation in a coopera-

The Japanese Defense Posture

tive system for the protection of maritime transportation. Since the sea lanes traverse such a vast area, no individual nation can hope to protect its transportation routes singlehandedly. It is necessary, therefore, that friendly nations cooperate to provide for the security of these vital waterways. Such efforts would prove mutually beneficial to Japan, the U.S., and other nations in the Asian/Pacific Basin region.

The importance of Japan's ability to guard and protect the three straits around the Japanese homeland has been stressed above. Realistically speaking, however, Japan as a nation dependent upon sea-borne trade must concern itself with other waterways as well. Approximately 80% of Japan's total exports and 60% of its imports move by sea through the Western Pacific, west of the Bonin Islands. Hence this area and its sea lanes are vital to Japan's survival, in peacetime as well as war. Japan also has important interests in areas beyond the Western Pacific. Most of Japan's oil comes from the Persian Gulf area, transported through sea lanes of crucial importance between Japan and the Middle East, including the Strait of Malacca. Despite these realities, the Japanese government has thought it possible to adhere to the basic concept of limiting the operational sea area of the Maritime SDF to waters in the immediate vicinity of Japan.

The issue of the defense of the sea lanes in the open seas so far has been outside the purview of the Japan-U.S. security system. Neither the security pact nor the Japanese Constitution makes any specific provision for maintaining the security of these waterways. Japan now cannot simply assume that the U.S. in all circumstances will be fully capable and willing to bear the brunt of responsibility in this regard. In fact, according to the U.S. Senate Report of the Pacific Study Group to the Committee on Armed Services,[1] the U.S. has no legal obligation to protect the open sea lanes. One high U.S. official has also noted the possibility that the capabilities of the U.S. navy are inadequate to defend the sea lanes in the Western Pacific because of lack of ships. Thus the issue of possible Japanese cooperation with the U.S. to share the burden of protect-

---

[1] "United States-Japan Security Relationship—The Key to East Asian Security and Stability," Report of the Pacific Study Group to the Committee on Armed Services, United States Senate, March 22, 1979, p. 11.

ing maritime transportation in the open seas remains unresolved between the two countries. Japan and the U.S. should reach agreement on this essential matter, in such a manner that Japan can be persuaded to assume a larger share of this defense responsibility, especially in the case of an emergency.

It is our view that the inherent rights of self-defense give Japan the right to protect its sea-borne trade on the high seas, and to cooperate with the U.S. in this endeavor. However, while the Japanese government acknowledges that collective self-defense is a right recognized internationally by Article 51 of the United Nations Charter, the government's negative position with respect to the dispatch of ground troops abroad in effect seems to have expanded erroneously so as to preclude the exercise of this right, thus making precarious theoretically a larger Japanese role in defense of the maritime transportation routes. Not all persons subscribe to this latter interpretation, however. An alternative view is that the government's stance in admitting the theoretical right of self-defense thereby also implies the right of *accomplishment* of collective self-defense, for without the ability to exercise such a prerogative, the admission of the right is in-and-of-itself meaningless.

The Role of Japanese Economic Assistance

In view of its huge economic capacity, Japan can assist the economic development of individual countries and the region as a whole through contributions of capital, technology, and personnel. Such measures will assist individual nations in building a firm foundation for national self-defense and will help to strengthen political and economic well-being in the region.

The member states of the Association of Southeast Asian Nations (ASEAN) are of great economic significance to Japan for the supply of oil and other raw materials and in view of the importance of maintaining the safety of the sea lanes which pass through the Southeast Asian subregion. Consequently, the maintenance of close and friendly relations between Japan and the ASEAN countries, fortified by Japanese contributions to the political stability, military security, and economic development of these nations, is essential for the security of Japan itself.

Relations with the People's Republic of China

It is possible that the normalization of relations between Japan and the PRC may enhance the security of Japan by facilitating Peking's contribution to the balancing of Soviet power in the area and to the reduction of Soviet pressure from the north. From the viewpoint of the Asian/Pacific region as a whole, however, the following destabilizing possibilities must be considered:

1. The PRC's planned modernization of its economy may prove to be a very difficult task to achieve. The PRC's failure in this endeavor would lead inevitably to a domestic struggle of power, resulting possibly in a change of foreign policy toward the West as well as toward the Soviet Union.
2. The possibility of a restoration of closer Sino-Soviet relations cannot be denied.
3. The improvement of Japanese-PRC and U.S.-PRC relations may push Vietnam even more fully toward the Soviet Union. In this contingency, the Vietnam-PRC confrontation may become more severe and may involve neighboring nations.
4. Japanese economic aid to the PRC may exert an adverse influence on the economies of the ASEAN nations. It should be remembered that the economic stability and development of the ASEAN states are indispensable for the security of Japan.
5. In response to the improved ties among Japan, the U.S. and the PRC, Moscow may increase military support to North Korea and Vietnam, resulting in increased instability and security problems in both subregions. (The USSR already has increased military pressures in the occupied Japanese northern islands.)

There are thus several different possible foreign policy courses upon which Peking may embark. Chinese decisions in this respect will flow not only from Peking's motivations but also in response to the movements and behavior of other nations toward the PRC. Consequently, all nations concerned must mold carefully their relations with the PRC, with the security of the Asian/Pacific region as a whole always in mind. Whatever may occur, it is and will remain very dangerous for the non-communist nations of the region to place too much emphasis on the benefits of normalization of relations with the PRC and therefore reduce their own defense efforts.

THE TENSIONS ON THE KOREAN PENINSULA

Hogan Yoon

The Korean peninsula, divided into the communist Democratic People's Republic of Korea (DPRK) in the North and the Republic of Korea (ROK) in the South, is one of the world's potentially most dangerous areas of international conflict. The conflict between the two Koreas, a source of serious strain to regional stability, is complicated by the fact that nowhere else in the world do the interests of the major powers—i.e., the U.S., the Soviet Union, the People's Republic of China (PRC), and Japan—more clearly (and sometimes dangerously) intersect. Sino-Soviet rivalry in the area appears to be deepening, and the Soviet Union seems to have embarked on a path of continuous expansionism, as evidenced by the increased buildup of Soviet naval and air forces in the Western Pacific in recent years. In view of these considerations, the geopolitical and geostrategic location of the two Koreas is of

---

The analysis contained in this paper is that of Ambassador Yoon and does not necessarily reflect the views of the Government of the Republic of Korea.

extraordinary significance. A sudden change in the international configuration of power operating with respect to the peninsula would cause instability within and between North and South Korea and result in spill-over effects impacting on the regional, if not global, order.

Two primary national goals of the ROK government have been to protect and enhance the safety and security and the economic welfare of its 37 million people, and simultaneously to work toward the ultimate goal of peaceful reunification of the two Koreas. In pursuit of these goals, the ROK has consistently worked toward the reduction of tension on the Korean peninsula, a precondition for restoration of the mutual trust which will be an essential foundation for the process of peaceful reunification. It is the view of the ROK that such reunification can occur only through a gradual and evolutionary process of mutual accommodations and adjustments.

In contrast, the North Korean communist regime led by Kim Il-sung has not abandoned its long-declared goal of reunification of the peninsula under Kim's brand of communism. The ROK has advanced various constructive proposals which invariably have met with North Korean refusal or disruption: 1) unconditional resumption of direct talks between the responsible authorities of South and North Korea; 2) a tripartite conference (jointly proposed by the late President Park Chung-hee and President Jimmy Carter at the conclusion of the latter's visit to Seoul in the Summer of 1979); 3) Red Cross talks to facilitate the resolution of humanitarian problems; and 4) revival of the now-dormant South-North Coordinating Committee, which was established by the Joint Communique of July 4, 1972. North Korea's efforts to destabilize the South through subversion and small-scale violence have failed, as have schemes to diplomatically discredit the Seoul Government in the international arena. Yet all indications are that Kim Il-sung is dedicated unswervingly toward the attainment of his objective—the so-called "revolutionary resolution" of the Korean issue—by whatever means necessary, including the use of arms.

North Korea recently has been engaged in a military buildup of such proportions as to dangerously upset the precarious power balance in the Korean peninsula. Reliable reports produced recently by U.S. intelligence sources reassessing the current North

The Tensions on the Korean Peninsula

Korean armed strength indicate that North Korean ground forces have increased from 450,000 to between 550,000 and 600,000 (compared to 520,000 for the ROK); the number of brigades has increased from 29 to 37; the number of tanks has grown by 35%; and artillery tubes and armored personnel carriers have increased by about 20%. The widely-held notion that the ROK holds superiority in ground forces while the North maintains the edge in air and naval forces has thus been completely overturned. Consequently, the ratio of military strength between the South and North (at least in terms of gross numbers) has tipped dramatically in favor of North Korea. It can be concluded that North Korea now possesses armed forces far in excess of its defensive needs, thereby posing a greater military threat to South Korea than had previously been estimated.

The U.S. military presence in South Korea continues to play a vital role in deterring possible North Korean armed aggression and in maintaining the balance of power on the Korean peninsula. It is true that the strength of the U.S. Second Infantry Division stationed in Korea is not of great potency when considered solely in terms of numbers of soldiers involved. Nevertheless, the mere presence of the forces will result in automatic U.S. military engagement in case of war, in accordance with the provisions of the ROK-U.S. Mutual Defense Treaty. The sophisticated weaponry and equipment of the Second Division together with the ROK armed forces will be sufficient to repel the initial thrust of the enemy in a full-scale attack. The mission of the U.S. troops in Korea is not only military but also political and psychological. In peacetime the presence of the troops as a deterrent and stabilizing force is a source of self-confidence and comfort for the ROK armed forces. The presence of the troops has contributed to the relative security and stability which have enabled the ROK government to rebuild the South Korean nation and achieve rapid economic development during the past three decades. Furthermore, the importance for the security of Japan of the U.S. presence in Korea cannot be minimized, as the Japanese themselves are well aware.

The most obvious and practical way to safeguard the security of South Korea is through the continuation of a firm U.S. commitment to the defense of the ROK, backed by a strong and flexible U.S. military presence. For a time in the mid- and late 1970s, however, there was a fear among concerned Asian observers that the U.S., being wary of another Vietnam-type experience, was abandoning or reducing its strategic and security role in the Asian/Pacific region, as evidenced by the closing of the American bases in Thailand and the 1977 decision of the Carter Administration to withdraw the U.S. ground forces from Korea. In the absence of a meaningful quid pro quo from Seoul's North Korean adversaries, it was clear to many in South Korea and elsewhere that the unilateral U.S. withdrawal from the ROK would make no contribution to stability and peace in the Korean peninsula and instead would result in increased tensions in the area.

While U.S. policy did seem somewhat obscure and shaky in the wake of the Vietnam debacle, it now appears to have regained its purpose, and the U.S. has reiterated its intent to remain a Pacific power and to help shape the course of international politics in the region. The South Korean government is particularly encouraged by the decision of the Carter Administration to hold in abeyance further withdrawal of U.S. combat forces from Korea, for this step will reinforce deterrence against aggression and provide tangible evidence of American steadfastness and firm resolve. The ROK-U.S. Combined Forces Command, established and put into operation in late 1978, has made a significant contribution to the improved effectiveness of combined ROK-U.S. defense capabilities. The U.S. has also gradually strengthened the level of air and naval forces in the Pacific region, alleviating the fear that the U.S. might disengage from or lessen its concern about the area.

In the absence of a permanent solution to the Korean question, it is basically in the interests of the big powers to maintain the status quo on the Korean peninsula. North Korea's major military allies, the Soviet Union and the PRC, each have their own reasons for maintenance of a working relationship with the U.S. and avoidance of a major conflict with Washington. This fact may lead to policies of restraint with respect to North Korea's aggressive designs and to a reduction of tensions on the peninsula in the long run.

Two recent and major international events which are bound to have far-reaching implications for the Northeast Asian subregion are the normalization of diplomatic relations between the U.S. and the PRC and the conclusion of a treaty of peace and friendship between Japan and the PRC. The PRC's recent moves for closer economic and strategic ties with the U.S. and Japan can be interpreted as having the dual purpose of a) enhancing the country's national capabilities in its monumental struggle with the Soviet Union, and b) effecting as quickly as possible the modernization and economic development which were so long sacrificed during the upheaval of the Cultural Revolution. In pursuance of these major goals, regional stability is currently of crucial importance to the PRC, at least until such time as Peking becomes strong enough to cope with external threats impinging upon the country.

For these reasons, it would be strategically and economically imprudent for the PRC to jeopardize the looming strategic and economic ties with the U.S. and Japan by precipitating another military conflict on the Korean peninsula. However, it is difficult to predict what attitude the PRC will take with regard to neighboring countries once the goals of modernization and achievement of sufficient national strength are accomplished. The U.S. therefore must proceed with utmost caution in expanding its process of cooperation with the PRC. In the course of improving its relations with the PRC, the U.S. should ask Peking to take a more positive role in finding a peaceful solution to the Korean question, since the PRC—which participated in the Korean War and signed the current Armistice Agreement—is also an involved party. As a quid pro quo for the establishment of economic and other cooperative relations with the U.S. and Japan, the PRC should exercise its influence with Pyongyang and attempt to contribute to the creation of an international environment conducive to direct talks between South and North Korea.

In order to cope with the potential threat from the North and to increase the prospects for peace and stability on the Korean peninsula, it would be desirable for the ROK and the U.S. to jointly pursue the following policies as interim measures, pending ultimate solution of the Korean question:

1. Continued stationing in South Korea of a sufficient level of U.S. forces;
2. Over-all strengthening of the U.S.-ROK security arrangements;
3. Expansion and promotion of U.S.-ROK economic cooperation and mutually beneficial trade relations;

4. Continued maintenance of the Armistice Agreement and the UN Command on the Korean peninsula;
5. Sustained efforts for the resumption of the North-South dialogue for the reduction of tensions on the peninsula;
6. Conclusion of a non-aggression agreement between the North and the South; and
7. Consideration of cross-recognition of both Koreas and simultaneous admission of both Koreas to the United Nations.

In the immediate future, the ROK will continue to pursue its own Force Improvement Plan which comprises modernization of arms and equipment, including assemblage of advanced tactical aircraft such as the F-5E and the F-5F. As a way of revamping its overall armed strength the ROK will continue to develop its defense industry through the introduction of advanced technology. Some increases in military spending will inevitably be necessary to implement these plans, and it is expected that the ROK will raise annual military spending next year by almost $500 million from currently budgeted levels. The rise is equivalent to 1 percent of Korea's gross national product and will increase defense spending from a 1979 level of $3 billion. This latter figure represents 5.6% of the South Korean Gross National Product, whereas as much as 25% of the North Korean GNP may be spent on defense.

The most important priorities in the short-run view are the prevention of an outbreak of war, continued efforts to ensure the stabilization of the situation on the peninsula, and—through the reduction of tensions and restoration of mutual trust between the two Koreas—the creation of conditions conducive to eventual peaceful reunification. In the interest of achieving these goals, the ROK is willing to pursue initiatives for improved relations with such countries as the PRC and the Soviet Union.

Along with the gradual buildup of its military capabilities, South Korea will continue to expand and strengthen its economic base, since a strong economy is an essential ingredient for an adequate and viable national defense posture. One of the remarkable features of the 1980s will be the emergence of newly industrialized countries, among them the Republic of Korea, which will play an increasingly important role—politically, strategically, and economically—in the community of nations. The ROK has successfully laid a firm foundation for a self-reliant economy, and will be ready and willing to take up this challenging role, in the context of a growing awareness of economic interdependence and regional consciousness among the nations of the Asian/Pacific region.

As for long-term policies, it will be desirable for the ROK, the U.S., and possibly Japan to work toward the formation of a regional security arrangement for Northeast Asia, while maintaining mutually beneficial economic and trade relations. For its part, Japan can make a considerable contribution to the security of the Asian/Pacific region through a willingness to cooperate politically and economically with the countries of the area, including the ROK.

There are several ways in which Japan can enhance the security of Northeast Asia, even in the absence of a revision of the Japanese Constitution, which seems an unlikely prospect at this time. It must be unmistakably recognized by both Japan and the ROK that the security of South Korea is essential to the security of Japan. Diplomatic cooperation is needed from Japan in avoiding any policy toward North Korea which may adversely affect South Korean security. In view of South Korea's heavy defense burden, a strengthening of bilateral economic cooperation between South Korea and Japan would be helpful. Japan and South Korea are highly dependent upon the sea lanes of communication for the import of oil and other crucial raw materials, and the protection of these waterways therefore is of utmost importance to both countries. In this connection, the strengthening of naval capabilities and the institution of more effective regional naval cooperation among the U.S., Japan, and South Korea should be seriously considered in the future.

In emphasizing the need for cooperation in the Asian/Pacific Basin, we need not think in terms of engaging in bloc politics or building military alliances. What is required is movement out of the current stage of international confrontation into a climate of peaceful international cooperation. With this goal in mind, the ultimate long-term aim should be the development of cooperative endeavors which eventually can embrace all the nations in the Asian/Pacific region.

COMMENTARY

Frederick Chien

Several elements can be identified which have served to increase instability in recent years in the Asian/Pacific region. The communist victories in Vietnam, Laos, and Kampuchea have contributed to the heightened insecurity. The perceived withdrawal of the United States from Asia also has had a destabilizing effect, especially the announcement (now rescinded) of the Carter Administration in 1977 that the U.S. would undertake a phased withdrawal of its ground forces from the Republic of Korea. This announcement had a seriously adverse psychological impact on the non-communist Asian states and increased aggressive intentions on the part of the North Korean government. Another destabilizing factor has been the Chinese communist (People's Republic of China)/Japan and the PRC/United States rapprochements.

A number of analysts have claimed that the conclusion of the Treaty of Friendship between the PRC and Japan contributes to the power balance in the region (by helping the U.S. to counterbalance the Soviet presence) and will result in a reduction of Soviet pressure from the North. In fact, however, the improved relationship between the PRC and Japan has helped to *increase* the Soviet military presence in the Asian/Pacific region.

The Soviet Union in recent years has engaged in a military buildup in the Northern Pacific, along the South China Sea, and in the Indian Ocean. This buildup has been fueled by a growing apprehensiveness in Moscow, generated by the fact that the Japan/PRC treaty and the subsequent American normalization of relations with Peking appear to constitute an anti-Soviet entente formed by the United States, the PRC, and Japan. From the point of view of the Soviet Union, there now exist two NATOs, one on its western flank and the other on its eastern. Among other considerations, the increased Soviet military presence poses a direct threat to the sea lanes in the region, a source of concern for virtually all Pacific Basin nations.

It is often assumed that the current rift between the Soviet Union and Communist China will continue, and national policy-makers make important decisions based on this assumption. However, two elements have emerged in recent months which may be conducive to gradual changes in the relationship between these two countries.

The first factor is the U.S. normalization of relations with Peking. By acceptance of the latter's three demands,* the United States went out of its way to accommodate the desires of the PRC. This development served as a clear indication to the Kremlin that the hitherto relatively stable triangular relationship among Moscow, Peking, and Washington had changed and that its two arch-enemies were moving closer together, thus posing a direct threat to the Soviet Union. In order to accomplish a breakthrough from this undesirable state of affairs, the Soviets can be expected to do everything possible to try and drive a wedge between the newly established partnership of the U.S. and the PRC. One possible course of action which the USSR may follow is to mount an attempt to bury the hatchet with the PRC by making some concessions on the issue of the contest for leadership in the international communist movement.

The second factor is the Sino-Vietnamese border war which

---

* The three demands were U.S. withdrawal of recognition from the Republic of China on Taiwan, the withdrawal of all U.S. troops from that island, and termination of the U.S. mutual security pact with the ROC.

occurred early in 1979. It was generally expected that as the Sino-Vietnamese war continued, the Soviet Union somehow would become involved. That the Soviet Union did not do so naturally will be taken into consideration by the Chinese communist leaders.

One month after the conclusion of the Sino-Vietnamese border clash, the Chinese communists proposed to the Soviet Union that a new round of negotiations between Peking and Moscow be held. The new round of negotiations began in September 1979 and ended recently. Little of great significance seemed to transpire during the sessions; but toward the end of the negotiations, the chief Chinese communist delegate paid a visit to Soviet Foreign Minister Gromyko. It has been learned that inconclusive discussions were held in the meeting with respect to working out a replacement for the treaty of alliance between the PRC and the Soviet Union which was due to expire in April 1980. [The treaty now has lapsed and has not yet been replaced.]

In spite of the PRC's verbal barrage against the Soviet invasion of Afghanistan, several developments have occurred in recent months which may indicate some thaw in the Moscow-Peking rift. Firstly, the PRC after a hiatus of considerable length sent a new ambassador to Moscow in April 1980. Secondly, a top Soviet expert on Chinese affairs, Mikhail Kapitsa, secretly visited Peking in late March 1980. Thirdly, on April 8th the PRC changed the name of the street where the Soviet Embassy is located from Anti-Revisionist Road to Old East Gate Street. Finally, trade between the two nations has been growing steadily.

It is true that the Sino-Soviet dispute has been of a quite hostile nature since 1969. However, in view of the several considerations discussed above, it is not necessarily the case that the rift will continue in the future. This possibility must be taken into serious consideration in the formulation of the policies and strategies of the nations of the Pacific Basin region.

Much attention has been drawn to the moderate attitudes which currently seem to be prevalent in the PRC. Whether this climate of moderation continues will have a very significant impact on the future security of Northeast Asia. The PRC has experienced four cycles during its thirty years of history. Each cycle has been composed of two stages: a lengthy period of internal regimentation and oppression, accompanied by an attitude of belligerence and hostility toward the outside world; followed by a very brief period of internal relaxation of control and a smiling campaign toward the external world.

The first cycle began in 1950 and continued until 1957. The lengthy period of regimentation was marked by the rectification movement and participation in the Korean War; the brief period of relaxation began with the Bandung Conference of 1955 and culminated in 1957 with the very short-lived One Hundred Flowers campaign. The second cycle covered the years 1958 to 1965. The oppressive period was reflected by the Three Red Banners, including the People's Commune, the Socialist General Line, and the Great Leap Forward, and by the offshore bombardment of the Matsu-Quemoy Islands. By 1963, however, Liu Shao-chi was advocating a four-modernization program (the forerunner of the current four-modernization campaign), and in 1963 and 1964 Liu Shao-chi and Chou En-lai paid extensive visits to Asia and Africa. The third cycle, which commenced in 1966 and ended in 1972, was characterized in the first period by the Cultural Revolution and the Red Guards and in the second by "ping-pong diplomacy," which began in 1971. The fourth cycle was marked first by the harsh control of the Gang of Four, beginning in 1973, and then by a period of moderation which began in 1978 with the four-modernization program, the normalization of relations with the United States, and a smiling campaign to the countries of Asia and Western Europe.

This study of the last three decades might lead one to believe that another cycle is about to begin. It therefore is of dubious advisability for any country to base its policy on the assumption that the current attitudes in the PRC will continue.

The most important course for countries in both Northeast and Southeast Asia is the movement toward self-reliance. If a nation cannot defend itself and must rely on other countries for its defense, it is doomed. The Republic of Korea has taken significant measures toward self-reliance; particularly noteworthy is the South Korean force improvement plan. One problem is that the leading countries in Asia, particularly Japan, seem unwilling to spend more on defense.

It is also necessary that the interdependence of countries in the Pacific Basin region and the importance of regional cooperation be

Commentary

recognized. The White Paper published by the Japanese Defense Agency in July 1978 pointed out for the first time Japan's concern with respect to the security of the Korean peninsula. This Paper also acknowledged that Japan is aware of the importance of a safe and secure Republic of China, given the strategic position of the island of Taiwan, its close geographical proximity to Japan, and the role of the Taiwan Strait as a very major sea route for Japan. To my knowledge, this was the first time the Japanese government had published a paper drawing attention to the importance of the Korean peninsula and the Republic of China to the security of Japan.

Non-communist countries in the Asian/Pacific Basin region must recognize that we share the same plight and the same future problems—we are all in the same boat.

REPORT OF COMMITTEE #2

The members of Committee #2 considered and made recommendations with respect to the broad range of issues falling under the general heading of "Political/Military Dimensions of Northeast Asian Security."

Co-chairmen:
Dr. Kim Se Jin,
*Director General, Office of Research,
Institute of Foreign Affairs and National Security,
Ministry of Foreign Affairs,
Seoul, Republic of Korea*

Professor Harry Gelber,
*Head of Department of Political Science,
University of Tasmania,
Hobart, Australia*

I. The Japanese Defense Posture and the Soviet Challenge in Northeast Asia

Perceptions of the Threat

The challenge to security in Northeast Asia includes the following components:

    a. Soviet political pressure based on Soviet military deployment in the Japanese Northern Territories [the occupied four northern islands] and elsewhere;

b. The capability of the Soviet Union to mount a small-scale invasion of Japan from the Northern Territories;
c. A constantly increasing threat to the sea lanes of communication, based on an expanding Soviet naval buildup, the Soviet use of naval and air bases in Vietnam, the Soviet deployment of the Backfire bomber in Asia, and the changes in the regional military balance which have accrued in favor of the Soviet Union;
d. The major threat which might arise if U.S. security commitments were to be weakened; and
e. The threat which would arise from renewed warfare on the Korean peninsula.

Requirements for an Effective and Viable System of Territorial Defense of the Japanese Homeland

The requirements include:

a. A buildup in defense capability sufficient to counter the political pressure caused by the Soviet military deployment in the region;
b. Improved surveillance and early warning systems and greater mobility to cope with a small-scale invasion;
c. Increased anti-air and anti-submarine warfare forces for the security of the sea lanes in the Western Pacific, preferably coupled with regional cooperation with other Pacific Basin countries for protection of the sea lanes;
d. A further military buildup designed to improve Japan's capability to defend the major straits, control the sea around the homeland, and defend the homeland territories;
e. Closer cooperation with the Republic of Korea in the economic realm, thereby indirectly enhancing the security position of the ROK;
f. Continued U.S. assurances that it will honor its treaty commitments; and
g. Japanese help in facilitating an effective and stable utilization of the U.S. military bases in Japan.

Further Considerations

1. The major weaknesses in Japan's general defense capability are both legal and material. Some re-examination of the present legal constraints is desirable. The climate for public acceptance of increased defense spending is constantly improving; and in this sense, Soviet

efforts to exert political pressure by military deployment have been counter-productive.
2. Such developments as the appearance of Soviet Backfire bombers in the Soviet Far East, the deployment of the new Soviet SS-20 mobile missile in East Asia, and evidence that Najin in the extreme northeast of North Korea is being developed as a potential Soviet warm water base are all indicative of the increasing Soviet naval, air, and ground capabilities in Northeast Asia.
3. The requirements for the maintenance and strengthening of the U.S.-Japan security system include evidence that Japan will contribute more to its own and regional defense and the preservation of a credible American deterrent in the Asian/Pacific region.
4. Some of the potential security implications of the Japanese rapprochement with the PRC are already evident in the increasing Soviet military buildup in the Far East. At the same time, Japan has no intention whatsoever of strengthening the military capabilities of the PRC.
5. Japan can contribute more actively to the development of a cooperative system for the protection of maritime transportation by providing future technical support and export of equipment, conducting combined practical training and exercises, and promoting mutual understanding by means of combined academic symposia and an exchange of military students.
6. The emergence of Japan as a significant military, but not militant, power is now acceptable in the Western Pacific, and Japan could play an appreciable part in the preservation of regional security in the Asian/Pacific area in the 1980s.

II. The Tensions on the Korean Peninsula

1. With respect to the improvements required of the South Korean armed forces for the provision of an effective and viable system of territorial defense, the ROK must develop a demonstrable capacity to deter North Korean aggression. In view of the recent disclosures about North Korean military strength, this capacity is not likely to be achieved in the early 1980s. In the long-term it is essential that the ROK should become capable of producing all conventional weapons needed for its own defense. Friendly powers in the region must increase their support toward the achievement by the ROK of a self-reliant defense capability.
2. The imbalance between the respective defense efforts of North and South Korea, in view of the reports that the North may allocate

close to 25% of its GNP for defense spending, carries serious implications for the short term. In the long term, the Republic of Korea's far superior rate of economic growth will neutralize North Korea's aggressive potential.
3. The PRC's support for Pyongyang's policies and North Korea's heavy dependence on the Soviet Union for political support, economic aid, and sophisticated weaponry carry both positive and negative implications for South Korean and regional security. Both the PRC and the Soviet Union have limited political influence in Pyongyang. The principal current danger is that Pyongyang has the capability to sustain a major offensive against the South for a substantial period of time without reinforcement from the Soviet Union or the PRC.
4. There is no likelihood of a political settlement between the two Koreas in the foreseeable future.
5. The now modified Carter Administration decision in 1977 to withdraw American ground forces from South Korea had a number of consequences. The decision raised doubts about the credibility of the U.S. commitment to South Korean security and raised the dangerous possibility that Pyongyang might be tempted to attack the South on the assumption that the U.S. response would be limited and ineffective. The decision to suspend the withdrawal has reduced the concern and possibly the dangers, but the U.S. ground forces should be retained in South Korea for the indefinite future.
6. The U.S. Second Division serves as a tripwire, and as such it is a vital ingredient of the military balance on the Korean peninsula. It also plays an important role as a balancer in Northeast Asia against the military strength of the Soviet Union.
7. The American and South Korean military and political policies most likely to increase the prospects for peace and stability on the Korean peninsula in both the short and the long term are a credible U.S. military deterrent against North Korean aggression, a stable and democratic government in Seoul, and continued South Korean economic progress.
8. With respect to the relationship between the defense of the ROK and the defense of Japan, it should be recognized that the two countries have become interdependent and a threat to one poses a threat to the other. Cooperation between the two nations should be as close as is constitutionally possible.
9. With respect to the means whereby South Korea can make a meaningful contribution to the defense of Northeast Asia and the Asian/Pacific area in general, the ROK's main role at this time is to

strengthen its own defenses against attack from the North. As its economy continues to develop, the ROK increasingly will develop the capacity also to contribute to regional security in general and to the protection of the sea lanes of communication in particular.

III. Additional Points

1. To ensure its continued development and stability, the Republic of China has several security requirements. One requisite is the maintenance of ROC air and naval superiority over the Taiwan Straits. For the maintenance of that superiority, the ROC needs a continued and unimpeded supply (primarily from the United States) of sophisticated defensive weaponry of a high performance nature.
2. As a concluding point, it should be emphasized that the security arrangements herein suggested for Northeast Asia cannot be considered in a vacuum, but should be seen as part and parcel of the security requirements of the broader Asian/Pacific region, including Southeast Asia and Australasia.

Chapter 3

ECONOMIC DIMENSIONS OF SECURITY IN ASIA AND THE PACIFIC

Issues And Questions To Be Addressed: 3

The organizers of the Pattaya conference set forth the following paragraphs—which outlined some of the more specific problems to be addressed, both formally and informally, during the course of the conference—as a guide for conference participants. While conferees in their formal papers, discussion sessions, and committee reports were free to range over a wide range of subject matter and concerns, and not all the suggested questions were answered fully or directly, the "Issues and Questions to be Addressed" served to provide a framework and direction for the deliberations of the conference.

Trade and Investment in the Asian/Pacific Region—Meeting the Needs of the Developed and the Developing Nations

The Asian/Pacific hub of economic activities consists of a wide variety of interactions among the nations of the region. Some countries serve as important sources of raw materials; others are crucial exporters of manufactured articles; and all the states serve as markets for the exports of other nations in the area. The Western Pacific region is undergoing a period of rapid and dynamic development, which can be seen in the economic growth rates of the individual countries and also in the expansion of trade among the various states. In fact, regional economic growth since the early 1960s has been the highest among the many regions of the world, averaging almost 6% per year.

Mutual trade brings reciprocal benefits to and sustains the economies of both the developed and the developing nations. In recent years, however, strained political and economic relations have emerged among the countries of the region, arising from various pressures to restructure trade policies and tariff regulations. The most serious problems involve the trend toward protectionist measures and trade restrictions (both tariff and non-tariff barriers) throughout the industrialized world. Because such policies have a negative effect on export-oriented manufacturing activities in the lesser developed countries, protectionism is a serious enemy to growth; and the World Bank has warned that rising protectionism in the West could prove to be the major threat to the continued economic improvement of the developing countries. Additionally, excessive protectionism—which leads to less productivity and more inflation at home—is self-defeating in the long-run for the industrialized nations, for only by increasing their exports can the developing countries earn the foreign exchange to import more goods from the developed nations.

All countries in the Asian/Pacific area must face the necessity of harmonizing international economic relations and working out accommodations between the needs of the developed and the developing nations. In the absence of such harmony, it can be expected that serious economic disturbances will arise which will affect the political relations and stability of the region. Some progress has already been made in the promotion of more cooperative economic relations among the ASEAN states and between ASEAN and Japan, the U.S., Australia, and New Zealand, but additional work is required in the areas of economic aid, facilitation of trade, and expansion of the flow of investment.

A new factor has arisen with the emergence of the People's Republic of China as an active economic force in the region. Particularly noteworthy is the possibility of growing cooperation between Japan and China, formalized in an eight-year pact signed in February 1978 designed to split U.S. $20 billion equally in two-way

Issues and Questions to be Addressed

trade between 1978 and 1985, with Japan supplying equipment and technology and China supplying coal and oil.

- What is the relationship of economic growth and development in general, and trade and investment in particular, to domestic and regional security and stability?
- What are the trade and investment policies which will further the development and growth process in the developing nations without damaging the interests of the industrialized countries? For example, what are the possibilities of preferential tariff systems to assist developing countries in the export of manufactures?
- What are the advantages to be gained from complementarity in economies (e.g., among the ASEAN states, between Australia and parts of East Asia, and between China and Japan); and what are the possibilities of developing complementary import and export markets and trade partnerships?
- What can the countries of the Asian/Pacific Basin learn from the experience of the European Economic Community?
- How can Japan and the U.S. best mitigate the economic and political strains in their relations flowing from disagreements over trade-related matters?
- Can a system of international commodity agreements be achieved which, in an overall sense, will benefit both producers and consumers?
- To what extent can the development process be facilitated by trade and investment, as a complement to foreign aid?
- In general, what forms of economic assistance and cooperation can be developed among the nations of the Asian/Pacific region so as to contribute to the increased prosperity and security of the area?

Energy Resources, Raw Materials, and the Safety of the Sea Lanes of Communication

The sea lanes of communication are the sinews of an economically and strategically interdependent world, for the sea is still the most practical and economical, and sometimes the only means of transporting large volumes of cargo. Since most of the world's imports and exports travel by sea, both the developed and the developing nations of the Asian/Pacific Basin are dependent upon free use of the world's oceans and sea passages for assured access to markets, finished and semi-finished manufactured goods, and sources of raw materials (including oil and other energy resources, metals and minerals, wheat, rice, natural rubber, palm oil, jute, and a variety of other essential commodities). Assurance of naval access to the sea lanes is also of critical importance in the contingency of military conflict in the region.

Several of the world's most heavily-travelled sea routes pass through the Asian/Pacific region. The tanker route from the Persian Gulf oil states crosses the Indian Ocean and then penetrates the Malacca or Lombok Straits, continuing into the South and East China Seas and the Sea of Japan. This route supplies the major portion of the fuel requirements for the non-communist states of the region. The dry cargo route via the coast of South Africa, across the Indian Ocean, and through the straits between the Pacific and Indian Oceans serves as the main link between continental Europe and Southeast Asia and Japan. Australia's geographic location places it in close proximity to the major access routes in the Indian and Pacific Oceans, and there are major Australian and New Zealand shipping routes throughout the Indo/Pacific area.

While American naval strength has declined, Soviet naval forces in the Indian and Pacific Oceans continue to increase steadily; and the Soviet Union has developed a deep water navy capable of putting Russian sea power athwart the region's vital trade and naval routes. The USSR has introduced at least fifty Backfire bombers in East Asia which could interdict shipping and strategic choke-points in the area, disrupting the flow of trade which sustains the economies of both the developed and the developing nations. As Admiral Gorshkov himself has stated, "Naval forces can be used—in peacetime—to put pressure on enemies, as a type of military demonstration, as a threat to interrupting sea communications, and as a hindrance to ocean commerce."

- What steps can be taken to defend against the possibility of overt or covert military attack on the ships traversing the sea lanes?
- How can the dangers of political or economic blackmail, harassment, or interdiction—especially in the straits and channels which serve as potential chokepoints—be reduced?
- What additional threat to the sea lanes is posed by Soviet utilization of naval facilities in Vietnam?

Issues and Questions to be Addressed

- How can nations committed to the freedom of the seas for commercial usage cooperate to protect maritime transportation in the Asian/Pacific region and around the globe?
- How viable and desirable is the possibility of a cooperative Indian/Pacific Ocean naval task force, composed of various national naval units, to protect East and Southeast Asian sea lanes for commercial shipping?
- What steps can be taken by the nations of the region to mitigate the effects of rising fuel prices and the possibility of another oil crisis in the future?
- What are the prospects for the further discovery and development of oil and other energy resources within the Asian/Pacific region itself, so as to reduce dependence on imports of exhaustible supplies from distant nations?

Conference Papers

Professor Sun Chen,
Department of Economics, National University of Taiwan, and Vice Chairman, Council for Economic Development and Planning, Taipei, Republic of China

Dr. Munir Majid,
Leader Writer, New Straits Times, *Kuala Lumpur, Malaysia*

Ambassador Alejandro Melchor,
Executive Director, Asian Development Bank, Manila, Philippines

TOWARD REGIONAL COOPERATION AND PROSPERITY

Sun Chen

Today's world is one of growing interdependence. Technical progress has raised the minimum scale of production for economic efficiency, making each country dependent on others for markets, raw materials, capital, and/or technology. The quarter century through 1973 was a period of relative world harmony which facilitated trade expansion, capital flow, and technology transfer. These developments in turn made it possible for the world economy to grow at a rate unprecedented in history. While some countries remain poor in terms of per capita income, many which were underdeveloped in the early post-war period have now risen to the middle-income group. Through large exports of mostly labor-intensive products, several nations in this latter group have come to pose a potential challenge to even the developed countries.

The oil crisis in late 1973 and the subsequent worldwide recession in 1974–1975 seemed to corroborate to some extent the long-

---

The author wishes to thank Miss Chang Sieu Liang for her able assistance in compiling the data and Mr. T. K. Tsui for the editing of the paper.

standing warning about the limits to growth. The annual economic growth rate of the twenty-four Organization for Economic Cooperation and Development (OECD) countries, which averaged 4.8 percent for the period 1960–1973, dropped to only 2.4 percent in 1974–1978, or 4.1 percent if the two recession years are not included. According to a report by International Monetary Fund staff members, the number of non-oil producing developing countries with both high growth and low inflation shrank from twelve in 1967–1972 to two in 1976–1977, while the number suffering from both low growth and high inflation rose from six to twenty-two.

An increasing number of protectionist measures have been implemented by the developed countries to protect domestic markets from being "flooded by cheap goods" from the developing countries. In fact, however, these measures will not spur the growth of the developed states. Economic growth is a process of persistent increase in labor productivity resulting mainly from technical progress and structural improvement. Therefore, protection of low-productivity industries, by forestalling changes in structure, retards rather than promotes growth. The developing nations will certainly suffer from such moves, and may be forced to turn to inward-looking policies to develop import-substituting industries behind high tariffs.

Protectionism also fuels already serious inflation in both the developed and the developing countries. People arguing in favor of protection too often fail to realize the price stabilizing effect of imports from abroad. With the average manufacturing wage rate in the developed countries five to ten times that which is found in the developing countries, the developed nations have little hope of substituting domestic products for imported products in labor-intensive categories without worsening inflation.

World Bank President Robert S. McNamara warned against "the new protectionism" in a speech to the United Nations Conference on Trade and Development in Manila early in 1979. He pointed out that it clearly would be a mistake for the developing countries to turn inward. Considerable potential exists for the developing nations to increase their exports to the developed countries by diversifying their products and upgrading their export structures, Mr. McNamara noted; and, he went on, opportunities also exist for the developing states to increase the volume of trade among themselves. Mr. McNamara argued that the deterioration in the current world trade environment has not been caused by a situation in which the developing countries have swamped the markets of the developed countries with low-priced goods, but rather by the loss of economic dynamism in the developed states themselves.

Policies of protectionism and retreat from the international market will achieve nothing but a reduction in production efficiency and further contraction of world demand. Therefore, it is most important that every country, whether developing or developed, assume a positive attitude toward trade, liberalizing imports and promoting exports, so that world economic activity will expand rather than contract. Regional cooperation among the Asian/Pacific countries would serve as a good start toward the achievement of these aims.

The eleven Asian/Pacific Basin nations represented at this conference—Japan, the Republic of Korea, the Republic of China on Taiwan, the Philippines, Indonesia, Singapore, Malaysia, Thailand, the U.S., Australia, and New Zealand—constitute 15.5 percent of the world's total area and in 1978 accounted for 15.4 percent of its total population. That same year they exported 27.1 percent of total world exports and imported 28 percent of total world imports.

The countries in this region vary in many respects. There are countries whose per capita Gross National Product (GNP) exceeded U.S. $7,000 in 1978 (the United States, $9,736; Japan, $8,530; and Australia, $7,737); most of the other states fall in the middle income group, with per capita GNPs which average around U.S. $1,000. There are resource-poor countries, such as Japan, Singapore, the Republic of Korea, and the Republic of China on Taiwan, that nevertheless have achieved rapid economic progress. Additionally, there are resource-rich countries, such as Malaysia, the Philippines, Thailand, and Indonesia, which have not yet attained a very high per capita GNP but have demonstrated great potential for future development.

Despite these differences, the developing countries of the region all have experienced rapid growth since the 1973 oil crisis. Their average Gross Domestic Product (GDP) growth rate for 1974–1978 registered 7.6 percent, ranging from 6.3 percent for the Philippines to 10.2 percent for the Republic of Korea. These performances compared favorably with those of the developed nations and other developing countries, with the exception of some of the Middle East oil-exporting states. [For data on the principal economic indicators, trade, principal export and import commodities, primary resources, and manufactured products of the Asian/Pacific countries, please see Tables 2, 3, and 4.]

Data on the intra- and inter-regional trade of the Asian/Pacific Basin countries in recent years is shown below in Table 1. More than 61 percent of the total exports of the area went to other regions in both 1973 and 1978. Only slightly more than 38 percent went to countries within the region. The regional distribution of imports was similar to the distribution of exports, with 60.5 percent in 1973 and 61.9 percent in 1978 from the rest of the world, and 39.5 percent and 38.1 percent from within the region.

More detailed information concerning the 1978 intra- and extra-regional trade of individual countries in the Asian/Pacific region can be found in Table 3. In the case of individual countries, the rather high proportion of both export and import trade conducted with countries within the region seems inconsistent with the 38.2 percent average (for percentage of the region's exports which are exported to other regional nations) shown in Table 1; this occurs because the heavy weight of the United States in trade dominates the result of the calculations for the individual countries. Exports from individual countries to other countries within the region would be significantly reduced as a percentage of their individual total exports if the United States were to be excluded from the data. When the United States is excluded, the proportion of the region's total exports which are exported to nations within the region becomes 33.8 percent in 1973 and 29.4 percent for 1978. In 1978, the U.S. exported U.S. $26.3 billion to the region and imported U.S. $47.2 billion from it, resulting in a huge trade deficit of U.S. $20.9 billion.

The analysis reveals that much room exists for the further development of intra-regional trade in the Asian/Pacific Basin area in general and among the countries other than the U.S. in particular. Intra-regional trade should be promoted through arrangements to strengthen regional cooperation. In this regard, the Association of Southeast Asian Nations (ASEAN) has laid down a solid foundation upon which development can take place. In recent years, ASEAN has been successful both in promoting trade between member countries and in negotiating with neighboring developed countries. An extension of this process to include other

TABLE 1 Intra- and Inter-Regional Trade of the Asian/Pacific Countries

	Export To				Import From		
	World	Asian/Pacific Area Total	Asian/Pacific Area Except U.S.	Rest of World	World	Asian/Pacific Area	Rest of World
Dollar Amount							
1973 (U.S. $billion)	141.5	54.3	23.7	87.2	143.2	56.7	86.6
1978 (U.S. $billion)	321.1	122.7	52.2	198.4	343.1	130.8	212.2
Average Annual Growth Rate (%), 1974-1978	17.8	17.7	17.2	17.9	19.1	18.2	19.6
Percentage of Trade (Export or Import)							
1973	100.0	38.4	33.8	61.6	100.0	39.5	60.5
1978	100.0	38.2	29.4	61.8	100.0	38.1	61.9

Sources: 1) *International Financial Statistics*, 1979.
2) *Direction of Trade Yearbook*, 1979

TABLE 2 Principal Economic Indicators of the Asian/Pacific Countries

	U.S.	Japan	R.O.C.	R.O.K.	Singapore	Thailand	Malaysia	Indonesia	Philippines	Australia	New Zealand
Area (1,000 Km²)	9,363	372	36	99	1	514	330	2,027	300	7,687	269
Share of World (%)	6.9	0.3	0.03	0.07	0.0007	0.4	0.2	1.5	0.2	5.7	0.2
Population in 1978 (millions)	219	115	17	37	2	45	13	140	46	14	3
Share of World (%)	5.2	2.7	0.4	0.9	0.05	1.1	0.3	3.3	1.1	0.3	0.07
GNP (U.S. $billion) in 1978	2,127.60	980.06	24.67	47.35	7.65	21.73	14.94	41.67	23.17	108.31	15.24[a]
Per Capita GNP (U.S.$) in 1978	9,736	8,530	1,451	1,279	3,827	483	1,149	298	504	7,737	4,899[a]
GDP Growth Rate (%) in 1978	4.4	5.6	12.8	11.6	8.6	8.7	7.4	7.5	5.8	2.5	−0.1[c]
Average Rate 1974-1978	2.5	3.6	8.8	10.2	6.9	7.4	7.0	6.9	6.3	2.6	1.4
Inflation Rate (%) in 1978	7.7	3.8	5.8	14.4	7.6	4.9	8.1	7.9	9.7	7.9	11.9
Average Rate 1974-1978	8.0	11.3	12.5	17.9	5.9	9.6	6.7	19.2	12.2	12.7	13.8
Unemployment Rate (%)	6.0	2.2	1.0	3.2	3.9[a]	5.0	6.3	—	5.6[b]	6.3	2.0[a]
Distribution of GDP											
Agriculture (%)	3.2	3.1	12.0	21.9	1.6	27.1	24.8	34.7[a]	26.1	5.0[a]	12.0[b]
Manufacturing (%)	33.8	58.6	40.3	38.0	22.0	21.3	18.8	11.9[a]	24.2	32.0[a]	31.0[b]
Service (%)	63.0	38.3	47.7	40.1	76.4	51.6	56.4	53.4[a]	49.7	63.0[a]	57.0[b]
Distribution of Employment											
Agriculture (%)	3.5	10.9	24.9	38.4	1.9	75.0	45.0	61.2	48.0	—	10.5[b]
Manufacturing (%)	—	35.4	39.3	23.1	29.4	6.0	12.0	38.8	11.0	—	34.1[b]
Service (%)	96.5	53.8	35.8	38.5	68.7	19.0	43.8	—	41.0	55.4	
Net Value of Direct Foreign Investment											
(U.S. $billion) in 1978	−168.08	−2.81[a]	0.43	0.15	0.42	0.05	0.60	0.39	0.17	1.74	−0.002
Cumulation 1974-1978	−42.74	−9.1	0.37	0.37	2.62	0.51	2.82	0.54	0.61	4.45	0.70

156

TABLE 2 Principal Economic Indicators of the Asian/Pacific Countries (*Continued*)

Current Account Balance									
(U.S. $billion) in 1978	−13.89	17.5	1.7	−1.1	−0.75	−1.19	−0.02	−1.22	−1.22	−3.89	−4.0
Cumulation 1974-1978	−3.45	2.67	1.34	−5.13	−3.64	−3.43	0.46	−2.69	−4.28	−11.08	−4.31

Sources:
1) The World Bank, *World Development Report*, 1979.
2) Key Indicators of Development Member Countries of the Asian Development Bank, 1979.
3) *International Financial Statistics*, 1979.
4) *Taiwan Statistical Data Book*, 1979.
5) *Monthly Digest of Statistics*, 1979.
6) *Overseas Chinese Economy*, 1977-78.
7) The Bank of Korea, *Monthly Economic Statistics*, June 1979.
8) The Bank of Japan, *Economic Statistic Annual*, 1978.
9) *Survey of Current Business*, September 1978.

Notes:
a 1977
b 1976
c 1977/78 Fiscal Year

TABLE 3 Foreign Trade of the Asian/Pacific Countries (1978)

World (U.S. $billion)	U.S.	Japan	R.O.C.	R.O.K.	Singapore	Philippines	Thailand	Malaysia	Indonesia	Australia	New Zealand
Export and Import	326.8	178.3	23.8	27.7	23.1	8.4	9.5	13.3	18.3	30.1	7.2
Share of World Trade (%)	13.5	7.4	1.0	1.1	1.0	0.3	0.4	0.5	0.8	1.2	0.3
Export	143.7	98.4	12.7	12.7	10.1	3.3	4.1	7.4	11.6	14.4	3.7
Share of World Trade (%)	12.1	8.3	1.1	1.1	0.8	0.3	0.3	0.6	1.0	1.2	0.3
Import	183.1	79.9	11.1	15.0	13.0	5.1	5.4	5.9	6.7	15.7	3.5
Share of World Trade (%)	14.9	6.5	0.9	1.2	1.1	0.4	0.4	0.5	0.5	1.3	0.3
Balance	−39.4	18.5	1.6	−2.3	−2.9	−1.8	−1.3	1.5	4.9	−1.3	0.2

Region (U.S. $billion)	U.S.	Japan	R.O.C.	R.O.K.	Singapore	Philippines	Thailand	Malaysia	Indonesia	Australia	New Zealand
Export and Import	73.5	82.2	15.4	17.8	12.0	5.7	5.2	8.5	13.9	15.7	3.7
Share of Region's Trade (%)	22.5	46.1	64.7	64.7	53.6	65.3	55.3	63.9	75.5	55.3	51.4
Export	26.3	46.9	8.1	7.3	5.0	2.4	2.1	4.8	9.6	8.4	1.9
Share of Region's Export (%)	18.2	47.8	64.2	58.6	52.7	68.4	52.0	65.4	83.3	58.3	49.6
Import	47.2	35.3	7.3	10.5	7.0	3.3	3.1	3.7	4.3	7.3	1.8
Share of Region's Import (%)	25.6	44.2	66.3	70.4	54.2	61.7	57.9	61.8	61.9	52.3	52.7
Balance	−20.9	11.6	0.8	−3.2	−2.0	−0.9	−1.0	1.1	5.3	1.1	0.1

Sources: 1) *International Financial Statistics*, 1979.
2) *Direction of Trade Year Book*, 1979.

TABLE 4 Principal Export and Import Commodities, Primary Resources, and Manufactured Products of the Asian/Pacific Countries (1978)

Principal Export Commodities (% of Total Exports)	Principal Import Commodities (% of Total Imports)	Primary Resources	Manufactured Products
United States Capital Goods (32.0%) Grain and Soybeans (13.0%) Automotive Vehicles (10.1%) Chemicals (7.2%) Non-metals (5.9%)	Fuels and Lubricants (24.9%) Automotive Vehicles (14.1%) Foods, Feeds, and Beverages (8.9%) Consumer Durables (8.9%) Non-electrical Machinery (7.1%)	Coal Petroleum Soybeans Grain Lumber	Automotive Vehicles Aircraft Chemicals Computers Machinery
Japan Motor Vehicles (15.9%) Iron and Steel Products (12.2%) Vessels (7.4%) Scientific and Optical Equipment (3.5%) Radio Receivers (2.7%)	Petroleum, Crude and Partly Refined (29.5%) Wood (5.2%) Coal (3.9%) Iron Ore (3.1%) Petroleum Products (2.9%)	Coal Fish Rice Potatoes	Motor Vehicles Iron and Steel Products Vessels Scientific and Optical Equipment Radio Receivers
Republic of China Textile Products (25.2%) Electrical Machinery (15.9%) Machinery and Metal Products (8.1%) Plastics and Plastic Products (7.0%) Plywood, Wood Products, and Furniture (6.9%)	Petroleum (14.4%) Electrical Machinery and Apparatus (12.1%) Machine Tools (11.8%) Basic Metals (10.0%) Chemicals (8.6%)	Bananas Sugar Pineapples Tea Coal	Textile Products Electrical Machinery Machinery and Metal Products Plastics and Plastic Products Plywood, Wood Products, and Furniture
Republic of Korea Textiles (31.3%) Electrical Machinery (11.0%) Ships and Boats Other Than Warships (6.5%) Footwear (5.7%) Iron and Steel Products (5.4%)	Petroleum and Petroleum Products (15.4%) Wood (4.4%) Organic Chemicals (3.7%) Raw Cotton (3.0%) Ingots of Iron or Steel (2.8%)	Anthracite Tungsten Concentrate Kaolin Talc Limestone	Fibers and Textiles Plywood Rubber Products Television Receivers Radios

TABLE 4 (*Continued*)

Principal Export Commodities (% of Total Exports)	Principal Import Commodities (% of Total Imports)	Primary Resources	Manufactured Products
Singapore Petroleum Products (22.9%) Rubber (10.7%) Office Machines and Other Electrical Machinery (9.9%) Telecommunications Apparatus (4.6%) Clothing Other Than Fur (2.9%)	Petroleum (21.1%) Office Machine and Other Electrical Machinery (7.9%) Crude Rubber (5.3%) Other Machinery and Equipment (5.0%) Woven Textile Fabrics (3.3%)	Tobacco Flowers Coconut Meats	Petroleum Products Machinery and Electrical Products Textiles Wood Products Rubber Products
Philippines Coconut Products (25.9%) Wood (9.9%) Copper (7.6%) Sugar (6.3%) Copra (4.0%)	Crude Petroleum (17.7%) Machinery Other Than Electrical (14.7%) Transportation Equipment (8.3%) Base Metals (7.6%) Electrical Machinery (3.8%)	Coconuts Bananas Wood Copper Sugar	Textile Wood Products Paper and Pulp Shoes Transportation Equipment
Thailand Tapioca Products (13.1%) Rice (12.6%) Rubber (9.7%) Tin (8.7%) Corn (5.1%) Sugar (4.8%)	Crude Petroleum (15.2%) Base Metals (10.3%) Chemicals (8.7%) Petroleum Products (5.8%) Electrical Appliances (1.9%) Paper and Paper Board (1.1%)	Tapioca Rice Pineapples Corn Sugar Tin	Textiles Cement Paper and Pulp Wood Products Petroleum Products

Malaysia

Rubber (21.1%)
Logs and Timber (14.9%)
Petroleum (13.2%)
Tin (11.8%)
Palm Oil (11.0%)

Machinery and Transportation
  Equipment (34.8%)
Food, Beverages, and Tobacco
  (16.2%)
Mineral Fuels (14.4%)
Chemicals (8.5%)
Crude Petroleum (6.8%)

Rubber
Palm Oil
Tin
Wood
Petroleum

Textiles
Wood Products
Paper and Pulp
Electrical Machinery
Electrical Products

Indonesia

Crude Petroleum and Petroleum
  Products (63.9%)
Jungle Wood (8.5%)
Rubber (6.2%)
Coffee (5.5%)[a]
Tin Ore (2.3%)[a]

Crude Petroleum and Petroleum Products
  (11.7%)[a]
Rice (10.9%)[a]
Machines (Industrial and
  Commercial) (9.6%)[a]
Cement (0.4%)[a]
Fertilizer (0.4%)[a]

Petroleum
Wood
Rubber
Palm Oil
Tin

Textiles
Fertilizer
Cement
Steel
Paper and Pulp

Australia[b]

Coal (11.9%)
Wool (10.6%)
Meats (9.2%)
Wheat (8.4%)
Iron Ore (7.5%)

Machinery (16.7%)
Transportation Equipment (11.7%)
Petroleum and Petroleum Products
  (10.3%)
Electrical Machinery and Apparatus
  (8.5%)
Textile Yarn, Fabrics,
  Made-Up Articles (6.1%)

Coal
Wool
Meats
Wheat
Iron Ore

Steel Products
Textile Yarn
Tires
Cement
Metal Products

New Zealand[c]

Meats and Meat Preparations (23.7%)
Wool (20.1%)
Butter (7.9%)
Pulp, Paper, and Paper Board
  (4.7%)
Hides, Skins, and Pelts (4.0%)

Machinery and Transport (33.6%)
Manufactured Goods Classified
  Chiefly by Material (22.3%)
Apparatus (8.5%)
Mineral Fuels, Lubricants, and
  Related Materials (14.4%)
Chemicals (13.1%)
Food and Live Animals (4.6%)

Meats
Wool
Butter
Hides, Skins, and Pelts
Coal

Meat Products
Textile Yarn
Cement
Tires
Automotive Vehicles

Sources: Same as for Appendix 1
Notes: [a]1977
  [b]1977/78 Fiscal Year
  [c]1976/77 Fiscal Year

countries in the Asian/Pacific region certainly would magnify the effect of regional integration.

In addition to institutional arrangements in connection with regional cooperation, tariff and non-tariff barriers should be reduced to facilitate intra-regional trade expansion. In this connection, it has long been the policy of the Republic of China on Taiwan gradually to liberalize imports and reduce tariffs in order to promote production efficiency by introducing competition from abroad.

One basic requirement for successful regional cooperation is that member countries have the ability to adapt themselves promptly to disadvantageous conditions. Without the ability to adapt, a country that faces foreign competition may have little choice but to turn to protectionism. The ability to adapt in turn depends upon technical progress and structural change. Arrangements therefore should be made for the facilitation of capital flow and technology transfer from the rich to the poor and from the more developed to the less developed countries. Since technical progress and structural change are always slow and gradual processes, it is understandable that in many instances only a so-called "orderly" expansion of exports is tolerable to importing countries.

While political disturbances and economic disorder have engulfed almost the entire world, the Asian/Pacific Basin area for the most part has maintained peace, order, and prosperity. Regional economic performance, as measured by the growth rates of countries in the area, has outshone that of any other region in recent years. When considered together, the non-oil exporting countries of the developing world over the past three years suffered annual deficits of U.S. $20 to $30 billion in their current account balance-of-payments. During the same period, however, the balance-of-payments position of the developing countries within the Asian/Pacific region showed signs of great improvement. There is no reason why the vigorous growth enjoyed by the region in the past will fail to be sustained in the future. In fact, some of the developing countries of the region have been referred to by development economists as "newly industrializing countries." Other nations in the area have shown great potential for future development. As Europe and North America approach full economic maturity, there exists a good opportunity for the Asian/Pacific Basin to become the focus of world development.

REGIONAL SECURITY THROUGH TRADE AND INVESTMENT

Munir Majid

I. Introduction

That one of the best forms of regional security arrangements can be attained through an interlocking, mutually beneficial system of economic cooperation is a fact often not sufficiently appreciated.

If such a system involves cooperation between capitalist developed states and developing nations, some ideologists are likely to characterize it as an example of "economic imperialism," pointing to alleged collusion between foreign capitalist interests and the local comprador class. However, states claiming to be socialist which are at different levels of development also engage in economic cooperation, at least ostensibly for mutual benefit (although the benefits derived from the Soviet-sponsored COMECON may not be so mutual, in point of fact). Whatever ideologists may say, the point is that in all societies, cooperation between and among groups for economic gain is a fact of life. The mark of a true society—within, between, or among states—is the existence of a set of implicitly understood norms of cooperation, in economic and other matters, which generate valuable benefits and provide for all members a stake in the continuation of the society and its way of life.

The coming to independence of Asian and African states challenged the system of uneven advantage inherent in the colonial relationship. Although the colonized countries had gained from this relationship in several ways—e.g., through the development of their economic and social infrastructures and the introduction of new technology, particularly in the fields of agricultural production and mining—these benefits paled in comparison to the riches extracted by the colonial powers.

During the first phase of the post-colonial period, the newly independent states for the most part took a doctrinaire approach toward economic relations with their erstwhile colonial masters. During the 1950s in Indonesia, for example, real fear existed for the safety of foreign investment and even foreign nationals. Instability in the political realm continued during the process of nation-building through appeals to symbols and abstractions. The new states in their enlivened nationalism challenged the colonial order so strongly that a new basis for economic relations with the former colonial powers was difficult to forge.

Although this first phase largely has been supplanted, there is no question of a return to the status quo ante of the colonial relationship. The second (and current) phase of the post-colonial period is characterized predominantly by the desire for trade with and aid and investment from the developed countries in connection with the internal development process. The developing countries now place much emphasis on the achievement of mutual advantage. Furthermore, economic interactions are expected not only to lead to tangible material returns but also to contribute to the attainment of the socio-economic objectives of the developing political economies.

The developing nations also strongly desire to participate in all stages and dimensions of international trade, rather than being confined to their traditional role as exporters of raw materials and importers of industrial products. The desire to process, insure, and transport some of their available raw materials for export is growing. The newly industrializing countries (NICs), most of which are located in the Asian/Pacific region, have demonstrated sectoral diversification in their rising exports of manufactured goods.

Terms of trade which are weighted against primary producers no longer will be tolerated. Developing countries which have become significantly dependent on the export of manufactures strongly oppose protectionism in developed markets. Serious problems will exist in the trading relationship between the developed and the developing nations if the terms of trade for the latter are not improved and if market access is denied. The developed economies, in the Asian/Pacific region and elsewhere, correctly may perceive contradictions in the demands of the developing countries. On the one hand, the developing states demand various forms of market intervention so as to secure export earnings (e.g., through the buffer price mechanism and export controls) and, on the other, express strong belief in free trade. This phenomenon is not a new one, however, as international trade never really has been free. What is significant is that while the mix of contradictions in times past has favored the developed economies, the developing nations now desire a mode of involvement which takes their interests more fully into account.

II. Trade

Trade in Commodities

The basic dynamics of trade between the developing and the developed countries have been characterized by exports of raw materials from the former and exports of manufactured products from the latter. The developing countries are overwhelmingly dependent for their economic development on foreign exchange earned from primary produce. It therefore is imperative that such earnings be sufficient in real terms for the sustenance of growth.

Prices of primary commodities have tended to fluctuate violently, however, with a resulting stop-go impact on development which in turn has a deleterious effect on political stability. The first priority for the developing countries is the ensurance of stable primary commodity prices. These nations propose to achieve this goal through stabilization schemes mounted in cooperation with the consuming countries (mainly the developed economies). Such schemes have been discussed for well over a decade, with Dr. Raul Prebisch, the first secretary-general of the United Nations Conference on Trade and Development (UNCTAD), being an illustrious champion in the early 1960s. However, progress has been extremely slow, with only a few exceptions (e.g., the various International Tin Agreements).

Fresh impetus came in 1976 with UNCTAD's Integrated Program for Commodities and the Common Fund.* Of the eighteen commodities listed under the Integrated Program, however, agreement has been reached only on one: the natural rubber price stabilization agreement concluded in October 1979. Additionally, although an agreement in principle was reached in Geneva just before UNCTAD V took place in May 1979, there remain many details still to be worked out. Understandably, the primary producing economies (including the Association of Southeast Asian Nations [ASEAN] countries in the Asian/Pacific region) are becoming restless and disturbed. If progress in the realm of commodity stabilization is not forthcoming, it is likely that the atmosphere surrounding the relations between the developed and the developing nations will be further adversely affected. In the Asian/Pacific region, this development primarily would affect relations between the ASEAN countries and Japan.

Malaysia, Indonesia, and Thailand together account for over 80% of the world's exports of natural rubber and almost 70% of the world's exports of tin. Malaysia, Indonesia, and Singapore together account for 80% of world palm oil exports, and the Philippines, Malaysia, and Singapore jointly account for about 70% of the world's exports of coconuts, copra, and coconut oil. The ASEAN countries also account for substantial shares of the world's exports of rice, sugar, and forest products. This trade is concentrated with Japan, the United States, and the European Economic

---

* *Editor's Note:* At the UNCTAD IV conference in 1976, countries from the developing world proposed the adoption of an Integrated Program for Commodities, which would establish international stockpiles for key commodities financed through a Common Fund, as well as provide for expanded compensatory financing and processing opportunities for raw materials producers. Resistance by industrial nations to such comprehensive approaches for dealing with supply problems was evident in their response to this proposed program. The governments of the industrialized states instead prefer to approach commodity problems on a case-by-case basis and to minimize interferences with market forces to the extent possible. See Ronald L. Meltzer, "Contemporary Security Dimensions of International Trade Relations," in Klaus Knorr and Frank N. Trager, eds., *Economic Issues and National Security* (Lawrence, Kansas: Regents Press of Kansas, 1977), p. 222.

Community; hence the possible venom which might arise from an uncooperative relationship would tend to be directed at these major trading partners, undoubtedly also with adverse impact on the producer economies.

Japan, in particular, might find itself bearing the brunt of ASEAN frustrations. Japan's relationship with the five ASEAN countries continues to be governed by the raw materials/manufactures matrix of exchange, a legacy of the 1960s. While Japan wishes to secure the goodwill of the ASEAN states, leading to a stable supply of primary resources and access to ASEAN markets, Tokyo has not sought adequately to meet ASEAN grouses. Tokyo, for example, has failed to make a firm commitment to the establishment of commodity price stabilization arrangements. More specifically, Japan's ASEAN trading partners have proposed that a scheme be set up between themselves and Japan to stabilize export earnings, rather like the STABEX scheme between a number of African, Caribbean, and Pacific countries and the European Economic Community (EEC).[1] This proposal, however, has yet to gain the full support of Japan.

In addition to the growing frustration over the slow progress with respect to the establishment of commodity price stabilization schemes, dissatisfaction flows from other sources in an inflationary world of unstable exchange rates. The real earnings gained even from commodities currently obtaining relatively high prices are being eroded by the ever-increasing prices which must be paid for manufactured imports. The point of view can already be heard that even stabilization arrangements cannot secure real value today for raw material exports. It now seems that stabilization schemes alone are not adequate, but must be accompanied by built-in inflation clauses or, at the least, by strictly defined periodic reviews of the reference prices.

Trade in Manufactures

Developing countries also have sought to protect and expand their economies through the process of industrialization. This process has taken place largely at the levels of low and intermediate tech-

---

[1] STABEX is a stabilization fund established at the first Lomé Convention in 1975. Applying chiefly to tropical products, it was intended to supply insurance cover against the effect on export earnings of a fall in these commodity prices.

nology, and has usually started as import substitution. Domestic markets, however, have not been large enough to support rapid industrialization utilizing the economies of scale. The markets of fellow developing countries also have been largely inaccessible, since these economies have embarked on their own import-substitution programs. The lack of integrated policies and priorities has impeded the development of regional markets, and inadequate technology has prevented the production of more sophisticated products.

Where manufactures from the developing nations have penetrated developed markets, such trade often has been rudely checked by a rising tide of protectionism among erstwhile free-trading states. In some instances, the developed markets are so well protected by tariff and non-tariff barriers that the entry of products from the developing nations is barred entirely. In the realm of trade in manufactures, the question of protectionism constitutes the major problem between the developing and the developed nations.

Market access for the products of the developing nations will free developed economies from inefficient industries and give their consumers the benefits of comparative advantage.[2] Political constraints are such, however, that the logic of economics often does not predominate. Structural change is not achieved without pain, and the leaders of the developed political economies are not certain that they can manage its consequences without incurring serious social instability. Policies of protection thus are developed under different guises: e.g., "voluntary export restraints," "orderly marketing arrangements," "organized free trade," government aid to industry, and even currency depreciation.

The developing countries—in the Asian/Pacific region, primarily the ASEAN states—are being denied access to the markets needed for their manufactures at this early stage of their industrialization programs. The ASEAN countries particularly expect Japan to be sympathetic to their situation and requirements, in view of Japan's position as a fellow Asian nation which success-

---

[2] A country has a *comparative advantage* in the production of those commodities in which it is relatively most efficient. If each country specializes in the products in which it has a comparative advantage, international trade will be mutually profitable.

fully has ascended the industrial ladder and as a fellow sufferer of devious protectionist tactics in Europe and North America. It is of crucial importance that Japan take a bold step in opening its market to goods from the ASEAN nations.

Japan, however, to a large extent has not been helpful and itself has erected barriers and hindered access. Under the Generalized System of Preference covering both agricultural and industrial products,[3] the cuts offered are not significant, and export items of significance to the ASEAN countries are excluded (e.g., canned pineapples, coconut oil, plywood, fish, and palm oil kernel). Furthermore, safeguard mechanisms—i.e., quotas and ceilings—are in operation to restrict imports.

It is true that since the advent of the oil price crisis every advanced political economy has found it increasingly difficult to maintain high rates of employment. As the advanced industrialized economies wrestle with their continuing employment problem, their leaders seek quick solutions. In the process they often fail to realize the real nature of the problem and to recognize that other economies face similar difficulties.

Protecting inefficient industries is not the way to secure full employment. In virtually all countries the labor force continues to grow. At the same time, general opinion holds that public sector employment (the main employment absorber in the 1960s) is already too high, a stance reflected by wide-spread complaints about public sector deficits and high taxation. As a consequence, the pressure on the private sector to absorb employment has been increasing. Within the private sector, the importance of manufacturing relative to other activities now is more widely acknowledged, and it is now realized that manufacturing is the major source of real wealth. It is recognized further that manufacturing constitutes the major international competitive sector, and that a country's success in this realm can protect employment against imports and even expand it through exports.

Access to the markets of the developed economies is a crucial

---

[3] Many countries in the industrialized world have instituted various preferential schemes commonly known as a generalized system of preferences (GSP), which result in unilateral cuts in tariffs on products imported from the developing world. In fact the various schemes have been replete with exceptions both as to the nature and quantity of goods covered and the countries to which the preferences apply.

requirement for the current and future well-being of the developing states. It must be remembered, however, that policies which encourage and support the import of raw materials but restrict the import of manufactured products will abort the attempts of these latter countries to develop their manufacturing sectors, especially in the absence of agreements establishing stable prices for raw materials. The growing industrializing economies, such as those in the ASEAN nations, can suffer irreparable damage by foreclosure of the manufacturing option.

III. Investment

The developing countries now very much encourage the flow of investment from the developed nations, and such investment in fact is actively solicited for industrial and development projects. The time when foreign investment was regarded a priori as suspect and demeaning has passed. At least with respect to the non-communist Asian/Pacific countries, gone too are the days when making a foreign investment entailed a risk beyond that normally incurred. Many of the non-communist developing states in the Asian/Pacific region in fact are parties to the Convention on the Settlement of Investment Disputes Between States and Nationals of Other States reached in 1965 under the auspices of the World Bank. To a large extent foreign investment no longer engenders at the local level such adversarial reactions as vituperative popular attack and even outright nationalization.

The possible scope for investment flows between the capital-exporting and -importing countries in the Asian/Pacific region therefore is encouraging, and returns can be expected to be worthwhile and reasonably secure. The developing economies in this region are among the fastest growing in the world, and funds for investment will gravitate to the region as the investment returns in the older, advanced economies decline. The three "growth potential" blocks in the region—ASEAN, the People's Republic of China (PRC), and Indochina—have different attractions and priorities. Of the three blocks, ASEAN is perhaps the most attractive, with its open economies, relatively skilled and cheap labor, well-developed infrastructure, abundant natural resources, and enormous growth potential.

Constraints, however, do exist, which affect the direction and composition of investment but not its safety. In Malaysia, for example, certain equity sharing and employment requirements must be met under the Industrial Coordination Act and in line with the objectives of the New Economic Policy. The goal is that by 1990 foreign, bumiputran, and non-bumiputran interests[4] respectively will control 30%, 30%, and 40% of the Malaysian economy. Within the context of this overall ratio, the foreign share can be higher in some industries than in others. The ratio requirement tends to be more strictly pursued in industries which produce for the domestic market, whereas greater flexibility is allowed in those industries which are aimed at foreign markets. Furthermore, the Malaysian government has indicated a willingness to make exceptions based on the merits of individual cases. While some investors may complain, the inflow of foreign investments and interests demonstrates that Malaysia's socio-economic policies do not act as a deterrent.

The ASEAN countries as a group strongly desire to attract investment in areas related to raw materials processing. After generations of being denied the value which is added in the processing stages—some of which have involved only the simplest technology—developing economies now want to reap these benefits. Foreign investment and assistance in the establishment of such processing industries will be welcomed and will generate local goodwill toward the foreign interests.

On the other hand, foreign attitudes which are indifferent to local aspirations will cause resentment. Current resentment is strongest against the multinational oil companies, which are seen as concerned only with extracting quick profits and which appear to show no interest in sharing worthwhile technology or assisting in the development of downstream activities. It even has been suggested that some oil companies working in the developing nations apply untried technology in offshore exploitation, thus using the developing countries as a testing ground, with the cost of such experimentation borne solely by the resource-owner. Even the suspicion of such a practice imparts to the oil multinationals a bad reputation.

---

[4] The *bumiputras* are ethnic natives (i.e., Malays). *Non-bumiputras* are the immigrant races in Malaysia.

Japanese investment in the Southeast Asian subregion has been increasing. However, it is felt that Japanese investment does not involve any significant transmission of technology and imparts low value added. Some critics furthermore believe that Japan is employing industrial practices beyond its shores which do not satisfy minimal pollution requirements in Japan itself. Finally, the feeling has increased that Japanese investment is taking place in industries enjoying preferential treatment offered by developed countries—thus cashing in on what is designed to encourage local capital and entrepreneurial skill.

On the other hand, the ASEAN countries, while tending to blame Japan, have not covered the ground adequately themselves to attract the right kind of Japanese investment. Japan, for example, can hardly be held responsible for the delay in establishing the five ASEAN industrial projects announced in Bali in 1976. The projects in fact involved a hodge-podge of schemes designed to serve various national interests, and their economic feasibility (or lack thereof) was not taken sufficiently into account.

With respect to international economic interactions, the People's Republic of China represents the new frontier. While the extent of its full potential is still largely unknown, the importance of the PRC in terms of sheer size is obvious. Viewed in a positive light, the PRC constitutes an important market for ASEAN raw materials. The vast Chinese market may also be expected to absorb some of the manufactured goods and agricultural technology which the ASEAN economies have to offer. Possibilities do exist for the development of a fruitful triangular economic relationship among the developed countries of the Asian/Pacific region, the developing ASEAN states, and a stirring Chinese giant. Much depends on the factor of political stability in the PRC and how the Chinese and ASEAN economies complement one another.

While ASEAN thus far has not been deprived because of the PRC, ASEAN and the PRC will be in competition for foreign investment. It may be assumed, however, that as long as ASEAN remains an attractive investment proposition, funds will flow its way. The fear that ASEAN and the PRC will compete over investment presupposes the production of directly competing manufactured products for foreign markets. If this were to occur, the PRC might choose to exploit its abundant supply of labor in labor intensive production. The PRC for political reasons also might be granted favored treatment for its exports to developed economies. Under such circumstances, ASEAN might find it difficult to compete.

It is clear that greater thought must be given to the impact a developing China will have on international economics in the Asian/Pacific region, particularly with respect to the manufacturing sector. Attention must be paid to the question of how China's manufactured products will be absorbed, given the fact that its huge potential market is relatively undeveloped and is already being coveted by various nations as it begins to grow. It is possible that, at least in some respects, the problem of markets in the area may be deepened and exacerbated.

As a final consideration, there is no reason why an economically resurgent Indochina, particularly Vietnam, should not be able to engage in beneficial trade and investment relations with Japan and ASEAN. (Such Vietnamese relations with the PRC may be impossible for political reasons.) Notwithstanding the turmoil on the Indochinese peninsula, ASEAN should keep all its options open with respect to such possibilities, as Japan has done.

IV. Conclusion: The Economic Basis of Security

Tremendous opportunities exist in the Asian/Pacific region for trade and investment. The states of the region—particularly the developing economies—constitute the center of economic growth in the world today.

The potential of the region's developing states must be tapped in such a way that there are no feelings of exploitation. Furthermore, in their relations with the developed nations, the developing economies are becoming more insistent that adequate attention be paid to meeting their internal needs, from social restructuring to the establishment and maintenance of internal security. In general, the developing economies are seeking a pattern of development which will serve to broaden their domestic economic bases, so that they can be more resilient and withstand the adversities of the world economy.

The nations of the region share a desire to collaborate, but there exist important differences between the developed and the developing states with respect to the details of such collaboration. On the whole, the climate for investment in the ASEAN countries is extremely good, for example; however, the foreign investor and the capital-importer still lack a complete appreciation of one another's respective needs and modes of usefulness. When the developing countries observe the developed economies changing the rules of international trade (upon which they have long insisted) to suit their immediate interests, they worry about the basis of international exchange. When they see promises about commodity stabilization not kept after nearly two decades of consideration, they question the value of engaging in cooperation.

The developed economies may operate under the assumption that the developing states have no real alternatives but to interact with them in the realms of trade and investment—and they well may be right. The real point to be emphasized is that if the problems outlined in this essay are not addressed the benefits of cooperation may be lost to both the developed and the developing nations through conscious or unconscious choice. The developed economies must think in terms of the important resources and strategic sea lanes which could be denied them in such a contingency, as well as the loss of investment already expended.

If a world of ever closer, mutually advantageous economic interdependence can be constructed in the Pacific Basin region, in terms of the protection of real common interests the mutually reinforcing strength of that system will have a force far greater than the stationing of garrisons.

ENERGY RESOURCES, RAW MATERIALS, AND THE SAFETY OF THE SEA LANES OF COMMUNICATION: An Organic Approach Toward a New Security Framework

Alejandro Melchor

I. Toward a New Security Foundation: A Theoretical Framework

The structural dynamics of international forces in the world or in a given region at any point in time may be seen as falling somewhere along a continuum which has as its extremes *bipolarity* at one end and *organicity of structure* at the other. In terms of this framework, in the years since World War II the configuration of world power has shifted from the largely bipolar world structure of the Cold War toward a more organic world structure.

The postwar economic recovery of Europe and the phenomenal growth of the economies of Japan, the Republic of Korea, the Republic of China on Taiwan, Singapore, Hong Kong, and the Organization of Petroleum Exporting Countries (OPEC) nations have created new centers of economic power. The Sino-Soviet rift, the rise of Islamic fundamentalism, and the emergence of the non-aligned bloc have resulted in the formation of additional centers of political power. (It is important to note that although some of its members in fact are as aligned as many other states, basic to the philosophy of the non-aligned movement is a desire to avoid being drawn into conflicts between the two superpowers.)

The postwar process of decolonization, which continues to the present, has resulted in the establishment of a number of new nation-states, many of which are concerned less with the ideological struggle between the two superpowers and more with the business of economic development and the evolution of viable political systems responsive to their individual cultures and needs. More nations are now involved simultaneously in the process of nation-building, in more different cultural contexts, than at any other time in history.

As a result of these developments, the number of political choices and alternatives open to nation-states has increased, and international alignments have been formed on the basis of commonalities of interests and security concerns which do not exactly conform with the bipolar Cold War logic. The growth of international trade and the increased diversity of available trading partners undoubtedly have enhanced the stability of the global system. The transformation of the structure of bilateral relations toward organic exchange and mutual benefit has resulted in a reduction in the perceived threats to security.

The recent decision of the People's Republic of China (PRC) to join the mainstream of international trade; the PRC's conclusion of bilateral trade treaties with Japan, France, West Germany, Canada, and the United States; and the normalization of relations between the PRC and many countries have contributed in important ways to the establishment and maintenance of stability in the Asian/Pacific region and the world in general. Under these new conditions, it is less likely that the PRC will decide to participate in serious conflicts or confrontations, since such activity might distract attention from or delay the country's aggressive industrialization plans, or deny the benefits Peking expects to gain from multibillion dollar trade and investment relations with Japan and the West.

A mutually beneficial trade relationship is an organic relationship, since feedback forces—in the form of penalties incurred—come into play whenever one of the parties acts to destroy or deviate from the relationship. The dynamic logic of a mutually beneficial structure calls for the maintenance of stability and efforts to increase the mutuality of the structure.

Structures which are non-mutual or unequally beneficial are less stable because feedback forces are unequal and asymmetrical. The patron-client relationship which often exists between developed and less developed countries serves as an example. Because the maintenance of the relationship brings fewer rewards to one party than to the other, the relationship is less dynamically stable.

The attainment and/or enhancement of security can be viewed as a search for workable institutions and mechanisms which can manage multifarious and often conflicting interests and transform them into inherently stable systems. Specifically, the challenge is to neutralize potential zero-sum game situations, and to adopt imaginative and farsighted means to transform non-mutual relationships into mutually beneficial ones which are more effective in stabilizing a regional system and/or the world order. Another component of enhancing security may consist of identifying investment and other economic opportunities which can be put to work despite differences in priorities, ideologies, or social systems.

II. World Shipping and Trade in Energy and Raw Materials: Some Structural Measures Toward Greater Stability

Since the start of the Industrial Revolution in England some two hundred years ago, a world economy has been evolving which increasingly depends on trade in energy resources and raw materials and on the sea lanes for transport of these objects of trade. This trend can be expected to continue for the remainder of this century. During the twenty-first century, two important modifications of the present situation are likely to occur. Firstly, oil—the most exportable energy resource—will become scarce and therefore prohibitively expensive within the first half of the century, according to many experts. Secondly, increasing supply-side difficulties emanating from the sources of energy and important industrial raw materials are likely to shift conceptions of development away from material productivity in the industrial sense and toward a "post-industrial" world economy, which will emphasize the primary and tertiary sectors, and in particular the information and knowledge industries.

However, for the immediate future it is of crucial importance for the security of all participants that the expanding world trade and shipping system be stabilized. In this connection, two corollary propositions are suggested: 1) the security of the sea lanes must be recognized as a global concern, and 2) in the long-term view, the security of the world trading and shipping system is best ensured by structural solutions that effect greater system stability.

The structure of the present world trading and shipping system leaves much to be desired, especially with regard to energy trade. Oil accounts for more than 90% of world energy consumption, upon which the maintenance and growth of the world economy is basically dependent. The transport of oil comprises 43% of the world gross tonnage of shipping. The world trading and shipping system is beset by a number of structural imbalances:

1. As of 1976, trade (including both imports and exports) involving developed market-economy countries accounted for 85% of total world trading activity. The figures in this respect for the developing, OPEC, and centrally-planned countries were 38%, 17%, and 12% respectively. Of total imports of raw materials, 74% was imported by developed market-economy countries, 12% by developing countries, only 2% by OPEC countries, and 10% by countries with centrally-planned economies. Of total imports of mineral fuels* (the source for many countries of a considerable degree of vulnerability and insecurity), 77% was imported by developed market-economy countries. The figures for the developing countries, OPEC, and the centrally-planned countries were 19%, less than 1%, and 3% respectively.
2. In the Asian/Pacific area, energy and raw materials account for large

---

* The mineral fuels consist mostly of crude oil.

fractions of the imports of the United States (28% and 16%), Japan (44% and 35%), and Singapore (27% and 19%).
3. In 1974, 61% of the gross tonnage of maritime fleets was owned by developed countries, not counting the 24% which is registered with open-registry countries. In contrast, developing and socialist countries owned only 6% and 8%, respectively.** As of mid-1979, the gross tonnage of the Soviet Union's maritime fleet comprised 5.5% of the world total.
4. With respect to the question of who trades with whom, it can be observed that in 1976, 39% of world trade took place among the developed countries, 5% among the developing countries, and 4% among the socialist countries. The greater bulk of the latter is transported via land routes. Trade between OPEC and the non-oil producing developing countries comprised only 3% of the total world trade in 1976.

This imbalanced pattern of world sea-borne trade is not conducive to stable relationships among world trading partners. Both short-term measures and long-term planning are indicated so as to reduce structural imbalances in the system. The following testimony by U.S. Assistant Secretary of State Harold Saunders before the House Committee on Foreign Affairs in July 1979 suggests one such action.

> Over the next few years, water issues will increasingly occupy the attention of the political leadership of the region. The Margarin Dam and questions of water management in the West Bank have made the availability of water a matter of crucial importance in the Arab-Israeli negotiations. However, there is an even broader perspective. Water has always been a scarce resource in the Middle East. As incomes rise and development takes place, demand for water for personal consumption, agriculture, and industry increases. In many areas, however, there are few remaining underdeveloped water resources. The pressure of rising demand for a fixed and limited supply of a resource even more vital than oil would have far-reaching political significance—both as a cause of conflict and as an imperative for cooperation.

** Unless separate figures for OPEC are cited, the OPEC countries are included in the data compiled for the developing nations.

Approximately one hundred Very Large Crude Carriers (VLCCs) leave Japan every month under ballast to travel to the Persian Gulf area to acquire a cargo of crude oil for Japan's energy needs. It would be possible for these VLCCs on their back-haul to carry fresh water from a number of watering points in Southeast Asia at no additional freight cost, aside from the time involved in diverting and loading the vessels. The fresh water then can be discharged at Persian Gulf ports, and any contamination or odor can be removed by available technology at a cost considerably lower than that for desalinated water. Aside from providing selected Middle East countries with a reliable, dependable, and cheap supply of water, such a scheme would greatly stabilize Japan's supply of crude oil by providing a two-way flow of commodities. Additionally, foreign exchange revenues would be provided to the developing countries which would serve as suppliers of the water.

Japan—a populous, resource-poor island nation—is extremely vulnerable to a naval blockade at any point along the sea routes which carry the nation's oil, food, and other raw material requirements. In order to reduce the vulnerability of its sea lanes of communication, Japan could make arrangements with neighboring coastal states in the region for the cooperative policing of the sea lanes so vital to international shipping. No nation sensibly can expect to effectively protect its own international shipping singlehandedly. A number of activities lend themselves to mutual cooperation and complementation—e.g., joint planning; mutual sharing of equipment, technology, and information; and coordinated training and exercises—and can obviate the need for a formal treaty, which may serve only to create suspicion and needless rigidity.

The establishment of non-naval patrols or maritime constabularies to engage in search and rescue operations, perform weather surveillance, provide for safe navigation for ships at sea, as well as enforce an ever-increasing number of conventions and national regulations with respect to the environment, fisheries, and other aspects of offshore resources, will be part of the operating environment of shipping in the immediate future. These activities will entail considerable budgetary outlays from the developing coastal nations.

Assistance to these nations from Japan and other Organization for Economic Cooperation and Development (OECD) countries to enable them to procure the equipment necessary for these tasks will redound to the mutual benefit of Japan and the coastal states of Southeast Asia. Southeast Asian nations might prefer this solution to that of increasing the budgets of their navies for the same purpose, and would certainly find it preferable to the establishment of a greater naval presence of maritime powers in their waterways.

In short, all measures designed to correct imbalances and distortions in world trade and shipping must be calculated in a manner that makes these measures building blocks toward organicity.

III. The Non-Communist States of the Asian/Pacific Region: The Challenge of Transforming Dangers into Opportunities

The Many Dimensions of Security

When the long-term planning horizon extending into the twenty-first century is considered, the Pacific Basin region offers one of the best opportunities in the world for peaceful trade and progress. Among the factors which can be put forward in support of this projection are: 1) the relative political stability of the governments in most of the nations located in and around the Pacific Basin; 2) the broad similarities among the non-communist states with respect to world-views and types of economic and political systems; 3) the fact that vast resource-rich areas remain untapped, and an abundant supply of relatively cheap labor and substantial markets for manufactured goods and services are available; and 4) the fact that in no other region of the world does the United States enjoy as great an advantage over the Soviet Union in terms of military presence and political influence.

It must be recognized clearly that the operational security framework most familiar to Europeans and Americans is not an adequate foundation for a new security framework for the non-communist states of the Asian/Pacific region. The unique political, economic, social, and cultural aspects of these nations must be taken into account. From the point of view of the United States, the search for a new security foundation for the Pacific Basin region accordingly will be more difficult and challenging than the search for security arrangements with its NATO allies in Europe. The major perceived security threat in both cases is the Soviet Union. It was noted above that the non-communist nations of the Pacific Basin region share broad similarities in important respects. In the case of NATO, however, the U.S. and the Western European countries share a much greater degree of commonality with respect to historical, cultural, economic, political and ideological assumptions, leading to an ease in handling security questions in operational military terms—an approach less appropriate to the diversities of the Asian/Pacific region and the problems these countries face.

Any consideration of the concept of security should take into account a number of interrelated political, economic, social, cultural, and psychological aspects. Before a new security foundation for the Asian/Pacific region can be realistically formulated and accepted by all concerned, fundamental questions and premises—approached from the viewpoints of both the developed and the developing nations—first must be addressed, leading ideally to a regional consensus of basic assumptions. A new security foundation must take into account the threats perceived and vulnerabilities experienced by the developed non-communist states, and the aspirations of the less developed states for economic development and greater political control of their national destinies in the context of their own cultural milieus.

When considering the political and economic realities of the Asian/Pacific region, special attention must be paid to the challenges faced by the young nations in the Southeast Asian sub-region and the emerging newly independent states in the Pacific. Despite optimistic projections with respect to the growth of the non-communist developing states of the region, most of these countries are still in search of the most viable political system which will be responsive to their needs and are far from achieving the goal of self-reliance. The soundness and workability of any new security foundation among the non-communist states in the region will depend, in part, on how well it takes into account the political, economic, and cultural problems and aspirations of these nations.

Resources, Raw Materials, and Sea Lanes

Economic Policies as an Underpinning Force for Greater Security

The economic and trade foundation of NATO is the European Economic Community; a similar relationship prevails between the Warsaw Pact and COMECON. A new security foundation for the Pacific Basin area should be based on and reinforced by imaginative and farsighted cultural, economic, and trade policies which stimulate the mutually beneficial organic relationships discussed at the beginning of this essay. As a source of support and stabilization for the new security framework, these policies will contribute to progress toward a number of important goals.

Rationalization of the economic and trade interests of the developed states. While the developed non-communist states often identify themselves as one distinct group transcending race, culture, tradition, language, and historical antecedents, significant differences still exist among them. Serious but only partially successful attempts have been made to resolve these differences through bilateral or multilateral negotiations, including through non-official channels. Trade treaties, the Trilateral Commission, and OECD serve as a few examples. Such divergences, in an interdependent world, do reverberate far and wide, affecting not only the developed market economies but also the less developed countries. There is thus the need to rationalize the economic and trade interests of the developed non-communist states as a source of stabilization and support for any new security foundation for the Asian/Pacific region.

Strengthening the less developed states by facilitating the achievement of their realistic aspirations. The less developed non-communist states for many years have provided the developed states with cheap labor, critical raw materials, markets, and profitable investment opportunities. Additionally, many of them sit astride the sea lanes vital to international trade. The countries of Southeast Asia, for example, not only command the choke points that link the Indian and Pacific Oceans but also offer markets and raw materials for the industrialized world. Southeast Asia's singularly extensive continental shelves may become the Pacific Basin's major source of oil, minerals, and aquatic resources in the coming decades. The subregion's potential for providing energy resources when most other sources in the world will have been nearly depleted or rendered politically insecure should not be underestimated. During the past few decades, however, the continuing validity of the assumptions underlying this traditional role of the less developed countries has come to be questioned. Conditions now must be created to ensure that the less developed states attain their legitimate aspirations. Indications are that for any new foundation for Asian/Pacific security to be viable and live up to expectations, the old assumptions must be exchanged for new ones more responsive to present realities.

Laying the basis for denying fertile grounds to revolutionary movements. Measures which improve the internal strength of the less developed non-communist states correspondingly will decrease the chances of success of revolutionary movements which seek the overthrow of the social systems of these new nations. Domestic instability invites external intervention. Revolutionary movements which seek to seize political power and governments which fear the loss of their power would rather collaborate with external forces than forego their ambitions. Any new foundation for the security of the Asian/Pacific region must enhance the internal stability of the non-communist states and diminish the prospects of revolutionary upheaval and external intervention.

The development of values which can generate a regional consensus. To facilitate their interests, the colonial powers often attempted to transform the values of the colonized states so that they would match their own. This historical legacy has created for many new nations an identity crisis which must be resolved as they aspire to a more dignified sovereign existence. In this context, any new foundation for the security of the Asian/Pacific region must be based on a regional consensus which takes into account the heterogeneity of the region, and which recognizes unity in diversity rather than unity based on a value system represented by a few nations.

If the new foundation for security comes to terms with the thrusts and orientations suggested above, no outside power reasonably can expect to acquire the capability to effectively mobilize any countervailing collective security system.

IV. Concluding Remarks

What is necessary is the transformation of a) an ultimately self-defeating scramble among the developed countries for markets, energy resources, raw materials, and control of the sea lanes, into b) a situation of opportunities based on an organic framework which ensures stability and security by the very nature of the structure of the relationships among participating nation-states. Saburo Okita, an eminent internationalist and [at this writing] Japan's Foreign Minister, has called for a dynamic international division of labor accompanied by an enlightened revision of existing economic and trade policies. Okita's proposal recognizes the requirements and perceptions of developing countries, allows for the planned transfer of technologies and industries no longer competitive in Japan's high labor environment, and provides for the restructuring of the Japanese economy toward technology-intensive industries. This scheme allows for industrial growth in developing countries while maintaining complementarity with the Japanese economy.

A close look at present conditions in the Asian/Pacific region suggests a number of potential realities. In the long term, it well may be the case that the future of the non-communist countries in the area will be determined less by the potency of the particular threats they face (e.g., the Soviet Union) than by the strength of their collective political resolve to: 1) re-examine the premises of the existing security environment and develop, if necessary, new premises more responsive to their collective aspirations; 2) rationalize economic and trade interests among the developed states; and 3) respond to the legitimate developmental goals of the developing nations. The existence in the region of economic and other opportunities for both the developed and the developing nations cannot be denied. The challenge to all parties lies in the need to evolve acceptable ways of transforming differing perceptions and interests into a basis for the achievement of stability in the region.

REPORT OF COMMITTEES #3 AND #4

The members of Committees #3 and #4 met together at the conference and as a group considered and made recommendations with respect to the broad range of issues falling under the general heading of "Economic Dimensions of Asian and Pacific Security."

Co-chairmen:
The Honorable Bernard Chen,
Deputy Minister of Defense, Singapore

Dr. Tomatsu Takase,
Professor, Kyoto Sangyo University, Kyoto, and Energy Consultant, Tokyo, Japan

I. Trade and Investment: Meeting the Needs of the Developed and the Developing Countries

1. Protectionism is a self-defeating measure which is detrimental to the growth of trade and investment. In the long run it affects the economies of the developed countries as much as it does those of the developing nations. The need to reduce protectionism must be emphasized urgently. It is recognized, however, that any liberalization process must take into account such domestic constraints as concern about employment and economic growth rates. Liberalization therefore must be implemented in stages and with constant consultation between the developed and the developing countries to ensure that the process will be smooth.
2. Most developing countries in Northeast and Southeast Asia have outgrown the need for soft loans from the developed countries. The

emphasis now should be placed on investment and the transfer of technologies to the developing states. Additionally, the industries thus sponsored must be made viable and feasible; especially important is access for the resulting products to markets in the developed nations.
3. Japanese financing in the region's developing countries through multilateral agencies is welcomed. However, it is essential that such multilateral agencies should be regional rather than global in operation, thereby ensuring that regional interests are not neglected. In the case of the member nations of ASEAN, the Association itself is such a suitable agency. As a prerequisite for the success of this collective financial scheme, individual ASEAN countries must place emphasis on regional interests rather than on narrow national interests. It is inevitable that some sacrifice may have to be accepted by certain individual countries for the collective benefit of ASEAN, which in the long run will benefit all the member countries. The effectiveness of a strong common stand was demonstrated amply in the recent air travel issue between ASEAN and Australia. The failure of several of the initial ASEAN industrial projects reflected the opposite consequences which result from the lack of a strong common stand.
4. The fear of Japanese economic domination of the region can be alleviated by the following measures: a) Japanese financing in the developing countries conducted through multilateral agencies rather than on a bilateral basis, and b) greater local participation in the various projects financed by Japan.
5. The increasing trade and investment between Japan and the People's Republic of China will divert a certain amount of finance away from other developing countries in the region. Additionally, the PRC may pose serious competition to the exporting industries in these states. These perceived threats can be minimized through rapid and sustained economic growth in Japan and the other developed countries, which will generate sufficient resources for additional financing and increase the size of markets. It is recognized that any attempt to impose constraints on exports from industries in the PRC would be unrealistic; furthermore, fair play and competition must prevail.

II. Energy Resources, Raw Materials, and the Safety of the Sea Lanes of Communication

Prefatory remark: The portion of the committee sessions devoted to discussion of these issues was characterized by the expression of

Report of Committees #3 and #4

highly diversified points of view. While the following general conclusions can be drawn from the sessions, they do not represent a consensus of views.

1. Measures must be taken to keep open the vital sea lanes of communication, so as to ensure the free flow of energy resources and raw materials.
2. An administrative arrangement—which would perform such functions as patrols against oil pollution, financing of a monitoring agency, etc.—should be formulated to ensure the safety of the sea lanes. ASEAN can serve as a coordinating agency in such an arrangement with respect to the sea lanes in that subregion. The operating costs of such a system should be borne by a fund derived from charges levied on the users of the sea lanes.
3. Perceptions with respect to the degree of seriousness of the Soviet threat varied considerably among the committee members. It was pointed out that overreaction on the part of the non-communist countries may be counterproductive. The organization of a formal regional security framework thus is undesirable, and moreover is beyond the capability of the ASEAN countries. On the other hand, the conduct of joint naval exercises involving the U.S., Japan, and the ASEAN states is an alternative which can demonstrate the will for collective defense. However, the effectiveness of such exercises will be in doubt unless a major role is played by the developed countries.
4. In view of the military weaknesses of the ASEAN countries vis-a-vis the military might of Vietnam and the Soviet Union, the security of the Asian/Pacific region is linked closely to the possession by the U.S. of the political will to take an active leadership role in the region.
5. In view of escalating oil prices and limited oil resources, alternative sources of energy must be found. The possible sources of energy in the region are coal, solar and thermal power, hydro-electricity, and nuclear power. Regional cooperation in the search for oil and the exploration of alternative energy resources is essential for the stability of the region. Countries which possess the technology for exploration and exploitation should be encouraged to export such technologies. Additionally, the Asian countries will welcome any Japanese offer to finance the storage of reserved crude and certain refined products. Stockpiling of petroleum and refined products will enhance the stability of the region and assure the existence of supplies in case of an emergency.
6. Given the current price of oil, nuclear energy has become a relatively

cheap source of power. This situation is likely to prevail during the next decade or two. Under these circumstances, it is particularly regrettable that the excessively stringent environmental regulations imposed by the U.S. nuclear regulatory agency already have stymied one major development of nuclear power in the region—namely, in the Philippines. The committees recommend that the ASEAN countries should take a collective stand toward the United States and should demand a revision of the rules which make it extremely difficult for countries in the region to develop their own nuclear power industries.

7. The production and distribution of food in the region constitute a problem which is as important, but not necessarily as acute, as the oil problem. This issue was not covered in the committee sessions, but it is recommended that the problem be undertaken for further study in future conferences.

Chapter 4

POLICY PROPOSALS AND ASIAN AND PACIFIC SECURITY

Issues And Questions To Be Addressed: 4

The organizers of the Pattaya conference set forth the following paragraphs—which outlined some of the more specific problems to be addressed, both formally and informally, during the course of the conference—as a guide for conference participants. While conferees in their formal papers, discussion sessions, and committee reports were free to range over a wide range of subject matter and concerns, and not all the suggested questions were answered fully or directly, the "Issues and Questions to be Addressed" served to provide a framework and direction for the deliberations of the conference.

It is imperative to examine how the nations of the Asian/Pacific region can cooperate together to strengthen their individual and collective abilities to cope with the manifold challenges to their security and stability. Several modes of regional cooperation are already in operation, and may serve as the foundation for enhanced collaboration in the future; on the other hand, international developments may demand the creation of new cooperative frameworks and institutions.

The non-communist countries of the region view continued U.S. economic, political, and military involvement in East Asia as essential to the area's defense and well-being, especially in view of the growing Soviet military presence in Asia, the uncertainty of long-range Chinese intentions, and the destabilizing events of 1979 in Indochina. Skepticism with respect to American diplomatic and military strength and dependability in the post-Vietnam war period still exists among these nations, however, and it remains for the U.S. to restore adequately the credibility of its international commitments and regain the trust of its friends. In particular, the U.S. commitment to the security of Japan and South Korea and to the Australia/New Zealand/U.S. (ANZUS) Treaty should be clearly articulated and strengthened. Also of crucial importance are concrete manifestations of U.S. involvement in the ensurance of Southeast Asian security, including economic and diplomatic support for the Association of Southeast Asian Nations (ASEAN) states, U.S. military assistance, and guarantees of continued sales of essential military equipment to American friends and allies.

Special attention should be drawn to the growing vitality of ASEAN, not only in the original areas of economics and cultural exchange but increasingly with respect to political and security interests as well. Under the pressure of the deteriorating situation in neighboring Indochina, this cooperative organization has created the means for the exertion of true regional diplomatic strength, has gone far toward the achievement of an independent and articulated presence in world affairs, and has developed mechanisms for the synchronization and coordination of policies of member countries on external matters of common interest. Outside the formal ASEAN structure, member states have established an extensive pattern of informal, bilateral security cooperation among themselves, with the ANZUS nations, and with Japan.

- What actions, decisions, and policy stances—both domestic and international—will constitute an adequate and realistic response to current (and likely future) security threats in the Asian/Pacific area?
- For the non-communist Asian nations, what kinds of defense capabilities and military postures are necessary as underpinnings to real individual and collective independence and strength? What level of U.S. military commitment and force deployments are required to maintain a credible regional deterrent?
- Given the inevitable differences in viewpoint among the various

Issues and Questions to be Addressed 195

nations, what are the problems of regional cooperation, and can these differences be surmounted?
- In view of the crucial importance of economic factors in the establishment and maintenance of both internal and external security and stability, how can the nations of the region best ensure an international environment conducive to continued national and regional economic growth and development?
- How can the ASEAN nations deter regional domination and/or interference in their internal affairs by any of the great powers active in Southeast Asia, and avoid being drawn into conflicts which might arise between or among the great powers involved in the region?
- What are the possibilities and problems of stronger Japanese security ties with the non-communist Southeast Asian states and with ANZUS?
- How can the Republic of China on Taiwan play a role as a positive force for stability in East Asia?
- Can the existing modes of cooperation in the region be expanded into a wider framework of security cooperation, or must new institutional arrangements be devised?
- What sorts of formal and informal planning and coordination—e.g., increased standardization of weapons systems, better intelligence sharing procedures, and joint training exercises—can be accomplished now, so as to prepare for future contingencies? In view of the troubled international environment in the area, is a formal, collective security agreement now a realistic and desirable option?
- Can Australia, Japan, and the U.S. profitably serve as the backbone of a new cooperative regional security framework, with other regional nations contributing at their chosen levels of commitment?

THE PACIFIC BASIN COMMUNITY:
Editor's Introduction

A considerable amount of attention has been directed in recent years toward the concept of a Pacific Basin community—i.e., a regional cooperative organization which might facilitate approaches to those needs which cannot adequately be met through existing bilateral, regional, and/or global arrangements. Through the efforts of the late Japanese Prime Minister Masayoshi Ohira and Australian Prime Minister Malcolm Fraser, studies on the topic have been initiated in these countries, and U.S. officials are also engaged in exploration of the idea. While several alternative proposals have been set forth with respect to the establishment of such a community, none has been precisely defined and delineated, and no broad consensus as yet has emerged regarding questions of membership, organization, and operational format.*

It can be expected that movement toward such a consensus will be difficult to achieve and that many obstacles inevitably will be encountered. Because the Pacific Basin has no historical record as a distinct region and no history of regional consciousness, it is

---

* Readers interested in the scope and variety of thinking surrounding the Pacific Basin community concept should refer to "The Pacific Community Idea," Hearings Before the Subcommittee on Asian and Pacific Affairs of the Committee on Foreign Affairs, U.S. House of Representatives, July 18, October 23, and October 31, 1979 (U.S. Government Printing Office, Washington, 1979).

not clear which countries should be included within its confines. In its broadest definition, the region might be viewed as encompassing the nations which border the Pacific Ocean, or have direct and easy access to it. Certainly the existence of a commonality of interests may be identified among many or even most of these nations, based largely (but not exclusively) upon the fact of growing economic interdependence. However, the Pacific Basin area also is characterized by an extraordinary diversity, which is manifested in strong cultural, religious, and racial differences; varying stages of economic development; and historical animosities. Intense political differences exist not only *between* the region's communist and non-communist states, but *within* the communist and non-communist sectors as well.

Some proponents of the Pacific Basin community concept have drawn attention to the problems, including difficulties in formulating effective action, which may emerge if the member states differ markedly in their basic values and/or types of political and economic systems. With this reservation in mind, several commentators have recommended that formal membership be restricted to those countries with market-oriented economic systems. Others, such as Tan Sri Ghazali bin Shafie (whose essay on the topic is included in this chapter), have expressed concern regarding the possibility that such a formulation might lead to a politically divided and economically estranged Pacific Basin based on a communist/non-communist cleavage. Ghazali states: "It is in terms of a creative force—bringing together ideologically, politically, and economically disparate societies—that I prefer to approach the Pacific Basin concept."

Other important questions remain unanswered as well. While the Pacific Basin community idea has been propelled mainly by economic considerations, opinions differ as to whether the goals of the community should be limited to the economic arena or expanded to include cooperative approaches to problems in such areas as environmental concerns, refugee issues, and regional security and stability. Even with so many key aspects yet to be resolved, however, the growing consideration being accorded the possibility of enhanced Pacific Basin cooperation must be viewed as a significant and welcome contribution to the search for more constructive political and economic relations among the nations of the region, however it ultimately may be defined.

Address

The Honorable Tan Sri Muhammad Ghazali bin Shafie,
Minister of Home Affairs, Kuala Lumpur, Malaysia

TOWARD A PACIFIC BASIN COMMUNITY: A MALAYSIAN PERCEPTION

Tan Sri Muhammad Ghazali bin Shafie

American, Japanese, and Australian circles have shown in recent months a perceptible quickening of interest in a Pacific Basin community concept. Although ideas of Pacific Basin cooperation have been mooted for well over a decade, renewed interest may be symptomatic of these uncertain times. The ASEAN countries have not been spared solicitations of their views with respect to this concept, which has been propounded in the main by their most important external economic and trading partners, who also happen to constitute some of the more important variables in their political-security considerations. ASEAN has not responded formally to these solicitations, but it is obvious that economic and strategic stakes require that due consideration be extended to the Pacific Basin community concept and ASEAN's approaches to it.

I therefore propose to share with you some of my thoughts on the Pacific Basin community concept, inasmuch as the concept touches on Malaysia's future as: 1) a developing nation attempting to attain national resilience through economic growth and social justice; 2) a member of the ASEAN regional community aspiring to regional resilience through political, social, and economic cooperation and the creation of a regional neutrality system (a Zone of Peace, Freedom, and Neutrality [ZOPFAN]); and 3) a responsible member of the global community anxious to contribute politically to a secure and peaceful world order through constructive nonalignment and neutralism, and economically to a New International Economic Order (NIEO).

Since Malaysia's basic perspective with respect to the challenges of these uncertain times is a globalist one, it is useful to summarize briefly the likely characteristics of the international system in the decades ahead. In the final two decades of the Twentieth Century, the countries of the Pacific Basin in common with the rest of the world will have to cope with an international environment that is profoundly revolutionary in nature. The revolutionary character of our age may be summed up by the following general propositions:

1. The strategic nuclear stand-off, meaning that military power cannot automatically be translated into political influence, has resulted in the emergence of new forms of power—notably economic and financial power, including the negative power of denial of natural resources.
2. Global political power has fragmented from a bipolar to a multipolar matrix, spawning new patterns of shifting political alliances with different coalitions forming around different issues.
3. Economic issues have gained primacy on the agenda of international politics, a result of global economic interdependence, especially in energy matters; this has led to the politicization of international economics, legitimizing the structural asymmetries in international power.
4. The interdependence of politics and economics in international affairs has added an economic dimension to the concept of national and international security.
5. The permeability of states to general global developments in terms of politics, economics, and ideas has increased, a consequence of the ever quicker pace of technological developments and the onset of the communication revolution.
6. The capability of states to contain political loyalites strictly within national boundaries has eroded; under the pressure of transnational

ideologies, conflicts among states merge with divisions within nations, resulting in the erosion of the traditional division between domestic and foreign policy.

These features of our revolutionary age exert a fundamental influence on the conduct of foreign policy by all states. States—both big and small, strong and weak—can no longer conduct their foreign policies as exercises unrelated to their domestic policies, and vice versa. Whereas in the past dominant powers could afford the irresponsibility of determining their foreign policies according to domestic political dictates, and subordinate powers likewise could afford the irresponsibility of making foreign policy the plaything of domestic political maneuvering, both now must face the hard and ironic truth that all nations are saddled with the difficult and unwanted responsibility for keeping the current divisive and imperfect international system afloat—if they wish to ensure their survival as distinct political entities within the system. All countries must sooner or later accept as axiomatic the fact that their foreign and domestic policies are inextricably interrelated and, for efficient and effective management, must be correlated in the context of an overall National Policy. In an interdependent world foreign policy must increasingly provide the strategic thrust of National Policy. A foreign policy that is not fully interrelated with domestic policy is self-defeating; conversely, a domestic policy that takes no account of international realities is similarly doomed to failure.

The difficult task of evolving integrated national policies to meet the challenges of a revolutionary age is one which is faced, without exception, by all states. The more developed and older states start, however, with the advantage of an inherently stable and secure polity, which may be based on the concept and reality of a homogeneous nation-state or on political institutions and rules hallowed by history and legitimized by long national popular acceptance. The problem faced by these states is one of educating their populations to accept constraints on selfish and hitherto relatively unfettered domestic demands, in the interest of maintaining a modicum of stability in the larger international system.

Developing emergent states have a far more difficult time. Their problem is the fundamental one of organizing a stable national consensus—often without the benefit of national homogeneity or truly legitimate political institutions—in order to realize the socio-economic benefits that statehood has been thought to promise. In the international system of the past, these states for all intents and purposes played no relevant or meaningful role, and consequently their national disorganization never was of great international significance. (However, such disorganization often did provide the excuse for external interference and intervention in the internal political processes of these states.) However, in our revolutionary age—when domestic expectations must be speedily fulfilled, and the developing nations have become drawn into the vortex of international instability arising from the unwillingness and/or inability of states to adjust to the fact of international interdependence—national disorganization becomes a prescription for disaster, not only for the developing countries themselves but also for the developed countries that are dependent upon them for the supply of natural resources.

The revolutionary situation posed by the rapidly changing relationship between man's infinite demands and the finite natural system has profound economic, social, and political consequences affecting the organization of global society. These consequences seem certain to affect every nation. The welfare of a state's population and its long-term survival as a stable political entity therefore must depend ultimately upon the nation's ability to adjust adequately to rapidly changing situations. In turn, global society—if it is to keep alive the hopes and aspirations of man—must depend upon the survival of separate nations which can maintain some degree of stability.

Under the impact of these developments, both the developed and the developing countries have tended to organize themselves into larger political-economic agglomerations, so as to better manage such variables as market considerations, technological developments, and geopolitical factors. These agglomerations become new centers of bargaining power both economically and politically; and, to the extent they prove successful, themselves stimulate geopolitical changes. It is possible for these groupings to exert a benign influence on the structure of global society by stimulating growth and efficiency, thereby increasing economic opportunities through a ripple effect; alternatively, if their inefficiency should generate political pressures toward economic exclusiveness inhibitive of global growth, they may exert an unfavorable influence.

If the Pacific Basin community concept is to be relevant in the decades ahead, it must adequately address itself to the emerging dynamics of the international system and the impact of those dynamics on the separate subregional and national systems of the Pacific Basin area. Furthermore, because the Pacific Basin is but a microcosm of the larger world, any concept of a Pacific Basin community must be compatible with and complementary to the notion of a universal global community. Unless the Pacific Basin concept is approached from these standpoints, it may embark on a course that could well prove tangential to its present direction.

The developed countries have hitherto been the exclusive proponents of the Pacific Basin concept in its various permutations, with their supporters among the developing countries generally reacting to or amplifying their perceptions. While it is not being suggested that this fact necessarily impairs the concept, it does raise the point of motive. Altruism or enlightened self-interest, while in decidedly short supply at the best of times, may play a role but are hardly credible in themselves as motivating forces for grand designs. The explanation can perhaps be sought in the *real-politik* considerations of the advocates, here outlined briefly.

For the United States, the Pacific Basin concept has inherent geopolitical and geostrategic attractions. Just as the U.S. has dominated the North Atlantic in partnership with the United Kingdom and/or West Germany in the recent past, so it will have the potential in the future for domination of the Pacific Basin in partnership with Japan and/or the PRC. At a time when American strategic power is in "rough equivalence" with that of the Soviet Union, a Pacific Basin arrangement would reinforce the relative position of the U.S., especially if the manpower of China could be brought into the equation. At a time of relative economic decline, economic partnership with Japan and the achiever states of Northeast Asia, Southeast Asia, and Australasia would similarly reinforce the economic security of the U.S. and provide a strong base for building political/economic/security relations with China, while further inhibiting Soviet economic growth potential.

For Japan, a Pacific Basin arrangement provides the framework within which: **a.** political influence built on economic foundations can be effectively exercised; **b.** continued access to the energy resources and other raw materials, the markets, and the strategic waterways of developing Asia and Australasia can be secured; and **c.** the American security umbrella can be kept intact.

For Australia, a Pacific Basin arrangement ties the country more securely with the American-Japanese security nexus against real or perceived threats from the Soviet Union. It also establishes Australia's economic connection with the industrial Pacific North, thus allowing for more confident Australian management of economic relations with developing Asia. Additionally, Australia's partial identification with the natural resources-based economies of Southeast Asia affords an opportunity for Canberra to play the perceived role of intermediary on behalf of these states in the councils of the developed. This enhances the perceived importance of Australia, and makes Australia feel less the junior partner in an arrangement dominated by economic giants.

The common strand that runs through the considerations of the three main proponents of the Pacific Basin concept is an overriding strategic preoccupation. However, the concept is presented primarily in economic terms. The economic objectives advanced for the Pacific Basin concept by its American, Australian, and Japanese proponents include:

1. Fostering the continued economic dynamism of the Pacific Basin through the promotion of closer links in trade, investment, and other areas which will stimulate new commercial and other economic opportunities;
2. Facilitating better and more extensive management of the increasing economic interdependence and the changing qualitative relationships between and among the Pacific Basin nations (and especially between the developed and the developing countries), thus enabling sources of friction to be articulated and perhaps ameliorated in an organized and constructive manner;
3. Encouraging greater rationalization of Pacific Basin economies in the longer term based on the principle of comparative advantage, thereby facilitating the process of structural adjustment within a wider regional perspective;
4. Contributing to the removal of constraints to growth in the Pacific Basin developing countries through the establishment of closer links

with these economies and the organized stimulation of trade, investment, and aid flows;
5. Providing a forum which on a regular periodic basis will encourage the development and focusing of relations among the Pacific Basin countries in the context of a larger milieu;
6. Enhancing the sense of well-being and security of the Pacific Basin countries through economic cooperation and growth and the advancement of cooperative politics; and
7. Providing for an exchange of views concerning the modalities and content acceptable to Pacific Basin countries with respect to economic relations with communist states.

These are valid economic aims and are in themselves unexceptionable. It is noteworthy, however, that the objectives as they have been framed could be as easily pursued outside the context of a Pacific Basin arrangement. Furthermore, the objectives as they often are articulated seem in effect to limit participation to market-economy countries, a fact which necessarily will determine to a great extent the nature and scope of the arrangement. The potential for a politically divided and economically estranged Pacific Basin based on a communist/non-communist cleavage would appear to be a natural concomitant.

There is thus a potential for a "bloc mentality" inherent in the Pacific Basin concept as it has been propounded by its American, Japanese, and Australian exponents. It is this potential which constitutes the crux of my trepidation in approaching the concept. At the outset of this paper a number of dynamics which are currently shaping the international system were set forth. These essentially economics-based dynamics offer prospects for new approaches to international relations based less on the confrontative political-security matrix of the past and more on the cooperative political-economic matrix which—in view of the unavoidable interdependence of the global economy—is inexorably taking hold. The fact that the free enterprise, market-economy countries have clearly demonstrated productive and growth capacities superior to those of the centrally-planned economies should encourage the adoption of economics-based strategies in dealing with internal and external communist challenges. Conversely, the relative absence in the communist states of public constraints with respect to the accrual of strength through massive arms spending would appear to put market-economy countries at a disadvantage in the pursuit of confrontative strategies. I do not believe that Malaysia would be willing to subscribe to a Pacific Basin concept that in effect is a recycling of a Pacific "containment" scenario, albeit with new combinations of antagonists, even if the arrangement were instituted in the name of economic enlightenment and with the promise of tangible economic rewards.

However, the Pacific Basin concept need not be the defensive reflex of prosperous but insecure nations attempting to preserve an advantageous status quo against a seemingly irresistible communist military tide driven by economic deprivation. It instead could be a creative force that builds upon the self-evident strengths of open societies to irresistibly draw stagnant closed societies into mutual interaction in cooperative socio-economic endeavors. It is in terms of a creative force—bringing together ideologically, politically, and economically disparate societies—that I prefer to approach the Pacific Basin concept.

To serve as a creative force which can encompass disparate nations, the Pacific Basin concept must be perceived as aiming at, and in fact have as its goal, an open—as opposed to a closed—arrangement. The Pacific Basin therefore must be defined in an essentially geographical manner rather than politically and/or economically. In this light the Pacific Basin would encompass all the littoral states of the Western and Eastern Pacific seaboards, the island states between the two seaboards, and those hinterland states which may experience a dominant Pacific pull.

To conceive of the possibility that countries from such a wide geographical region—one characterized by extremes of economic, cultural, and ethnic diversity—can be brought together in a spirit of community requires an extraordinary faith in the wisdom of man. Nevertheless, it should not be viewed as a concept impossible to achieve. Much depends upon the particular notion of community employed. A Pacific community founded upon common traditions and shared experience, or premised upon social and economic homogeneity, is clearly unattainable. However, a Pacific community which will slowly build up habits of cooperation, premised upon a recognition both of the diversity in the region and the fact of ultimate interdependence, has every prospect of success.

The new dynamics now operative in international relations will force greater interdependence upon the world. The attainment of peace and prosperity therefore will require the placement of a premium on cooperative strategies. The Pacific Basin encompasses the largest share of the world's population, the greatest concentration of economic and military power, the fastest growing subregions, and—in an overall sense—the greatest potential of all the regions of the world. By virtue of these facts, the Pacific Basin will by the turn of the century be the globe's political and economic center of gravity. In the absence of a common socio-political past, the regional interaction which has increasingly developed among the Pacific Basin countries has hitherto been sustained by sheer objective economic dynamics. If it is not sidetracked by artificial and divisive stereotyped impulses, the potential is accordingly very real for the further development of community, based on nurtured cooperative relations, which aims at common goals while maintaining the region's diversity.

The model for an open, cooperative Pacific Basin community can perhaps be found in the ASEAN experience. ASEAN is debatably the most successful of the Pacific Basin's several subregional groupings. In the space of a decade, the ASEAN arrangement has transformed a motley collection of bickering and even warring rivals—with no particular sense of commonality beyond the varying hurts imposed by colonization—into political and economic partners bound by a strong sense of community. While still perceiving themselves most importantly as citizens of their respective nations, it is natural today for nations of the ASEAN member countries to have a sense of belonging to and identification with the larger ASEAN community. Similarly, while still pursuing first and foremost their individual national priorities, the governments of the ASEAN states now habitually take into account the common ASEAN interest, seeing it not in the light of any contractual obligation but in the spirit of community. Rather than invoke agreements, the ASEAN partners extend help where it is needed, again in the spirit of almost telepathic community. There are no elaborate structures, no grand design, no military pact, and no economic blue print for ASEAN. The organization is guided by a Declaration which sets forth the simple objective of establishment of "a firm foundation for common action to promote regional cooperation."

In its essence, ASEAN is most importantly a "state of mind." Encapsulated therein is the promise of all that is possible.

If ASEAN were to provide the premise for a Pacific Basin community, what should constitute the founding principles of such an arrangement?

1. It must serve a valid and genuine need, for no arrangement which fails to do so will long outlive its creation. Pacific Basin countries at the outset must recognize collectively that the avoidance of conflict will require a commitment to work and cooperate together.
2. It cannot demand from Basin countries what they cannot give. No community arrangement which is premised upon and/or perpetuates inequality can be accepted. A community of equal sovereign states—enabling each to better maintain independence and sovereignty within the context of overall interdependence—is a fundamental necessity.
3. Community cooperation must be freely extended, based on the understanding that the serving of community interests also advances separate individual interests.
4. The arrangement should be loose and informal, without rigid rules of procedure and elaborate structural machinery. It should accordingly be able to absorb national differences as well as insulate itself from national pressures.
5. The arrangement should foster cooperation and eschew conflict. It should be a wholly neutral arrangement that attempts to harmonize the interests of all, operating by the approach of the "lowest common denominator."
6. It should be a regional arrangement with a global perspective, committed to globalism as a fundamental principle. In view of the contemporary context of global interdependence, issues solved at the regional level should be extended to the global level as well.

A Pacific Basin community concept framed on the above principles would have a far higher acceptability quotient than the patently non-universal political and/or economic Basin concepts currently being floated by various American, Japanese, and Australian proponents. A Pacific Basin concept that exacts a political price for the economic benefits promised will constitute a problem, at least for the ASEAN countries. A precondition essential for ASEAN acceptance is a guarantee that the arrangement will not impair the relations among the ASEAN nations themselves and

Toward a Pacific Basin Community

ASEAN's wider Southeast Asia, Pacific, and global links. Essentially, any Pacific Basin concept—if it is to be acceptable to ASEAN—must represent a natural extension of ASEAN's activities in the broader regional and global circles.

For such a development to be possible, the idea of community must take a stronger hold in the region. Economic dynamics have fostered increasing interaction in the Pacific Basin. ASEAN, for example, has entered into dialogues with Australia, Japan, the United States, and New Zealand on common economic concerns. However, this interaction has been fairly sterile in the sense that it has not been placed in the setting of, nor been accompanied by, nor occurred in the spirit of, an extended community. The accomplishments so far remain limited business arrangements which reflect little sense of a common future or even overall interdependence. It is unlikely that the situation will magically change if suddenly these dialogues are subsumed under the aegis of a Pacific community arrangement.

Present dealings between the developed and the developing Pacific Basin countries must be characterized by feelings of genuine concern and warmth if the idea of community is to emerge. To put it quite bluntly, it seems that the feeling of community is more evident among the developing nations of the region than it is among the developed countries, or than is the case between the developing and the developed components. For example, ASEAN's dealings with Burma and communist Indochina show more elements of community concern than do ASEAN's dealings with its developed partners.

Genuine support on the part of the developed Pacific Basin countries for cooperative endeavors among the developing nations of the region would constitute a good beginning toward development of a broader sense of community. This can find expression in support and financing for regional transportation and communications projects; regional research and training programs in various fields, such as anti-dadah (anti-drug abuse measures); regional facilities for search and rescue operations; a regional meteorological watch, to include early warning systems for natural and other disasters; regional machinery for blotting oil slicks and neutralizing other dangerous pollutants in the Pacific Ocean so as to preserve marine life; regional relief facilities; and other such noncontroversial activities. Such programs would be designed to meet universal needs devoid of ideological or political content, and would envisage the active involvement and participation of both communist and non-communist states. Unless such tangible signs are forthcoming of the developed nations' real concern for the future of the developing countries, the latter's reaction to the industrialized states' espousal of community cannot help but be tinged with skepticism or even cynicism. A Pacific community concept that promises little beyond the freezing of the present international division of labor and the entrenchment of the political and military divisions currently characteristic of the developed North will be quite distasteful to ASEAN.

On the other hand, a Pacific Basin community which is relevant to the aspirations of the developing South—for growth, stability, peace, and the orderly evolution of the regional and global systems toward a more equitable future—will be welcomed with unfeigned enthusiasm. By virtue of the economic and social structures of its member countries and its geographical setting, ASEAN has always been outward looking. If a Pacific Basin community can be conceived which truly will maximize the development of constructive political and economic relations among all the Pacific Basin countries, the present leaders of ASEAN, I am certain, would be more than willing to give their highest consideration to active participation in such an endeavor.

Conference Papers

Dr. Sompong Sucharitkul,
Director General, Treaty and Legal Department, Ministry of Foreign Affairs, Bangkok, Thailand

Professor Jun Tsunoda,
Department of International Relations, Asyama-Gakuin University, Tokyo, Japan

Admiral Kenichi Kitamura (Ret.),
Former Chief of Naval Operations, Tokyo, Japan

Dr. Douglas Pike,
Department of Defense, Washington, D.C., USA

POLICY PROPOSALS: A SOUTHEAST ASIAN VIEW

Sompong Sucharitkul

Any attempt to devise a plan for the defense of Southeast Asia or any other area is doomed to failure if it seeks to lay down absolute rules or prescribe a course of action for the states involved. The task of planning requires an appreciation of the complexities and uncertainties inherent in the multidimensional aspects of regional security. A cautious approach to the study of regional security, which is the only approach to be recommended, will reveal a high degree of relativity in every dimension of regional security issues.

The problem of construction or interpretation and therefore of identification of the subject matter under consideration does in fact contribute to the extreme delicacy of the task to be undertaken. Consideration of three main dimensions of security—the geographical, the philosophical/conceptual, and the time dimensions—illustrates these complexities.

Geographical Dimension

The identification, description, and definition of a geographical region may have an important bearing on policy-making and planning for the region's defense and security. It is often difficult to designate precisely the boundaries of a particular region; a region may be relatively well-defined with respect to the location and limits of its central core, but have a borderline which is blurred.

Southeast Asia is usually defined as including the five Association of Southeast Asian Nations (ASEAN) countries (the Philippines, Indonesia, Singapore, Malaysia, and Thailand), the Indochinese states (Vietnam, Laos, and Kampuchea), and Burma. On the outer ring of the main core of Southeast Asia, diverse neighboring states are watching developments within the subregion. On the front row of the ring side sit Bangladesh, Sri Lanka, Nepal, the People's Republic of China, North Korea, South Korea, the Republic of China on Taiwan, Japan, Australia, New Zealand, Papua New Guinea, Samoa, Brunei, and nearby island states.

The two superpowers, the United States and the Soviet Union, also have security interests in the area under consideration. As global powers, their presence and influence are inevitable, and they certainly have key roles to play in the maintenance of peace and security within the region. Other powers which can contribute to regional security in positive terms, especially in the realm of economic development, are Japan, Australia, New Zealand, the European Economic Community, and—probably to a lesser extent—India and Pakistan. A delicate balance must be maintained at all times in the interplay of interested outside powers. Unfortunately, no ground rules have yet been clearly prepared and set forth for adoption to guide and ensure the peaceful participation of these countries in strengthening the foundations for Asian and Pacific security.

Conceptual Dimension

A planner also cannot afford at any time to lose sight of the fact that the expression "security"—and its principal ingredient, "safety"—are themselves highly relative and susceptible to varying interpretations, depending upon the particular point of view

A Southeast Asian View

from which "security" and "safety" are discussed. For Thailand, for example, the notion of "security" implies the maintenance of the existing national sovereignty, political independence, and territorial integrity. It necessarily implies protection of the basic freedoms and fundamental liberties traditionally associated with the Thai people, as well as their safety and well-being.

The other states of ASEAN appear to share this notion of security, which leads to recognition of the equality of states and the equal partnership of the Association's members. The philosophy regarding regional security adopted by the ASEAN nations, based on good neighborliness and cooperation among equals, appears to offer the brightest prospect for political and economic well-being and a more durable peace. It presupposes interdependence, embraces close cooperation and coordination in a number of fields (political, economic, social, and cultural), and stands against relationships of domination, subjugation, or regional hegemony. The ASEAN concept of a Zone of Peace, Freedom, and Neutrality (ZOPFAN), set forth in the Kuala Lumpur Declaration of 1971, stands as eloquent testimony with respect to ASEAN's understanding of the expression "security."

The ASEAN notion of regional security, however, does not appear to be coterminous with the concept of security prevailing in other circles in Southeast Asia. Burma has consistently maintained a benevolent posture based on an isolationist type of neutrality, accepting cooperation only on a bilateral and universal (not regional) basis. In recent months, however, Burma has shown some signs that it does not reject all proposals of regional cooperation. While the Indochinese states are bound together in a close relationship, this grouping has not been established on a basis of equal partnership, for Vietnam is the unchallenged leader.

The possibility of a toning down of the differences between the concepts of security now prevailing in the ASEAN states and the Indochinese states should not be ruled out. For example, Vietnam has indicated that it would react more positively to the possible establishment of a zone of neutrality in Southeast Asia if the word "independence" were to be substituted for "freedom" in the title. Furthermore, both Thailand and the Indochinese states are active members of the Mekong Committee for the investigation and development of the lower Mekong Basin. The mighty Mekong in its role as an international watercourse may yet serve the positive purpose of uniting peoples who are compelled by sheer necessity to share their invaluable natural resources. A basis for possible cooperation thus exists, which could provide a healthy foundation for the security of Southeast Asia, once the countries of the region are able to come to share a common definition of "security."

Time Dimension

A third significant dimension relates to the measurement of the relevant time span. Time is an important factor which must be taken into consideration in any meaningful analysis of the problem of security, for security issues are not static. What was considered safe and secure yesterday may no longer be so today. What is described as constituting Southeast Asia today may be given a slightly different appellation tomorrow. While history reflects the past, and may be pertinent to future planning, it must be recognized that history does not necessarily repeat itself. If time is sliced thinly enough, variables may seem unchangeable and what is transitory may seem perennial. The passage of time, however, has clearly shown that no two nations can be tied together permanently, there is no perpetuity in alliance, and there is no permanency in either amity or enmity.

An analytical study of the problem of security for a region is meaningful only if it is confined to a particular span of time, and opinions of analysts will reflect the different vantage points of the time spans from which they view. For present purposes, the time dimension need not extend backward beyond a quarter of a century, i.e., to the time of Dien Bhien Phu and the establishment of the Southeast Asia Treaty Organization (SEATO). In fact, attention which is concentrated on the last two decades will indicate distinctly the current trends. Similarly, in view of the vicissitudes of international relations, planning cannot expect to remain valid beyond the next two decades. What appears to form a solid foundation today may turn out to be fragile and in need of further reinforcements in the years ahead. The relevant time span is thus no more than half a century, with special emphasis on the twenty years just passed and preparations for the twenty years to come.

ASEAN as a Foundation for Southeast Asian Security

The Association of Southeast Asian Nations (ASEAN) should be taken as a starting point in the regional quest for security and a more durable peace. ASEAN continues to expand its activities and gain in strength from year to year, and has fostered a compelling sense of solidarity never before attained in any part of Asia. In the economic realm, ASEAN is helping to pave the way toward progress and prosperity for individual members of the Association, and has provided an effective and attractive answer to the growing need for the development of sound and solid foundations for the growth of a strong regional economy. A collective political will to survive together as free and sovereign nations has been forged out of an instinctive awareness that mutual cooperation—based on good neighborliness and equal partnership—is the best alternative to relationships of domination, exemplified in the past (and, in some areas, in the present) by various forms of imperialism and colonialism. ASEAN has reduced tensions between and among its member states, thereby succeeding on several occasions in averting possible conflicts within the region. While maintaining its regional solidarity, ASEAN also has been characterized by a mutual tolerance for the inherent differences existent among its free and independent member nations, each state being equally sovereign and determined to preserve its individual identity as a nation.

The position which the ASEAN countries have reached today could not have been attained without experimentation, trials, and errors. Several endeavors in the realm of regional cooperation have been launched in the past, with varying patterns of membership and types of activities. Several have achieved some measure of success, but a few have not survived the test of time. For example, SEATO has been dissolved and the Asian and Pacific Council (ASPAC) has succumbed to a similar fate; nevertheless, both organizations have left some indelible marks which have outlived the organizations themselves, and some of their offspring (e.g., the Social and Cultural Center in Seoul, Republic of Korea and the Asian Institute of Technology [AIT] at Rangsit in Thailand) have been institutionalized on a more permanent footing. Other regional arrangements, such as the Ministerial Conference for the Development of Southeast Asia, also exist, although their progress and achievements have been limited. The Mekong Committee, for its part, is not altogether immune from political hazards, despite the willing support of some friendly helping hands with readily available funds with no strings attached.

Out of these trying experiences and instructive lessons, which have been costly in terms of time and money, ASEAN has emerged as a viable community and a realistic response to the challenges of its times. Its success notwithstanding, however, ASEAN has encountered a variety of criticisms, sometimes diametrically opposed, from a number of different quarters. The Association has been criticized for lack of speed, growth, and imagination; it has also been criticized for lack of deliberation, circumspection, and grounding on practical foundations. Fortunately, time and experience have proved the fallacy of such allegations, for the truth is that ASEAN has attained its natural growth pattern, which has been gradual and spontaneous, and the cautious and pragmatic approach adopted from the very start of the Association has proved rewarding.

As was stressed above, ASEAN's quest for security is based upon the collective political will of its member states to survive as free and sovereign nations. This will, in turn, rests upon the determination of the people in each individual state to preserve their heritage of freedom, even if this should require fighting and the sacrifice of lives. The ultimate willingness of the ASEAN nations to fight in defense of their independence and well-being, however, does not necessarily imply that ASEAN should plan to develop its military strength so as to match the might of other collective defense organizations. Collective security of the NATO or Warsaw Pact type presupposes inclusion of at least one member nation with enormous military strength; in the absence of such a power, collective security loses much of its meaning.

Without the participation of a regional or global military power—and such participation seems unlikely in present circumstances—any proposal to turn ASEAN into a military organization or collective security pact would be absurd and senseless. Furthermore, if a military power is one day invited to join the Association in order to boost ASEAN military strength, ASEAN will lose its originality and true identity. It nevertheless must be emphasized that the disinclination of the ASEAN member nations to reorganize ASEAN into a grouping with collective military roles and responsibilities in no way rules out or interferes with the possibilities and existent realities of military cooperation and close planning and collaboration on a bilateral basis between member countries, and with friendly countries on the outer ring of Southeast Asia.

What must be avoided is any further heightening of tensions and escalation of military forces in Southeast Asia. When countries face actual or potential military threats and/or subversive activities, a more salutary response must be sought than resort to individual or collective military action. In view of the beginning of a new decade, planners might give consideration to more novel approaches to security issues, in recognition of the fact that it is often inadequate and dangerous to anchor security to the development and use of sheer military might.

It is to be hoped that in many cases diplomacy can be put forward as a positive alternative to brute force. While the United Nations has sometimes been viewed as a nearly futile endeavor, there may now be reason for a glimmer of hope. A Charter review is now underway, including a study with respect to how the role of the U.N. might be strengthened. Among other recent accomplishments, the General Assembly has succeeded in adopting significant resolutions on the Kampuchean question. The existing machinery of international justice also appears to have matured.

Strong determination accompanied by sound planning can make it possible to avoid resort to the use of force. It is important that all countries in the region make useful contributions to the maintenance of regional security in Southeast Asia. Part of the answer is to be found in ASEAN, which forms a protective political shield providing a formidable obstacle to external threats. Especially significant is the collective will of the ASEAN states to ensure and safeguard security in a way which reflects their own interests, rather than security which serves the interests of an outside power. With these positive developments in mind, it is to be hoped, in the final analysis, that reason will prevail.

POLICY PROPOSALS: A NORTHEAST ASIAN VIEW

Jun Tsunoda and Kenichi Kitamura

I. Foreword

Other papers presented at the Pattaya conference have set forth the manifold challenges to the security of the Asian/Pacific region which exist as the new decade begins. In view of these challenges, the non-communist countries of the region can and should work both individually and collectively to strengthen their deterrent ability and the other components of defense and security.

Creation of an atmosphere of firm unity and cooperation among the nations of the region is essential. In order to proceed with the appropriate policies and measures for ensuring the security of free Asian/Pacific states it is essential that all parties work together with a positive will and the determination to gain mutual understanding. At the same time, in the search for unity it must be recognized that the particular situations prevailing in various regional countries may call for different approaches or solutions.

In order to work collectively, the countries of the region must address a number of specific questions. What sorts of individual and collective defense capabilities are necessary for the security of these nations? What sorts of defense structures should be adopted? What are the difficulties which must be faced in coordinating various policy positions? How can the United States, Australia, and New Zealand best contribute to the defense and stability of the area? Given the constraints imposed by Japan's so-called "Peace Constitution," with its various political and psychological implications,[1] and in view of lingering sensitivities arising from the Japanese role in World War II, to what extent and how should Japan cooperate in regional security matters?

II. The American Commitment to the Security of the Asian/Pacific Region

Since the Vietnam debacle doubt and uncertainty have increased with respect ot U.S. credibility in the region, along with fears that the U.S. may be withdrawing its involvement from Asian security matters. The Asian nations alone do not have sufficient strength to preserve the security of the Asian/Pacific region. Therefore, a U.S. presence in and general commitment to the Western Pacific is both desirable and necessary, and clear assurance from the U.S. that it will respond quickly to counter any military threat to the non-communist nations of the region is essential.

Given the importance of U.S. involvement, regional states therefore should cooperate with the U.S. so as to facilitate its continuing military presence and viability. It is true that nations which host U.S. military facilities or bases are susceptible to internal left-wing criticism or attacks. The U.S. military presence nevertheless carries political and psychological significance of a vital and positive sort. All nations which benefit from this presence must counter the internal socio-political attacks by lending their

---

[1] See Chapter 2's "Japan and the Security of Northeast Asia: Editor's Introduction," address by General Horie entitled "Northeast Asian Security: The Japanese Role," and essay by Admiral Kitamura and Professor Tsunoda entitled "The Japanese Defense Posture and the Soviet Challenge in Northeast Asia," especially pp. 111 to 119, for discussions of Japan's basic defense policy and the dynamics of Japanese domestic politics with respect to defense and security issues.

utmost support and positive encouragement to the U.S. commitment and involvement.

The U.S. "Swing Strategy"[2] has hazardous implications—military, political, and psychological—for Asian/Pacific security. One sure alternative to the "Swing Strategy" would be the construction of a larger U.S. fleet, including more carriers; such an option, however, entails certain difficulties with respect to U.S. domestic politics. In any case, if a suitable alternative to this strategy is to be found, other nations in the region must lend their support and cooperation to the United States and provide naval contributions of their own.

III. Required Defense Capabilities for the Non-Communist Nations of the Region

While establishment of a collective security agreement among the nations of the Asian/Pacific region seems desirable in many respects, in practical terms (at least in the short-run) it probably is not attainable. However, even though in the absence of a crisis it is rather difficult to achieve a level of motivation sufficient to act on such matters, efforts can be made to work out new and enhance existing bilateral and multilateral agreements and arrangements in the realm of security cooperation.

Countries might work together to study common defense matters, and basic steps should be taken to promote regular exchanges of information. Specific measures might include joint training maneuvers, efforts toward standardization of weaponry, military student exchanges, reciprocal naval visits, and frequent contacts among the various leaderships. These steps can promote better understanding among the nations of the region with respect to their various defense programs, with an emphasis on finding the means whereby defense efforts can be coordinated in an emergency. Such activities could be conducted on an informal

---

[2] See Chapter 2's paper by these same authors, pp. 105-06, for a description of the U.S. "Swing Strategy." It has been reported that the U.S. now has dropped this strategy in favor of a more flexible policy. In response to the recent destablizing developments in Southwest Asia, particularly in Iran and Afghanistan, the U.S. has moved a portion of its Pacific Fleet not to the Atlantic but to the Indian Ocean. The implications of the exercise of this option must be more carefully appraised.

basis rather than through the establishment of formal treaties.

Cooperation for security in the Western Pacific also should involve measures which will facilitate the procurement of needed ships, aircraft, and other defense equipment. In some situations advanced countries as a matter of economic policy and diplomatic strategy have exploited the security needs of developing countries through sales of expensive, sophisticated weapons. However, when Western Pacific nations agree in advance with respect to their specific defense needs, there will be no room for exploitation.

Nations in both Northeast and Southeast Asia repeatedly have requested Japan to export defense items. However, the Japanese government, being fully aware of the burdens of past history, has been steadfast in the maintenance of its policy prohibiting the export of any ships, aircraft, weaponry, or other hardware for military use. Since Japan cannot sell weapons, the U.S. and the European countries presently constitute the main available sources of sophisticated military hardware. A critical point which should be remembered, however, is that if a large-scale armed conflict should break out, it is likely that the sea lanes and therefore the defense supply lines of the Asian/Pacific region will be jeopardized and perhaps blocked. In view of this possibility, it is necessary that the countries of the region strive to develop some degree of defense production capability within the region. In conjunction with the United States, Japan has the financial, technological, and industrial capabilities to make a meaningful contribution toward such a program. It is also of crucial importance that other concerned nations should work out, within the context of their respective domestic economic development programs, the creation of a basic defense structure.

IV. Cooperation Toward Ensuring the Safety of the Sea Lanes

Because the common interests of the various states are more apparent in the realm of maritime security, cooperation in this area—especially with respect to ensuring the integrity of the sea lanes of communication—will be easier to accomplish than security cooperation on land. In a very real sense the lives of the people of the region depend upon the safety of the sea lanes. Nevertheless, it sometimes is difficult for the average citizen to appreciate his/her country's interest in such defense endeavors. For this reason, it is necessary that countries mount a special effort to gain the understanding and support of their citizenries in this regard.

The area covered by the U.S. Seventh Fleet is so vast that if anything occurs to draw the attention of the Seventh Fleet elsewhere—e.g., to the Persian Gulf area, in the case of the Iranian situation—the Western Pacific is left without adequate coverage. It is evident that countries friendly to the U.S. need to assume greater responsibility for guarding the sea lanes of communication as well as for local defense according to each nation's military capability. This would serve to ease somewhat the defense burden of the U.S. and would free U.S. resources, which then could be applied toward the building of more mobile striking power, in such forms as nuclear weapons and/or the production of additional carriers. With each nation taking a larger responsibility for the defense of its own locality, the U.S. can devote more attention to such large scale activities as securing the sea lanes and engaging in submarine-hunting reconnaissance. Australia and Japan, both of which are situated near important sea lanes, should recognize fully their security and defense responsibilities.

In order to achieve mutual cooperation the nations of the region need to create organizations for the exchange of information and the coordination of aspects of strategic defense. Through these efforts it will be possible to achieve some added degree of security short of forming a combined task force, which at present would be exceedingly difficult. The contribution which each country should make toward the collective security of the sea lanes should be determined according to the political, economic, military, and technological circumstances of each nation. Many suitable areas for cooperation exist, such as coastal patrols to ensure free passage in the straits.

The United States regularly sponsors world-wide naval symposia. U.S. sponsorship of a similarly styled symposium to explore the special needs of the Asian/Pacific nations would be beneficial. In early 1980 the U.S. sponsored joint naval exercises in Hawaii, with Japan, Australia, and New Zealand also participating in this training.[3] The U.S. regularly conducts joint naval exercises in the Japan Sea with the Republic of Korea, and also with Japan. How-

---

[3] See Chapter 2's "Editor's Introduction," footnote 5, p. 92, for a brief description of the RIMPAC exercise.

ever, combined U.S.-ROK-Japan exercises have never been conducted. The training in Hawaii may constitute a step toward the future realization of combined American-Korean-Japanese exercises.

V. Japan's Role in Regional Security: Contributions Despite Constraints

Japan needs to seek out appropriate new defense policies and adequately strengthen its own defense capabilities.[4] What are the specific steps which Japan could take, in the spirit of the U.S.-Japanese Security Treaty, which would be complementary to the furtherance of the American defense efforts in the region and would contribute productively to the individual and collective security of the nations in the area?

Despite the steadfast refusal of the Japanese government to export defense hardware, there are persons in Japan—concerned about the security of the region rather than about the benefits to Japanese industry—who support the requests of other Asian/Pacific nations for Japanese defense exports. At least to these people, it is clear that issues concerning Japan's security cannot be separated from such issues for the region as a whole, and Japanese security cannot be guaranteed apart from the security of the rest of the Western Pacific region. The Japanese export ban in fact involves a question of interpretation, for the ban is not explicitly set forth in the Japanese constitution.

Japan's first responsibility is to exert its best effort to ensure its own defense capability. As it now stands, Japan can engage in the defense of the three nearby straits and conduct anti-submarine and air defense around Japan. In performing duties for its own defense—e.g., guarding Japanese air space and the three straits (Sohya, Tsugaru, and Tsushima) against submarines—Japan can contribute to the security of the region as a whole. Potentially, Japan also could assist in securing the safety of the region's sea lanes of communication. Qualitative and quantitative improve-

---

[4] See Chapter 2's paper by Admiral Kitamura and Professor Tsunoda, especially pp. 112 to 119, for a more extensive discussion of the *indirect* and *direct* ways in which Japan can contribute to Asian/Pacific security, and a number of specific recommendations with respect to the improvements Japan should make in its defense posture.

ment of Japan's naval power is essential, however, for the protection of maritime transportation and the adequate conduct of anti-submarine warfare.

In general, Japan should: a) strengthen the capabilities of its ground, maritime, and air forces for the defense of the Japanese territories, including capacities in the areas of anti-air defense and defense of the major straits, and b) strengthen its anti-air and anti-submarine warfare forces for the security of the sea lanes in the Western Pacific. Japan also has a considerable capacity for shipbuilding, and might pursue the possibility of building ships which in one way or another could increasingly operate together with the U.S. Pacific fleet.

To hasten the realization of appropriate new Japanese defense policies, one development of tremendous value would be the enunciation by the non-communist Asian nations and the United States of clear statements regarding the sorts of defense policies they would like Japan to adopt, including their views with respect to the kind of defense cooperation they desire with Japan in this region. Japan must ascertain, for example, whether the Asian/Pacific states, including the U.S., would find acceptable an eventual Japanese decision to increase the country's naval strength. In view of the residual historical memories still latent in some parts of the region, Japan is certainly in no position to take a unilateral positive initiative with respect to such a project as constructing large ships similar to those of the U.S. fleet. Japan can proceed only to the extent that acceptance can be obtained from the other regional states, and then only under the condition that the future Japanese naval forces would be incorporated into an allied fleet, thereby precluding any possibility that Japan would utilize such forces unilaterally, except in the case of defending the Japanese homeland and the nearby sea lanes.

It is of crucial importance that the viability of the Japan-U.S. security system be maintained and strengthened. Article V of the Japan-U.S. Security Treaty reads: "Each party recognizes that an armed attack against either Party in the territories under the administration of Japan would be dangerous to its own peace and safety and declares that it would act to meet the common danger in accordance with its constitutional provisions and processes." This Article should be interpreted in a rational and practical manner, so as to allow the U.S. and Japan to act in cooperation to meet common threats which might arise. Within the context of this pragmatic interpretation, Japan and the U.S. should work toward the development and enhancement of cooperative and collective security measures in response to common security problems. Such cooperation would benefit every free nation in the Western Pacific region.

There remain some obstacles and resistance in Japan to the strengthening of Japan's defense posture. As a first step the Japanese must shift their thinking and attitudes toward a broader appreciation of Japan's interdependence in the region and the country's concomitant responsibilities. Despite the constitutional restraints with respect to its armed forces, Japan as a member of the United Nations clearly retains the inherent right of a country to exercise self-defense. Unless the basic goal of defending the nation can be accomplished, however, the spirit of the constitution will be rendered meaningless. If the country's right to self-defense is to be substantiated, Japan cannot put limitations on the Self-Defense Forces in such areas as troop strength and equipment which plainly ignore rational military thinking.

VI. The Relationship of Other Regional Nations to Japanese Security

The importance of the Korean peninsula to the security of Japan is a factor gaining increasing recognition, and in July 1979 the Director General of Japan's Defense Agency, Ganri Yamashita, made the first visit to South Korea by someone in his position in the post-World War II period. Many observers believe that if a medium- or large-scale armed conflict were to again break out between North and South Korea, Japan could not avoid involvement, in view of the possible American entanglement and potential Soviet and/or PRC countermoves.

It would be beneficial for the Republic of Korea (ROK) and Japan to discuss the means whereby these nations could cooperate to defend the Tsushima strait and carry out measures for coordinated naval and air defense. In order to implement exchanges of information and initiate cooperative defense measures, close communication between the leaderships of the two countries will be required. In view of the fact that the ROK and Japan each has a mutual security treaty with the United States, cooperation between these two nations might be profitably facilitated by the U.S. assumption of the role of coordinator.

Such cooperative endeavors between the ROK and Japan would not require a formal treaty as a necessary prerequisite; rather, agreement could be reached through regular, informal exchanges of views with respect to the ways in which the two countries could act together in emergencies to ensure the defense of their common straits and airspace. The ROK and Japan also should reach some understanding regarding the position Japan should take in the event of an attack on the South by North Korea, and regarding the action which should be taken to protect and preserve the sea lanes in the area in the event of a large-scale conflict involving the U.S. and the Soviet Union.

The Republic of China (ROC) also occupies an important strategic location with respect to the defense and security of the sea lanes in the Asian/Pacific region. A strong, free, secure, and friendly ROC can make an important contribution to guaranteeing the integrity of the sea lanes, especially if the nation will engage in cooperative endeavors for submarine-hunting air patrols and ocean rescues in its environs. Neither Japan nor the U.S. has formal diplomatic relations with Taipei at this time. Any attempt by either country to develop a special relationship with the ROC regarding security matters would surely result in problems with the People's Republic of China. However, the PRC eventually may grant tacit acceptance to the involvement of the ROC in cooperative activities for the security of the sea lanes if Peking can be convinced that the resulting benefits extend as much to Communist China as to the non-communist states and the region as a whole. It also is possible that the U.S., Japan, and the ROC might continue to conduct informal, non-governmental level information exchanges and joint academic studies with respect to the security of the sea lanes.

Other nations in the Asian/Pacific region also have an impact on Japanese security and well-being. Australia and New Zealand play important roles as suppliers of raw materials, manufactured goods, and services, and also serve as guarantors of the sea lanes in their respective areas. Given the fact that the U.S. has treaties with both Australia and New Zealand, the U.S. might serve—as was suggested above in the case of Japan and the ROK—as the sponsor and coordinator of joint studies and exercises which would help lead to the creation of closer, more practical relationships.

The ASEAN states are important suppliers of energy resources and raw materials, and are situated astride sea lanes—e.g., the Strait of Malacca—which are of essential significance. Enhanced cooperation among the ASEAN states, the U.S., Australia, New Zealand, and possibly other regional states for the protection of these sea lanes should be seriously considered. The continuing political, economic, and military security and well-being of the ASEAN states, along with the continuation of friendly stances on the part of these countries, are of vital importance to the security of Japan and every free nation in the Asian/Pacific region.

POLICY PROPOSALS: AN AMERICAN VIEW
U.S. Policy in Asia in the 1980s: Time of Change

Douglas Pike

The United States has never been able to articulate its Asian policy to the full satisfaction of all, partly because America's is a polycentric society, partly because Asia continuously springs surprise developments on the U.S., and partly because such is the way of the world, Asia being no neat place. Furthermore, of course, there often is value in deliberate ambiguity.

This condition of somewhat muzzy policies continues today, exacerbated perhaps by the dynamism and tempestuosity currently marking the Asian scene. However, what is more worrisome even than the inability of the United States to enunciate a fully worked-out policy for Asia in the 1980s is the existence of a fundamental uncertainty as to what will constitute the vital components of that policy. The U.S., for example, is not certain how important Asia will be in the general scheme of American foreign policy in the 1980s. Asia's perceived importance dropped sharply in American minds after the fall of South Vietnam—a trend which now has been halted due largely to the appearance of "the China card" on the table. Today's policy makers in the Carter Administration now seem to have agreed that Asia is indeed important, but no official seems able to articulate a precise view with respect to Asia's degree and manner of importance. Fundamentally, of course, this uncertainty reflects a larger problem—i.e., an insufficient consensus among Americans with respect to U.S. national interests around the globe. This problem seems to be rectifying itself, but only slowly.

Therefore, as will be argued throughout this essay, the United States currently is experiencing difficulty in defining its precise interests in Asia, but for the most justifiable of reasons: the U.S. recognizes that the current period is not simply a time of change (after all, the times are always changing) but also an era which is characterized by the emergence of new criteria for the determination of national interests. Such a situation of transition and uncertainty of course has a profound influence on the final product of the foreign policy process, the implementation of policy.

These circumstances reflect not a crisis in confidence but chiefly an inability—one shared by other nations around the world—to establish which factors will be central and which will be only marginal in the international relationships of the future. In any given instance, of course, the U.S. may have a clear preference with respect to possible outcomes—for example, the U.S. does not want to be hag-ridden by an Ayatollah Khomeini or spectator to a Kampuchean holocaust—and in some instances Washington may even be able to achieve whatever goals it has set for itself. Because of changing criteria, however, the U.S. fears that decisive American action will trigger serious secondary effects of a negative sort. For the most part this situation cannot accurately be associated with irresolution or weak leadership, as many critics charge, for it well may be that in the best Socratic sense, this lack of certitude is the beginning of wisdom.

Despite these changes, uncertainties, and ambiguities, one coherent and integrating criterion for determining U.S. national interests does seem to be emerging and can be expected to play a major role in defining and anchoring U.S. policy in Asia in the 1980s. This characteristic as yet can be only dimly perceived, but it is persistent; and bits and pieces of evidence for its emergence can be found scattered all across the Pacific. It seems quite probable

An American View

that as the U.S. moves deeper into the 1980s it increasingly will be guided—partly by design and partly in reaction to the rush of chaotic events—by a single over-arching principle: the desire to see established in Asia a condition of socio-political, economic, and military equilibrium within the framework (i.e., within the organizational structure) of some new type of international system. For those who find sloganized labels useful, this U.S. policy can be referred to as "Asian equilibrium through Asian regionalism." Unfortunately, the U.S. will be forced to pursue this objective within the context of a new and peculiar struggle for power in Asia, here labeled "engendered anarchy," which poses a new impediment to equilibrium.

Equilibrium

A chemical solution, such as salt dissolved in water, can serve as a metaphor for equilibrium as it is herein discussed. The solution, a product of several chemicals, is in equilibrium—i.e., in balance, relatively stable, lacking permanence yet not easily changed.

In earlier eras this general condition was referred to as a "balance of power" and in more recent years as an "ideological balance of power." To some degree components of this notion of "balance" remain in effect. Certainly it is in the interests of *all* Asian nations that no *single* state should come to dominate the Asian/Pacific region. If any one nation should threaten to attain such domination, it is in the interests of all other states in the region to oppose such a development. This imperative propelled the fight against Japan in World War II, was the perceived rationale for the actions of the United Nations during the Korean War, and constituted the basic reason why five Pacific nations sent troops to fight with the Americans in Vietnam. Furthermore, the desire to deny domination to any one nation is behind the fact that virtually all Asian states—whether or not they will admit it—wish long life to the Sino-Soviet dispute.

From the viewpoint of the United States a fairly stable equilibrium now exists in Asia, particularly in view of the new tilt of the People's Republic of China (PRC) toward the U.S. Recent activities on the part of the USSR—for example, the movement of Soviet naval vessels into Cam Ranh Bay—have had an effect on the fundamental balance, but to date the significance of these actions has been primarily symbolic. When measuring the relative state of equilibrium in Asia, the employment of a traditional balance of forces yardstick is misleading. The Asian/Pacific region, for example, simply cannot be viewed in the manner or terms applicable to the NATO/Warsaw Pact balance of forces.

Threats to the equilibrium of the Asian/Pacific region of course are always in evidence. In no particular order of importance, possible future threats include an expansionist Vietnam (particularly if Hanoi's ambitions extend beyond Indochina—perhaps, for example, into Thailand); outbreak of a Sino-Soviet war; a radical change in the policy of the PRC, resulting perhaps from an internal change of leadership; growing difficulties between Japan and the PRC with respect to the proper strategic posture to be taken vis-a-vis the USSR; and various internal problems arising within individual Asian nations, stemming from crises of leadership succession, indigenous and imported insurgencies, growing economic grievances, ethno-racial disorders, etc.

Anarchy: Threat to Equilibrium

The great enemy of the United States in Asia in the 1980s (and, indeed, the great foe for most nations everywhere in the years ahead) will be *anarchy*—i.e., *the absence of government.*

The plain fact is that the U.S. cannot cope with anarchy, whether it is induced deliberately (as in Kampuchea) or perpetuated by vested interests (as in Iran). For that matter, no country can cope adequately with anarchy, but most states faced with an anarchical situation in a neighboring area can simply wait it out, a luxury the U.S. (and the other superpower, the USSR) often cannot afford, since failure to act can be interpreted locally as an unwillingness to act, which in turn can trigger an avalanche of undesirable developments. The situation in Afghanistan in part has presented the Soviet Union with the problem of anarchy, at least in its incipient stage, and Moscow has chosen to act.[1]

---

[1] Moscow's solution for anarchy is the instant and massive application of force to reimpose if not government at least order; as of this writing, this response in the case of Afghanistan has neither succeeded nor clearly failed.

An American View

Ordinary anarchy—i.e., the temporary breakdown of a particular government—need not overly concern the U.S. Such a phenomenon is neither new nor unique—in fact, history can be seen as one long struggle to establish and maintain government—and when ordinary anarchy develops, it is temporary and for the most part self-correcting. However, anarchy in its new and more threatening form—*engendered anarchy*—is quite a different matter.

Engendered anarchy can manifest itself in two distinct forms. In the first form, it is deliberately induced as a tactic to bring about one stage in the process of social development. Not only the government but the entire social value system is destroyed in the hope and expectation that out of the resultant chaos will emerge a new and better (but largely undefined) system and set of values. This phenomenon does not constitute revolution in its ordinary sense, for engendered anarchy is broader in concept and intention and is essentially nihilistic, offering not some grand new social blueprint but anarchy itself as the way to a better existence. The Sandinista Front in Nicaragua and some aspects of Mao's Cultural Revolution in China are examples of this form of engendered anarchy.

Engendered anarchy in its second form might be called "perpetuated anarchy" (or possibly "existential anarchy"), for it involves destruction of the existing government followed by a continuation of the condition which has been created (i.e., the absence of government), in effect not permitting a new government to be established. Since nature hates a vacuum, it would seem that the substitution of nothing for something would give rise to an inherently unstable situation. However, two contemporary examples of this form of anarchy, in Kampuchea and Iran, have managed to endure for several years.

Anarchy within a country can lead both to confusion in which there is inadvertent suffering and a sort of libertarian freedom bordering on jungle law (which is to say, no law at all.) If anarchy were merely an internal matter the rest of the world could ignore it. However, anarchy at its deeper level is a destroyer of peace, within a state and/or between or among countries. In fact, the opposite of engendered anarchy is peace.

It must be clearly grasped that at a deeper level the phenomenon of engendered anarchy has nothing to do with government (absent or not) but rather with the changed nature of politics, both domestic and international. Most informed observers recognize that political relationships and the manner in which such relationships are conducted are undergoing radical changes. These observers, however, find it extraordinarily difficult to transfer recognition of these changes and the ensuing implications to general concerns about national security. They continue to think in terms of military hardware, fire power, and strategic geographic position, all the while talking vaguely about the "political" aspects of national security, putting the word "political" inside quotation marks to indicate special meaning but tacitly admitting they in fact do not know what that meaning is. With the advent in the twentieth century of the concept of *armed political struggle* (referred to as "people's war" in China), it became increasingly obvious that as a method of analysis the old geopolitical assessment of national power had become obsolete. The measurement of such indices as the size of a nation's armed forces and its industrial capacity was no longer adequate. An entire new dimension—having as its ultimate manifestation the capacity for engendered anarchy—now had to be measured.

No nation, the United States included, can ever again feel secure until it has come to understand and has learned to deal with this added dimension of national security. To date the U.S. has not advanced very far in this respect. Washington recognizes the reality of a situation of anarchy in Kampuchea or Iran but neither understands its dynamics nor knows how to deal with it. The U.S. instead finds itself in a surrealistic nightmare, trying to be rational about something implicitly irrational and attempting a systematic and legal approach to circumstances in which system and law have been deliberately excluded. With respect to these national security problems, within the halls of the U.S. government agreement cannot be reached even on a bureaucratic division of labor: the Pentagon sees its job as fighting wars, not treating anarchy; the State Department argues that it is neither structured nor trained to deal with non-governmental forces.

The rhetoric of this new condition of world politics is that of revolution, but such a rhetoric misleads. Revolt against authority is ancient and inevitable and in actual practice is simply one manifestation of the single immutable law of history: the inevitability of change. The source of difficulty is not a particular villain—e.g., an unreasonable revolutionary—but a malaise. The world is faced with an angry, snarling absence of consensus with respect to the nature and purpose of international (and national) institutions.

The breakdown which has occurred in fundamental relationships and in modes of behavior within these relationships constitutes no mere renunciation and proffering of some substitute (as would be the case in an orthodox revolution); rather, it represents only nihilistic intransigence. The current phenomenon of breakdown is anarchical, but in this case—in contrast to the views set forth by the nineteenth century classical anarchists in Russia—anarchy is not offered as a positive virtue. Engendered anarchy develops merely as a residue of negatives. The end result is a denial of law—and nothing could be more serious, for law is the greatest creation of human life, being mankind's most humanizing force and in many ways the only institution which distinguishes human activities from jungle life. It must be understood that what the phenomenon of engendered anarchy is *not* is a demand for the redress of grievances, nor is it a violent search for ways to end economic inequality or solve any of the other problems arising from the so-called "revolution of rising expectations."

The Chinese Cultural Revolution illustrates fairly well the phenomenon of engendered anarchy, in its shunting aside of the existing system without replacement and mobilization of spirit (chiefly youthful) dedicated to the notion of "permanent revolution" (or, as one Hong Kong Chinese so aptly described it, "life in the bottom of a malted-milk mixer"). The idea of a "cultural revolution" did not travel well, however, becoming entangled abroad with a multitude of extraneous phenomena associated with social change—e.g., an emphasis on civil and human rights, attention to the length of hair, the women's liberation movement, electronically amplified music, developments in race relations, the drug culture, youth contretemps, etc. Whatever their individual merits (or lack thereof), each of these focuses of attention or energy in some sense was a denial of or posed resistance to the system and thus was not counter to anarchy.

One characteristic of the condition of engendered anarchy is ubiquitous terrorism—not revolutionary violence, but jungle savagery whose only purpose is to justify further terrorism. It should be stressed, however, that such mindless terrorism is the result rather than the cause of engendered anarchy, in the same sense that the Jonestowns and Khomeinis of this world are not causes but merely symptoms.

The genesis of this condition lies clearly in the pernicious (and unintended) influences of the ideas inherent in collectivism. Indeed, these developments are the logical culmination of a system in which no one reigns but a committee/politburo rules; there must be total planning for all human activity; the abstraction called the masses rather than the individual person is the touchstone for social policy; and it is denied that personal choice is the central value which makes all other components of life worth doing, being, or having. The democratic societies have embraced much of this dehumanizing mass society syndrome in their approach to social problems and have inadvertently contributed to its perpetuation by tossing up a governmental process which automatically destroys faith in itself.

In the practical world of finite policies, the concept and tactic of *struggle* and two of its concrete forms, armed struggle and political struggle, must be addressed. *Political struggle* inhabits the grey area between politics and revolution. It is confrontational, operates outside any set of rules, and denies the value of compromise (and it is compromise which makes democracy possible). By its nature it must employ force; therefore, to the extent that it is political, it carries out politics with guns. *Armed struggle* is not warfare in the usual meaning of the term; rather it is activity in that netherworld between war and peace. It may resemble military action, usually in the form of guerrilla warfare, but it more commonly involves assassinations, kidnappings, bombings, and various other forms of intimidation.

The two forms of struggle always act in concert, as twin pincers or as hammer and anvil. In combination they form a potent challenge and represent a strategy for which there is no known and proven counterstrategy. These forms of struggle create difficulties enough when they are under someone's control; when they are out of control, the situation is worse and constitutes engendered anarchy.

At the moment, the best the U.S. and the other nations of the Pacific Basin region can do is to recognize clearly their currently limited capacity to deal with engendered anarchy and devote themselves to learning more about the phenomenon. These nations must isolate the early symptoms, experiment with remedies, and eventually learn to cope with this sort of anarchy.

Regionalism

"Regionalism," as used extensively in this essay, is a term of verbal shorthand which refers to supranational but geographically confined institutions and consciousness. Another term, often used by specialists, is "international system," which refers to the matrix of institutions, including regional institutions, above the nation-state level. In its psychological component, regionalism involves individual consciousness of the *region* as something distinct and meaningful, able to command if not loyalty then at least special feelings of identification. By creating specific functional organizations and developing supportive attitudes toward the institutions and the region itself, regionalism both materially and psychologically implies the value and utility of institutionalization.

It is likely that regionalism in general is destined to become one of the major forces shaping world history in the next century. Some observers place this emphasis on regionalism as a matter of political faith. Most of these individuals began with a devotion to the early simplistic experiments in international organization, i.e., the League of Nations and the United Nations Organization. When the hopes placed in these institutions to a great extent were dashed, these persons turned to regionalism in reaction. Too much had been expected from the idea and concrete manifestations of international organization, they now argued, and it was premature if not naive to believe that in one leap a "parliament of man" could be created to deal with transworld problems. Accordingly, the faith in international organizations held by these persons was scaled down and attached to the more manageable regional unit.

Other observers see regionalism as a coming historical force because it recommends itself so well in pragmatic terms. Being more rooted in reality, regional organizations are not as cumbersome as a group comprised of 140 member nations, and can deal effectively with problems which the U.N. cannot handle because of countervailing forces. (It is argued, for example, that some nations—e.g., in central Africa—must federate, for they simply do not have the necessary elements to become viable individual nations.) Eventually several (say, four or five) integrated regional groups, including one in the Pacific, may emerge. It is possible that in the distant future these regional groupings might unite, thus creating finally a single and effective worldwide confederation.

The regionalism which now is emerging is far broader than the concept's earlier form, which viewed regionalism as a function of respective states, leading to government-initiated and -operated institutions. Another change is that regionalism no longer is viewed chiefly in security and economic terms; rather, regionalism increasingly is seen to involve a complex matrix composed of both government and non-government organizations, interested not only in military, economic, and political matters but dealing also with social, educational, communicational, and legal concerns. Within the matrix can exist a wide variety of subgroups—some large and some small, some with broad abstract missions and some of narrow functional purpose. Organizations can exist within organizations, and some organizations might be composed of nothing but other organizations. All can overlap to form a vast spider's web of institutions which both enmeshes with responsibility and liberates by providing national and international benefits.

Regionalism in Asia in the 1980s and beyond may include the following components:

—Growth or creation of major governmental groups, such as the Association of Southeast Asian Nations, an Indochina Federation, the Australia/New Zealand/U.S. (ANZUS) grouping, a Northeast Asia League, and perhaps others.
—Development of a large number of differentiated organizations, along the lines of the Columbo Plan and the Mekong Development Scheme, to serve fairly narrow or specific purposes.
—Augmentation (and improved performance) of existing specialized international organizations, for the most part under United Nations auspices, such as the Food and Agricultural Organization (FAO), the World Health Organization (WHO), the United Nations International Children's

Educational Fund (UNICEF), and the United Nations Educational, Scientific, and Cultural Organization (UNESCO).
—Marked development of and increased activity and more systematic and comprehensive planning by the international lending agencies, such as the World Bank and the International Monetary Fund.
—Expansion of private capitalist multinational corporations and creation of regional private financing companies and marketing consortiums.
—Increased functional activity in education, medicine, and agriculture through, for example, creation of a University of Southeast Asia, a Tropical Disease Research Center, and a Southeast Asia Rice Experimental Station.

Also *possible* is the creation of a single pan-Asian organization. This would not be a supraregional organ but rather a sort of Pacific umbrella—a loosely formed secretariat to coordinate and facilitate the activities of the entire regional matrix.

Traditionally, the great enemy of regionalism in Asia has been nationalism (and sometimes ultra-nationalism)—i.e., the claimed right of each nation to do as it pleases, at least to the extent possible. This force remains operative and will pose the sharpest limits to the pace and effectiveness of the developing regionalism in Asia. Transfer of sovereignty is psychologically difficult, for it seems not only to entail loss but also to constitute a violation not justified even by great gain. This nationalist spirit can be tamed, however, as it has been tamed elsewhere (e.g., in Western Europe). Progress in regionalism comes through the gradual recognition by the peoples involved that great benefit can accrue from dampening down the fires of nationalism and that this can be accomplished without loss of national honor, as the ASEAN nations already have experienced in dealing with Japan. Asians for the most part are pragmatic peoples, and although they are proud they are not inclined to injure themselves seriously in a material way for the sake of an abstraction, such as nationalist sentiment.

Regionalism's second great enemy in Asia is the body of historical animosities—including internecine clan struggles, socio-ethnic antipathies, and local rivalries over territory or use of language—which have been deeply ingrained by the passage of centuries, leaving vast pools of suspicion and distrust. These animosities will dissipate, but only slowly. It is sometimes charged that regionalism "papers over" the fact of rivalry, leading observers to conclude erroneously that rivalry no longer constitutes a problem when in fact it merely has been obscured. It is also the case, however, that—as any international negotiator knows—one of the best methods for dealing with ingrained confrontational rivalry is to submerge it in a larger context, causing the disputants to take other factors, and not just their hostility, into account during the process of decision-making. For example, French-German antipathy still exists, but to a large extent it has been submersed in a broader concern, the joint French-German search for national security.

It is true that there exist a number of stumbling-blocks to regionalism in the Asian/Pacific region. The area's principal existing regional organization, ASEAN, is plagued by such built-in difficulties as Moslem separatism, conflicting claims on ocean and other resources, competing economies (since most are producers of raw materials), and suspected Indonesian ambitions, to name a few. However, while ASEAN still is young and shakey, it has grown remarkably since its creation in 1967. Whatever else might be said about ASEAN, it is a fact that the Association today is of far greater importance than at any time in its past, and counts for far more than did any previous regional organization in Southeast Asia, including the Southeast Asian Treaty Organization (SEATO).

U.S. interest in and natural gravitation toward Asian regionalism stem basically from an American sense of the limits of U.S. power. This sense is largely the result of what the U.S. has taken as the lesson to be learned from the Vietnam war. Given the self-doubts which arose from that debacle, the U.S. in its international dealings now tends to seek out those approaches which are cautious in nature. Because encouraging the development of and interrelating with regional groupings appears to constitute a relatively safe approach, it is viewed as preferable to the more risky route of unilateral action. In fact, however, the regional approach is more complex and therefore more difficult, and thus can be counted on to try American patience.

An American View

Some in the Asian/Pacific region seek to use regionalism as a cold war weapon; others (chiefly the Soviet Union) view it mainly as a force hostile or potentially hostile to their interests. Within the dynamics of the Sino-Soviet dispute, the PRC and the USSR each will engage in a process of pulling and hauling at regional groups in an attempt to form an alliance supportive of its intentions and outlook, but it is in the interests of all—including Moscow and Peking—that such a use of regionalism be avoided.

The most constructive attitude which the U.S. and other nations can take toward regionalism is to recognize and encourage its enormous potentiality. It is true that while much of the potential of regionalism is positive, it does have possible negative components as well, and regionalism will never be a simple, unmixed blessing. Great opportunities nevertheless are inherent in regionalism, and the U.S. should take advantage of these opportunities. Naming a special American envoy with Presidential rank as a sort of ambassador to the region would be both wise and practical, and would give impetus to regional development. This envoy could deal systematically with regional problems better than can the individual U.S. embassies in the region and could help facilitate the development and implementation of U.S. policies, since proposed actions are far more palatable if they are presented and defined at the regional level rather than relayed by imperial edict from Washington.

Finally, it seems that the greatest recommendation for regionalism in Asia—for the U.S. as well as for other nations—is that it offers the best available insurance for continuity, in the sense of the continuation of an orderly international system, at least at the regional level. Furthermore, if engendered anarchy does erupt and all else fails, regionalism provides the best mechanism for rectification. Regionalism does not provide immunity from engendered anarchy, but it is a form of innoculation against it, reducing its incidence and facilitating treatment when engendered anarchy does develop.

Appendix.
CONFERENCE PROGRAM AND PARTICIPANTS

CONFERENCE
on
NEW FOUNDATIONS FOR ASIAN AND PACIFIC SECURITY

December 12-16, 1979

Royal Cliff Hotel

Pattaya, Thailand

Conference Coordinator: Hugh McGowan

Conference Co-Sponsors:

Center for Strategic and International Studies	**Indonesia**
Faculty of Political Science of **Chulalongkorn University**	**Thailand**
Institute for Pacific Affairs (in formation)	**Japan**
John F. Kennedy Foundation of Thailand	**Thailand**
National Strategy Information Center	**United States**
The Pacific Institute	**Australia**

CONFERENCE PROGRAM

WEDNESDAY, 12 DECEMBER 1979

RECEPTION AND DINNER, hosted by Ministry of Foreign Affairs, Thailand

Addresses
—His Excellency Dr. Upadit Pachariyangkun, Minister of Foreign Affairs [at time of conference], Bangkok, Thailand, "The Strategic Outlook for Thailand in the 1980s"
—The Honorable Tan Sri Muhammad Ghazali bin Shafie, Minister of Home Affairs, Kuala Lumpur, Malaysia, "Toward a Pacific Basin Community: A Malaysian Perception"

THURSDAY, 13 DECEMBER 1979

FIRST PLENARY SESSION
POLITICAL/MILITARY DIMENSIONS OF SECURITY IN SOUTHEAST ASIA

Chairman: The Honorable Allan Griffith, Special Advisor to the Prime Minister, Canberra, Australia

Address
—The Honorable Dr. Thanat Khoman, Former Minister of Foreign Affairs [appointed Deputy Prime Minister in March 1980], Bangkok, Thailand, "Conflict and Cooperation in Southeast Asia: The New Chapter"

Papers
—Mr. Lim Joo-Jock, Institute of Southeast Asian Studies, Singapore, "The Indochina Situation and the Superpowers in Southeast Asia"

—Mr. Jusuf Wanandi, Center for Strategic and International Studies, Jakarta, Indonesia, "Internal and External Dimensions of Southeast Asian Security"

LUNCHEON

Address
—The Honorable Lt. General Ali Moertopo, Minister of Information, Jakarta, Indonesia, "International Politics in Asia and the Pacific: Uncertainties and Complexities"

SECOND PLENARY SESSION
POLITICAL/MILITARY DIMENSIONS OF SECURITY IN NORTHEAST ASIA

Chairman: Vice Admiral Tun-Hwa Ko, Vice Minister of Defense, Taipei, Republic of China

Papers
—Admiral Kenichi Kitamura, Former Chief of Naval Operations, Tokyo, Japan, "The Japanese Defense Posture and the Soviet Challenge in Northeast Asia"
—Ambassador Hogan Yoon, Consul General of the Republic of Korea, New York, N.Y., USA, "The Tensions on the Korean Peninsula"

Commentary
—The Honorable Dr. Frederick F. Chien, Vice Minister of Foreign Affairs, Taipei, Republic of China

ORGANIZATION OF COMMITTEES

Co-chairmen of Committee #1: Professor Chandran Jeshuran and Dr. Peter Polomka
Co-chairmen of Committee #2: Dr. Kim Se Jin and Professor Harry Gelber
Co-chairmen of Committees #3 and #4: The Honorable Bernard Chen and Dr. Tomatsu Takase

FRIDAY, 14 DECEMBER 1979

THIRD PLENARY SESSION
ECONOMIC DIMENSIONS OF ASIAN AND PACIFIC SECURITY

   Chairman: Dr. Snoh Unakul, Deputy Under-secretary of State, Bangkok, Thailand

Papers
- Professor Sun Chen, National University of Taiwan, Taipei, Republic of China, "Toward Regional Cooperation and Prosperity"
- Dr. Munir Majid, *New Straits Times*, Kuala Lumpur, Malaysia, "Regional Security Through Trade and Development"
- Ambassador Alejandro Melchor, Asian Development Bank, Manila, Philippines, "Energy Resources, Raw Materials, and the Safety of the Sea Lanes of Communication: An Organic Approach Toward a New Security Framework"

COMMMITTEE SESSIONS

RECEPTION AND DINNER, hosted by the John F. Kennedy Foundation of Thailand (courtesy of Dr. Thanat Khoman) and the Education and Public Welfare Foundation (courtesy of Mr. K. Y. Chou)

SATURDAY, 15 DECEMBER 1979

FOURTH PLENARY SESSION
POLICY PROPOSALS AND ASIAN AND PACIFIC SECURITY

   Chairman: Dr. Kernial S. Sandhu, Director, Institute of Southeast Asian Studies, Singapore

Panel
- Dr. Sompong Sucharitkul, Ministry of Foreign Affairs, Bangkok, Thailand, "A Southeast Asian View"
- Professor Jun Tsunoda, Asyama-Gakuin University, Tokyo, Japan, "A Northeast Asian View"
- Professor Harry Gelber, University of Tasmania, Hobart, Australia, "An Australian View"

—Dr. Douglas Pike, Department of Defense, Washington, D.C., USA, "An American View"

LUNCHEON

Address
—General Masao Horie (Ret.), Councillor, Japanese Diet, Tokyo, Japan, "Northeast Asian Security: The Japanese Role"

COMMITTEE SESSIONS

RECEPTION AND DINNER, hosted by Mr. (and Mrs.) Paul Sithi-Amnuai, President, PSA Company, Ltd., Bangkok, Thailand

SUNDAY, 16 DECEMBER 1979

FINAL SESSION

Chairman: Dr. Frank N. Trager, Director of Studies, National Strategy Information Center, Inc. and Professor of International Affairs, New York University, New York, N.Y., USA

Reports by Committee Chairmen

Conference Closing
—Dr. Frank N. Trager

LIST OF PARTICIPANTS

Lt. General Abhichart Dhiradhamrong
Advisor to the National Defense College
Bangkok, Thailand

Professor Heinz Arndt
Australian National University
Canberra, Australia

The Honorable Carmelo Barbero
Deputy Minister of Defense
Quezon City, Philippines

Professor B. D. Beddie
University of New South Wales
Duntroon, Australia

Mr. Michael Bianco
International Bank [based in Washington, D.C., USA]
Hong Kong

Lt. Colonel Donald Cann, USAF
Air Attache, Embassy of the United States
Bangkok, Thailand

Professor Chandran Jeshurun
University of Malaya
Kuala Lumpur, Malaysia

The Honorable Bernard Chen
Deputy Minister of Defense
Singapore

The Honorable Dr. Frederick F. Chien
Vice Minister of Foreign Affairs
Taipei, Republic of China

Mr. Chulchit Bunyaketu
Thai Oil Refinery Co., Ltd.
Bangkok, Thailand

Mr. James N. Creer
Abbott, Tout, Creer, and Wilkinson
Sydney, Australia

Captain Eng Juan Han
Ministry of National Defense
Singapore

Dr. Geoffrey Fairbairn
Australian National University
Canberra, Australia

Professor Harry G. Gelber
University of Tasmania
Hobart, Australia

The Honorable Tan Sri Muhammad Ghazali bin Shafie
Minister of Home Affairs
Kuala Lumpur, Malaysia

The Honorable Allan Griffith
Special Advisor to the Prime Minister
Canberra, Australia

Ambassador Hogan Yoon
Consul General of the Republic of Korea
New York, N.Y., USA

General Masao Horie (Ret.)
Councillor, Japanese Diet
Tokyo, Japan

Mr. Henry Kamm
The New York Times
Bangkok, Thailand

Mr. Peter Kelly
Federated Ironworkers' Association of Australia
New South Wales, Australia

Dr. Kim Se Jin
Ministry of Foreign Affairs
Seoul, Republic of Korea

Admiral Kenichi Kitamura (Ret.)
Former Chief of Naval Operations
Tokyo, Japan

Vice Admiral Tun-Hwa Ko
Vice Minister of Defense
Taipei, Republic of China

Dr. Kramol Tongdhamarchart
Chulalongkorn University
Bangkok, Thailand

List of Participants

Ms. Joyce E. Larson
National Strategy Information Center, Inc.
New York, N.Y., USA

Mr. Lim Joo-Jock
Institute of Southeast Asian Studies
Singapore

Mr. Hugh McGowan
National Strategy Information Center, Inc.
New York, N.Y., USA

Ambassador Alejandro Melchor
Asian Development Bank
Manila, Philippines

General Hans Menzi
Menzi and Co., Inc.
Makati, Philippines

The Honorable Noboru Minowa
Representative, Japanese Diet
Tokyo, Japan

The Honorable Lt. General Ali Moertopo
Minister of Information
Jakarta, Indonesia

Ambassador Haji Mohamad Ali Moersid
National Defense Security Council
Jakarta, Indonesia

Mr. Frank Mount
News Weekly [published in Australia]
Manila, Philippines

Dr. Munir Majid
The New Straits Times
Kuala Lumpur, Malaysia

Colonel Pat Akkanibut
Supreme Command Headquarters
Bangkok, Thailand

Senator Emmanuel Pelaez
Pelaez, Jalandoni, and Adriano
Manila, Philippines

Dr. Douglas Pike
Department of Defense
Washington, D.C., USA

Dr. Peter Polomka
Office of National Assessments
Canberra, Australia

Mr. Eric Rasmusen
Chemical Bank
Singapore

Dr. Kernial S. Sandhu
Institute of Southeast Asian Studies
Singapore

Mr. Robert W. Schwab III
Bangkok, Thailand

Mr. Paul Sithi-Amnuai
PSA Company, Ltd.
Bangkok, Thailand

The Honorable Dr. Snoh Unakul
Deputy Under-secretary of State
Bangkok, Thailand

Colonel Somkuan Suwan
Supreme Command Headquarters
Bangkok, Thailand

The Honorable Dr. Sompong Sucharitkul
Ministry of Foreign Affairs
Bangkok, Thailand

Dr. Sriboonrruang Chitkasem
Chulalongkorn University
Bangkok, Thailand

Professor Sumidro Djojohadikusumo
University of Indonesia
Jakarta, Indonesia

Professor Sun Chen
National University of Taiwan
Taipei, Republic of China

Professor Tomatsu Takase
Kyoto Sangyo University
Kyoto, Japan

The Honorable Tan Seng Chye
Charge D'Affaires, Embassy of Singapore
Bangkok, Thailand

The Honorable Dr. Thanat Khoman
Former Minister of Foreign Affairs
[appointed Deputy Prime Minister in March 1980]
Bangkok, Thailand

Group Captain A. E. Thomson, RNZAF
Defense Attache, Embassy of New Zealand
Bangkok, Thailand

List of Participants

Mr. C. C. Too
*Ministry of Home Affairs
Kuala Lumpur, Malaysia*

Dr. Frank N. Trager
*National Strategy Information Center, Inc.
and New York University
New York, N.Y., USA*

Professor Helen G. Trager (Ret.)
New York, N.Y., USA

Professor Tsai Chen-Wen
*National University of Taiwan
Taipei, Republic of China*

Professor Jun Tsunoda
*Asyama-Gakuin University
Tokyo, Japan*

His Excellency Dr. Upadit Pachariyangkun
*Minister of Foreign Affairs [at time of conference]
Bangkok, Thailand*

Mr. Jose de Venecia
*Landoil Resources Corporation
Makati, Philippines*

Mr. Barry Wain
*The Asian Wall Street Journal
[published in Hong Kong]
Bangkok, Thailand*

Mr. Jusuf Wanandi
*Center for Strategic and International Studies
Jakarta, Indonesia*

Mr. Denis Warner
*Journalist and Author
Victoria, Australia*

The Honorable Manuel Yan
*Ambassador, Embassy of the Philippines
Bangkok, Thailand*

Professor Datuk Zainal Abidin Wahid
*National University
Bangli Selangor, Malaysia*

National Strategy Information Center, Inc.

PUBLICATIONS

Frank N. Trager, Editor
Dorothy E. Nicolosi, Associate Editor
Joyce E. Larson, Managing Editor

BOOKS

New Foundations for Asian and Pacific Security edited by Joyce E. Larson, September 1980

Intelligence Requirements for the 1980s: Analysis and Estimates (Volume II of a Series) edited by Roy Godson, June 1980

Arms, Men, and Military Budgets: Issues for Fiscal Year 1981 by Francis P. Hoeber, William Schneider, Jr., Norman Polmar, and Ray Bessette, May 1980

Intelligence Requirements for the 1980s: Elements of Intelligence (Volume I of a Series) edited by Roy Godson, October 1979

The Fateful Ends and Shades of SALT: Past . . . Present . . . And Yet to Come? by Paul H. Nitze, James E. Dougherty, and Francis X. Kane, March 1979

Strategic Options for the Early Eighties: What Can Be Done? edited by William R. Van Cleave and W. Scott Thompson, February 1979

Arms, Men, and Military Budgets: Issues for Fiscal Year 1979 by Francis P. Hoeber, David B. Kassing, and William Schneider, Jr., February 1978

Arms, Men, and Military Budgets: Issues for Fiscal Year 1978 edited by Francis P. Hoeber and William Schneider, Jr., May 1977

Oil, Divestiture and National Security edited by Frank N. Trager, December 1976

Arms, Men, and Military Budgets: Issues for Fiscal Year 1977 edited by William Schneider, Jr., and Francis P. Hoeber, May 1976

Indian Ocean Naval Limitations, Regional Issues and Global Implications by Alvin J. Cottrell and Walter F. Hahn, April 1976

STRATEGY PAPERS

Raw Material Supply in a Multipolar World by Yuan-li Wu, October 1973. Revised edition, October 1979

India: Emergent Power? by Stephen P. Cohen and Richard L. Park, June 1978

The Kremlin and Labor: A Study in National Security Policy by Roy Godson, November 1977

The Evolution of Soviet Security Strategy 1965–1975 by Avigdor Haselkorn, November 1977

The Geopolitics of the Nuclear Era by Colin S. Gray, September 1977

The Sino-Soviet Confrontation: Implications for the Future by Harold C. Hinton, September 1976 (Out of print)

Food, Foreign Policy, and Raw Materials Cartels by William Schneider, Jr., February 1976

Strategic Weapons: An Introduction by Norman Polmar, October 1975 (Out of print)

Soviet Sources of Military Doctrine and Strategy by William F. Scott, July 1975

Detente: Promises and Pitfalls by Gerald L. Steibel, March 1975 (Out of print)

Oil, Politics and Sea Power: The Indian Ocean Vortex by Ian W.A.C. Adie, December 1974 (Out of print)

The Soviet Presence in Latin America by James D. Theberge, June 1974

The Horn of Africa by J. Bowyer Bell, Jr., December 1973

Research and Development and the Prospects for International Security by Frederick Seitz and Rodney W. Nichols, December 1973

Publications

The People's Liberation Army: Communist China's Armed Forces by Angus M. Fraser, August 1973 (Out of print)

Nuclear Weapons and the Atlantic Alliance by Wynfred Joshua, May 1973

How to Think About Arms Control and Disarmament by James E. Dougherty, May 1973 (Out of print)

The Military Indoctrination of Soviet Youth by Leon Goure, January 1973 (Out of print)

The Asian Alliance: Japan and United States Policy by Franz Michael and Gaston J. Sigur, October 1972 (Out of print)

Iran, the Arabian Peninsula, and the Indian Ocean by R. M. Burrell and Alvin J. Cottrell, September 1972 (Out of print)

Soviet Naval Power: Challenge for the 1970s by Norman Polmar, April 1972. Revised edition, September 1974 (Out of print)

How Can We Negotiate with the Communists? by Gerald L. Steibel, March 1972 (Out of print)

Soviet Political Warfare Techniques, Espionage and Propaganda in the 1970s by Lyman B. Kirkpatrick, Jr., and Howland H. Sargeant, January 1972 (Out of print)

The Soviet Presence in the Eastern Mediterranean by Lawrence L. Whetten, September 1971 (Out of print)

The Military Unbalance: Is the U.S. Becoming a Second Class Power? June 1971 (Out of print)

The Future of South Vietnam by Brigadier F. P. Serong, February 1971 (Out of print)

Strategy and National Interests: Reflections for the Future by Bernard Brodie, January 1971 (Out of print)

The Mekong River: A Challenge in Peaceful Development for Southeast Asia by Eugene R. Black, December 1970 (Out of print)

Problems of Strategy in the Pacific and Indian Oceans by George C. Thomson, October 1970 (Out of print)

Soviet Penetration into the Middle East by Wynfred Joshua, July 1970. Revised edition, October 1971 (Out of print)

Australian Security Policies and Problems by Justus M. van der Kroef, May 1970 (Out of print)

Detente: Dilemma or Disaster? by Gerald L. Steibel, July 1969 (Out of print)

The Prudent Case for Safeguard by William R. Kintner, June 1969 (Out of print)

AGENDA PAPERS

NATO, Turkey, and the Southern Flank: A Mideastern Perspective by Ihsan Gürkan, March 1980

The Soviet Threat to NATO's Northern Flank by Marian K. Leighton, November 1979

Does Defense Beggar Welfare? Myths Versus Realities by James L. Clayton, June 1979

Naval Race or Arms Control in the Indian Ocean? (Some Problems in Negotiating Naval Limitations) by Alvin J. Cottrell and Walter F. Hahn, September 1978

Power Projection: A Net Assessment of U.S. and Soviet Capabilities by W. Scott Thompson, April 1978

Understanding the Soviet Military Threat, How CIA Estimates Went Astray by William T. Lee, February 1977

Toward a New Defense for NATO, The Case for Tactical Nuclear Weapons, July 1976 (Out of print)

Seven Tracks to Peace in the Middle East by Frank R. Barnett, April 1975

Arms Treaties with Moscow: Unequal Terms Unevenly Applied? by Donald G. Brennan, April 1975 (Out of print)

Toward a U.S. Energy Policy by Klaus Knorr, March 1975 (Out of print)

Can We Avert Economic Warfare in Raw Materials? US Agriculture as a Blue Chip by William Schneider, July 1974